German
Grammar
HANDBOOK

Christopher Wightwick

German Grammar Handbook

The Author and Series Editor:
Christopher Wightwick is a former UK representative on the Council of Europe Modern Languages Project and principal Inspector of Modern Languages for England.

Other titles in the Berlitz Language Handbook Series:

French Grammar Handbook
Spanish Grammar Handbook
French Verb Handbook
German Verb Handbook
Spanish Verb Handbook

French Vocabulary Handbook
German Vocabulary Handbook
Spanish Vocabulary Handbook

Published by Berlitz Publishing Company, Inc.
400 Alexander Park, Princeton, NJ 08540 USA
9-13 Grosvenor Street, London W1A 3BZ UK

3rd printing August 1997
Printed in USA
ISBN 2-8315-1354-5

CONTENTS

C Actions and states: verbs and their uses

D   People, things and ideas: nouns and noun phrases

How to use this Handbook

This *Grammar Handbook* can be used in two main ways.

• If you want to get a *general picture* of some aspect of German grammar, start with the list of Contents on page iii. You can then read through the relevant sections of the text. The many *cross-references* [shown by ➤ plus a paragraph number] will lead you to other, related topics.

• If you want to find out about a *specific grammatical point*, look it up in the extensive General Index at the end of the book. This gives the paragraph numbers for all the important items of grammar and for many German structure-words. To help you to find what you are looking for, items are often listed more than once, under different headings.

The *Handbook* gives a great deal of information about grammatical forms and structures, but above all it is designed to show how they fit in with what you want to say or write. This shows in a number of ways.

• *Grammatical terms* are treated as convenient labels and used whenever necessary, but the Handbook does not assume that you already know what they mean. All terms are explained in everyday language in the most relevant paragraph, which is marked ⌞D⌟ (for Definition) in the General Index.

• The chapters are grouped into six parts (A to F), each of which deals with an area of language. This helps to show how various aspects of grammar are linked.

• Many *chapter and paragraph headings* use short descriptive phrases as well as grammatical terms.

• A key feature is the way in which grammatical points are *illustrated by examples* which make clear how they are used. Wherever it makes sense to do so, these sentences are linked together by a common context, and they often form short narratives or dialogues which help to fix them in the memory.

• The examples are drawn from a wide range of situations and occupations, so they provide you with a stock of useful expressions which you can adapt to suit what you want to say. If any construction is mainly used in more formal contexts, this is made clear in the text.

Finally, because all examples are translated into English, they provide a convenient way of testing your knowledge. Simply cover over the translation and try to produce the German original. If you get a structure wrong, check it in the text and try again later.

A
PUTTING IDEAS INTO WORDS

Classes of words: parts of speech

1a What kind of word is it?

It is often impossible to say what class a word belongs to (what *part of speech* it is) until it is used in a sentence. On the other hand, understanding a sentence may well depend on knowing what part of speech a word is, so it is useful to be able to recognize them. In this *Handbook* we define each part of speech mainly by what it does – what it refers to, and its function and position in the sentence. If you can also recognize a part of speech by its form, for example, by its endings, then this is described as well.

1b Content words and structure words

Four classes of word, the *content words*, contain most of the meaning of the sentence. The others, the *structure words*, do of course add to the meaning, but they do it mainly by the way they relate to the content words. There is some overlap between these two groups, but the distinction is useful all the same. The following table shows the two groups with their English and German names, the paragraph number where they are first defined, and some examples. The German terms are given for information – they are not used in the text.

Note German has two sets of grammatical terms, one derived from Latin, the other native German. The first set is much more like English, but the second set often gives a better idea of the function of a word than the Latin terms.

(i) Content words

Verbs
Verben, Zeitwörter [➤7a]
Meine Großmutter *spricht* und *liest* Deutsch.
My grandmother *speaks* and *reads* German.

Adjectives
Adjektive, Eigenschaftswörter [➤ch.24]
Sie findet sie *interessant* und *nützlich*.
Sie finds them *interesting* and *useful*.

Nouns
Substantive, Hauptwörter [➤19a]
***Sprachen* sind ihr *Hobby*.**
Languages are her *hobby*.

Adverbs
**Adverbien, Umstandswörter
[➤ch.28]**
Sie spricht *schnell* und *gut*.
She speaks *fast* and *well*.

(ii)   Structure words

Pronouns
Pronomina, Fürwörter [➤ch.25]
***Sie* schenkt *mir* oft *etwas*
Interessantes.**
She often gives *me something*
interesting.

Prepositions
**Präpositionen, Verhältniswörter
[➤27a]**
***In* diesem Buch kann man viel
über Sprachen lesen.**
In this book you can read a lot *about*
languages.

Exclamations
**Interjektionen, Ausrufewörter
[➤ch.26]**
***Na und!* Ich mag lieber Mathe.
*Auwei!***
So what! I prefer math/maths. *Oh
dear!*

Determiners
**Begleiter des Substantivs
[➤ch.23]**
***Mein* Lieblingsgeschenk ist *ein*
Buch über *alle* Völker *der* Welt.**
My favorite present is *a* book about
all the peoples of *the* world.

Conjunctions
Konjunktionen, Bindewörter[➤5a]
***Weil* sie Sprachen liebt, hofft sie,
daß ich sie studieren werde.**
Because she loves languages, she
hopes *that* I shall study them.

Getting it down on paper: spelling and punctuation

2a   Spelling and sounds

This chapter describes the main features of German spelling and punctuation. It does not deal directly with German pronunciation, as attempts to describe sounds on paper are more likely to be a hindrance than a help.

2b   The German alphabet

The order in which letters are listed in German dictionaries is the same as in English. The list below gives their pronunciation, using standard German spelling. Note that the **e** at the end of a letter name is pronounced as though doubled, as in the German word **See**. It is useful to know the German alphabet when spelling names and addresses, for example on the telephone.

A	a	J	jot	S	ess
(Ä	ä)	K	ka	(ß	scharfes S)
B	be	L	ell	T	te
C	ze	M	emm	U	u
D	de	N	enn	(Ü	ü)
E	e	O	o	V	vau
F	eff	(Ö	ö)	W	we
G	ge	P	pe	X	ix
H	ha	Q	ku	Y	ypsilon
I	i	R	er	Z	zett

Note   The three vowels with Umlaut (**Ää, Öö, Üü**) [➤2c(i)] are separate letters, with their own typewriter keys, but they are not listed separately in the alphabet. Similarly, **ß** is listed as **ss** [➤2c(iii)].

2c   The main spelling rules

In most ways German spelling is quite predictable. Even where there are irregularities they usually only affect a few words.
• Spelling rules do not apply to people's names.
• Important exceptions or inconsistencies are dealt with wherever they occur throughout the *Handbook*.

(i) Letters needing care

ä/e   Pronounced similarly, especially when short. Long **ä** is a more open sound than long **e**. Many words with **ä** are related to stems with **a**.

c   Used mainly in the combinations **ch, ck, sch** and **tsch**. By itself **c** is used only in foreign words, when it is pronounced like **k** before **a, o, u** and consonants, and like **z** or **s** before **e** and **i**.

f/v   Usually pronounced the same. **V** is used: in the many words with the prefix **ver-**; at the start of about a dozen other native German words (e.g. **Vater, Veilchen, Vetter, Vieh, viel, vier, Vogel, Vogt, Volk, voll, von, vor**); in foreign borrowings.

s/sch   The sound 'sh' is spelled **s** in words which start with **sp** (like **sprechen** or **Sport**), or **st** (like **stehen** or **Straße**). Otherwise it is spelled **sch**, as in **schwimmen**.

y   Only used in foreign borrowings. It is found as a vowel in words of Greek origin like **System** or **Physik**, when it is pronounced like **ü** or (by some people) **i**. In a few modern borrowings like **Yacht** or **Yoga** it is an initial consonant, pronounced like **j**.

b/d/g   Pronounced **p/t/k** respectively at the end of a word (though **-ig** is often pronounced **-ich**). This means that the pronunciation of many words changes when an **-e-** ending is added.

(ii) Long and short vowels

German vowels are pronounced long:

(A) Usually before a single consonant: **fragen, träge, leben, wider, bot, Öl, duzen, für**. The main exceptions are some one-syllable structure words [▶1b], like **das, in, mit, ob**. Before **ch** vowels are sometimes long, as in **Sprache** or **Buch**, but more often short: **lachen, Fächer, sprechen, sicher, kochen, Löcher, Küche**.

(B) When followed by **h** (which is then never pronounced): **fahren, fährt, gehen, ihr, ohne, stöhnen, Kuh, Bühne**.

(C) In the few words with double **a, e** or **o** and the many words with **ie**: **Paar, Meer, Boot, wieder**. Note that **aa** and **oo** + Umlaut reduce to **ä** and **ö**: **ein Saal - zwei Säle, das Boot - das Bötchen**.

(iii) Single and double letters

The following rules should be noted:

(A) **ck** is written instead of **kk** and (except in some foreign words) **tz** instead of **zz**: **Brücke, Katze** but **Jazz, Pizza** (**ck →** **k-k**: [▶3b(iii)]).

(B) Apart from endings and compounds, no German word contains the combinations consonant + double-consonant or double-consonant + consonant. Learners often write, for example, **der Artzt** for **der Arzt**, forgetting that **tz** counts as a double consonant.

(C) If two words make a compound which would result in triple-consonant + vowel, then one of the consonants is dropped. If the compound is split at the end of a line of running text [➤3b(iii)], then the missing consonant is brought back in.

das Be*tt* + das *T*uch	➔	das Be*tt*uch
vo*ll* + *l*aden	➔	vo*ll*aden
schne*ll* + der *L*äufer	➔	der Schne*ll*äufer
bre*nn*en + die *N*essel	➔	die Bre*nn*essel

Note   This does not apply to **ß + s**, as in **die Streßsituation**.

(iv)   ss or ß?

SS is always used when writing in capitals. Otherwise, **ß** is written instead of **ss**:

• always after a long vowel, including **ie** and the diphthongs (vowel combinations) **ai**, **au**, **äu**, **ei** and **eu**
• always before another consonant
• at the end of a word, including the end of part of a compound.

After a short vowel, therefore, **ß** reverts to **ss** before an **-e-** ending, but remains before an ending beginning with a consonant.

After long vowels	*After short vowels*
Fuß, Füße, Fußweg	küssen, küßt, Kuß, kußecht
groß, großes, Größe, Großhändler	gewiß, gewisser, Gewißheit

Note   **ß** is not used when **ss** is formed at the join between the two halves of a compound.

das Gla*s* + der *S*plitter	➔	der Gla*ss*plitter
die Rettung + joining *-s-*		
+ die *S*tation	➔	die Rettung*ss*tation

(v)   Capital letters

Capitals are used for the first letter of:

• a word at the start of a sentence, as in English;
• all nouns, not just the names of persons and places [➤19c];
• any other part of speech used as a noun. Especially with adjectives, the rules about capitalization are complex [➤24d(iii)].

beim Essen	while eating [➤10a(iii)]
eine Sechs	a six [➤30a(ii)]
das Für und Wider	the pros and cons
alles Gute!	all the best!
etwas Verdächtiges	something suspicious
das Ich und das Es	the ego and the id

2d *Punctuation*

The main punctuation marks in German are:

.	**der Punkt**
,	**das Komma**
;	**der Strichpunkt**
:	**der Doppelpunkt**
?	**das Fragezeichen**
!	**das Ausrufezeichen**
( )	**die Klammer (-n)**
„ "	**die Anführungsstriche (unten/oben)**
-	**der Bindestrich**

(i) *Periods/Full stops*

The period is used, as in English, at the end of sentences, and also:

• after ordinal numbers [➤30b]: **der 16. September**;
• after abbreviations like **Dr. Ing.** for **Doktor Ingenieur, bzw.** for **beziehungsweise** 'or', **vorm./nachm.** for **vormittags/ nachmittags** 'a.m./p.m.', but not after initial letters like **EG** for **Europäische Gemeinde** 'European Community' **USA, UNO**.

(ii) *Commas*

The use of the comma differs significantly from English.

(A) Its main function is to mark off each separate clause in a sentence from the next [➤4d]. Commas are therefore written:

• between main clauses with different subjects. Main clauses which share a subject are separated by either a comma or **und/oder**, but not both [➤5a(i)].

Wir standen alle auf, und ich holte meine Sachen und lud sie ins Auto.	We all got up, and I fetched my things and loaded them into the car.

• between the main clause and any type of subordinate clause. Subordinate clauses linked by **und** or **oder** do not have a comma between them.

Da Heiner noch nicht da war, fürchtete ich, daß er vergessen hatte oder daß sein alter Wagen eine Panne hatte.	As Heiner had not yet arrived, I was afraid that he had forgotten or that his old car had broken down.

• between the main clause and a **zu** + infinitive clause. Exceptions to this rule are given in paragraphs 8h(ii) and 10a(iv).

Ich versuchte mehrmals umsonst, ihn telefonisch zu erreichen.	I tried several times without success to get him on the phone.

• between the main clause and longer participle clauses [➤10b(v)].

Das Schlimmste fürchtend, ging ich zu seinem Haus hinüber.	Fearing the worst, I went across to his house.

(B) Commas are also normally written:
• between two or more adjectives before a noun if they are felt to be equally important, that is, if they could be linked by **und**.

Vor dem Haus saß Heiner in einem riesengroßen, knallroten Wagen. Es war das allerletzte amerikanische Modell.	In front of the house sat Heiner in a huge, bright red car. It was the very latest American model.

• to separate exclamations (but see (iii) (C) below), explanatory remarks and the like.

„Aber Heiner, um Gottes willen, hast du denn unseren Ausflug vergessen, Mensch?" rief ich.	"But Heiner, for heaven's sake, have you forgotten our outing, man?" I exclaimed.

• in decimals, where English uses a decimal point [➤30c(iii)].

„Magst du meine neue 3,5-Liter-Kutsche?" fragte er gelassen.	"Do you like my new 3.5-liter wagon?" he asked unperturbed.

(iii)   *Other punctuation marks*

(A) The semi-colon is rarely used in German. A comma or period is usually preferred.

Ich schwieg einen Augenblick, ich war nämlich sprachlos.	I was silent for a moment; I was in fact speechless.

(B) A colon, not a comma, is used to introduce direct speech.

Schließlich sagte ich: „Mann! Du bist mir aber einer!"	Finally I said, "Man! You really are something else!"

(C) Opening quotation marks are placed on the line, not above it as in English (see the examples given above). Hence the expression **Anführungsstriche unten/oben** for 'Open/close quotes'.

(D) Question marks are used as in English, at the end of direct questions [➤ch.6].

„Hast du unseren Ausflug wirklich vergessen?"	"Have you really forgotten our outing?"

(E) An exclamation point/mark is used:

• after exclamations and commands. If the command is more like a request, many Germans would now put a period [➤13b(ii)].

„Sei mir nicht böse, Karl!" sagte er. „Lies das!" Da reichte er mir einen Brief.	"Don't be angry at me, Karl," he said. "Read that!" And he handed me a letter.

• after the opening words of a letter, though a comma is now frequently used instead.

„Sehr geehrter Herr Klotz!" las ich. „Sie haben den ersten Preis im Lotto gewonnen!"	"Dear Mr. Klotz," I read. "You have won first prize in the national lottery!"

(F) Use of hyphens: ➤3b(iii).

Linking ideas together

3a Compound words or phrases?

All languages have ways of combining word meanings so as to express more complex ideas, either by joining two words together to form one compound word or by linking separate words to form phrases. German does of course employ phrases in this way, but the particular strength of the language is its capacity to make compound words.

3b Compound words

This section illustrates some of the ways in which compound nouns and adjectives are formed. Compound verbs, made either with prefixes or with particles, are dealt with in Chapter 16 (see references below). Compound adverbs are discussed briefly in paragraph 28b(ii).

Note 1) In any German compound, the last component plays the leading role. That is to say, it is the final part of the word that decides the gender (if a noun), takes endings and makes stem changes (if any).

2) The examples in paragraphs (ii) and (iii) below show some of the qualities of German compounds.

• The English equivalents sometimes use two words, sometimes one, perhaps with a hyphen. German compounds are written as one word, normally without a hyphen [but ➤(iii) below]. This can produce some very long words, but this is only really noticeable in writing.
• English often uses words of Latin or Greek origin (for example, 'anemometer, pugnacious, anemic') where German uses easily comprehensible combinations of everyday words.
• Especially with adjectives and adverbs, English often has to use a phrase to render the meaning of a German compound word.

➤ *for-* + get ➜ forget: verbs formed with fixed prefixes ➤16e(i).
get *up*: verbs linked to particles ➤16e(ii).
mis- + govern + *-ment* ➜ misgovernment: nouns formed with prefixes and suffixes ➤19g(iii) and (iv).
un- + read + *-able* ➜ unreadable: adjectives formed with prefixes and suffixes ➤24f(i) and (ii).

(i) *Nouns*

Compound nouns [➤19a] can be formed with any other part of speech, but noun + noun is the most common combination. After nouns ending in **-e** (and a few others) there may be a linking **-n-**; after some other nouns (e.g. feminine nouns ending in **-heit, -keit, -schaft** or **-ung**) a linking **-s-** is used.

Noun + noun

die Presse + die Karte	➜ **die Pressekarte**	press card
die Kasse + -n- +		
das Buch	➜ **das Kassenbuch**	cashbook
die Rettung + -s- +		
das Floß	➜ **das Rettungsfloß**	life-raft
der Wind + der Messer	➜ **der Windmesser**	anemometer
		(wind-speed meter)

Verb stem + noun

schreib- + der Tisch	➜ **der Schreibtisch**	(writing) desk

Adjective + noun

schnell + der Zug	➜ **der Schnellzug**	express (train)

Adverb + noun

sofort + die Hilfe	➜ **die Soforthilfe**	emergency aid

Preposition + noun

für + die Sorge	➜ **die Fürsorge**	care, welfare

Exclamation + noun

Pfui! + der Ruf	➜ **der Pfuiruf**	boo

(ii) *Adjectives*

Many compound adjectives come from the corresponding noun. In other cases the compound gives an adjective a particular slant which may be translated by a single English word but which is often best rendered by a phrase.

Noun + adjective

das Wasser + dicht	➜ **wasserdicht**	water-tight

der Streit + lustig	**→ streitlustig**	pugnacious, looking for a quarrel
das Blut + arm	**→ blutarm**	anemic
die Kreide + weiß	**→ kreideweiß**	white as chalk

Verb stem + adjective

lern- + begierig	**→ lernbegierig**	eager to learn
stink- + langweilig	**→ stinklangweilig**	deadly boring *(colloquial)*

Adjective + adjective

schwarz + weiß	**→ schwarzweiß**	black-and-white

Adverb + adjective

hoch + interessant	**→ hochinteressant**	most interesting
früh + reif	**→ frühreif**	precocious

Preposition + adjective

ohne + gleich + -en	**→ ohnegleichen**	unparalleled, like nothing else

(iii)   Hyphens

Hyphens have various functions in German. The precise rules are often complex and not at all important for learners. In general, hyphens are used:

(A) between syllables when a word has to be split across two lines in a piece of running text. (In the examples given below a vertical bar | is used to show the split, as these words would not normally have a hyphen.)

• Compounds are split at the join so that the new line starts with the second (or later) part.

Geschäfts|leute	business people
Miet|vertrag	lease
Mikro|wellen|ofen	microwave oven

• With simple words, including those with suffixes, the basic principle is that the new line begins with just one consonant or with the second of two separate vowels. **ck** splits into **k-k**. The diphthongs **ai, au, äu, ei** and **eu** are not split, nor are **ch, sch, ß** or **st**.

Öff|nung	opening	**Bäu|me**	trees
Bäcke|rei	bakery	**ber|sten**	burst
Ver|schie|de|nes	various things	**spre|chen**	speak
bö|ig	gusty	**wa|schen**	wash
freu|dig	joyful	**grü|ßen**	greet
lec|ker (→ lek-ker)	tasty	**küs|sen**	kiss
Fen|ster	window		

(B) to break up a compound which contains, for example, the name of a person or organization, an abbreviation, a figure or a prepositional phrase.

die Mercedes-Werke	Mercedes factory
die Fritz-Thyssen-Stiftung	Fritz Thyssen Foundation
die SDP-Fraktion	SDP (Social Democrat) party
der 10-Kilometer-Lauf	10-kilometer race
das Vor-sich-hin-Starren	staring into space

(C) to avoid repeating a part which two or more compounds have in common.

An- und Verkauf von Silber- und Goldwaren!	Silver and gold objects bought and sold!
Das ganze Hin- und Herlaufen hatte mich total erschöpft.	All that running backwards and forwards had completely exhausted me.

3c   Side by side: words in apposition

Sometimes we use one noun phrase immediately after another to give further information about it. This explanatory phrase is said to be in apposition. In German, the second phrase is separated from the first by a comma. It is normally in the same case as the first phrase.

Hans Wollmer, *der Präsident der Studentenvereinigung*, ist ein Freund von Dr. Bäumler, *dem Seminarleiter*.	Hans Vollmer, *the president of the student union*, is a friend of Dr.Bäumler, *the leader of the seminar*.

Note   1) This also applies to phrases introduced by **wie** 'as' or **als** 'than, as'. In this example, note how the change of case '**ich/mich**' affects the meaning.

Er kennt ihn viel besser als *ich/* als *mich*.	He knows him much better than *I do/*than *he knows me*.

2) With place names German often uses this construction where English has 'of'.

Ich bin auf der Insel Sylt geboren und in der Stadt Cuxhaven zur Schule gegangen. Jetzt studiere ich an der Universität Tübingen.	I was born on the island of Sylt and went to school in the town of Cuxhaven. Now I am studying at the University of Tübingen.

3d   Quantities, measurements and prices

(i)   Case usage

The use of case with measurement phrases varies greatly but depends mainly on how exact the measure is. [Plural forms: ➤(ii) below.]

(A) Container/standard measure (+ adjective) + noun: the whole phrase is in the same case.

In der Kohlenindustrie bleiben viele *Tonnen hochwertige Kohle* unverkauft.	In the coal industry many *tons of high-grade coal* remain unsold.

(B) Indefinite quantity (+ adjective) + noun: the quantity is followed by **von** plus the dative or, especially in writing, by a phrase in the genitive. If there is no adjective, then **von** can be left out; the whole phrase is then in the same case.

Eine *Anzahl unrentabler Bergwerke/von unrentablen Bergwerken* müssen mit der Stillegung rechnen. *Eine ganze Menge Bergleute* würden dann ihren job vertieren.	A *number of unprofitable pits* face closure. *A great many miners* would then lose their jobs.

(C) Nouns of number (**das Dutzend/Hundert/Tausend** and **die Million/Milliarde**) [➤30a(ii)] follow the usage of:

• (A) above if they are preceded by a number.

In unserer Region haben *zwei Millionen junge Leute* keine Arbeit.	In our region *two million young people* are out of work.

• (B) above in the plural without a number.

In manchen Städten gibt es *Tausende von jungen Arbeitslosen.*	In many towns there are *thousands of young unemployed.*

(ii)   Plural measures

Masculine and neuter nouns of number, measurement or value do not use their plural forms when they follow a number or another expression of quantity. **Die Mark** does not change either, but other feminine nouns of measurement do use their plural forms.

Sieben Glas Bier, vier Flaschen Wein und zwei Dutzend Bratwürste bitte! Bei 40 Grad Kälte braucht man mehrere Paar Handschuhe. Orangen - zehn Stück für drei Mark!	Seven glasses of beer, four bottles of wine and two dozen grilled sausages please! At 40 degrees of frost you need several pairs of gloves. Oranges - ten (pieces) for three marks!

B
PUTTING A SENTENCE TOGETHER: SYNTAX

Recognizing sentences

4a   What is a sentence?

A sentence is a spoken or written utterance which has a *subject* and a *predicate*. When talking, we often say things which are not sentences, for example, exclamations or isolated phrases which make perfect sense because we know the context. In writing, however, we usually use complete sentences. The way a sentence is put together is known as its *syntax*.

4b   The subject of a sentence

(i)   Generally speaking, the subject is the word or phrase whose action or state the sentence is describing. In other words, it answers the question **Wer/Was ist ...?** 'Who/What is ...?' or **Wer/Was macht ...?** Who/What is ... doing?.

Die meisten deutschen Familien besitzen ein Auto.	*Most German families* own a car.

➤   *It* is obvious that you'll get wet. *It*'s raining: impersonal subjects ➤25e.

(ii)   Sometimes the verb is in the passive [➤ch.15]. This means that, instead of doing the action, the subject is at the receiving end.

***Viele Leute* werden jeden Monat in Autounfällen verletzt.**	*Many people* are injured each month in car accidents.

(iii)   In commands the assumed subject is 'you'. In German the familiar forms **du** and its plural **ihr** are usually omitted, but the more formal **Sie** is always retained [➤13b].

Passen *Sie*/Paßt auf, wenn *Sie/ihr* am Steuer sitzen/sitzt!	Pay attention when you are sitting at the wheel.

4c   *The predicate of a sentence*

The predicate consists of the whole of the rest of the sentence, apart from the subject. Its essential element is the main verb, that is, a verb in one of the simple tenses [➤11b]. This verb agrees with the subject, that is, its form changes to match the subject. Chapter 7 describes the various types of verb and what they do.

Ihr Taxi *wartet*. Ihre Eltern *warten*.	Your taxi *is waiting*. Your parents *are waiting*.

Most predicates consist of more than this minimum. For example, they may contain adverbial expressions[1] [➤ch.28], objects of the verb[2] [➤8d] or non-finite verbs[3] [➤ch.10].

Das Taxi mußte *lange*[1] *auf Sie*[2] *warten*[3].	The taxi had to *wait*[3] *a long time*[1] *for you*[2].

4d   *Sentences and clauses*

There are three types of complete sentence:

• statements, which are the basic form;
• direct questions [➤ch.6];
• commands [➤ch.13].

All three must have a main clause. They may also have any number of subordinate clauses.

(i)   *Main clauses*

A main clause is a sentence which can stand by itself, though it may not make much sense unless you know what the speaker is talking about. [➤5a(i) for more examples.]

***Es hat lange auf Sie gewartet.* – Was? – Ihr Taxi!**	*It waited ages for you.* – What? – Your taxi!

(ii)   *Subordinate clauses*

A subordinate clause is always dependent on another clause, whose meaning it completes or expands. It is linked to the main clause by one of three types of word:

• a subordinating conjunction [➤5a(ii), 5c(ii)];

• a question word [➤5b];
• a relative pronoun [➤5d].

In the following example the subordinate clauses are in italics. [For further examples ➤paragraphs referred to above].

Ich konnte nicht länger bleiben, da mein Taxi schon auf mich wartete. Nachdem ich mich von allen verabschiedet hatte, verließ ich das Haus.	I could not stay any longer, *as my taxi was already waiting for me. After I had said goodbye to everybody*, I left the house.

Note   Because the finite verb is sent to the end of subordinate clauses [➤4e(iv)], they tend to be clumsier than in English and French. Germans will therefore often avoid them by using two main clauses containing suitable adverbs. [Avoiding relative clauses: ➤25j(viii).]

Mein Taxi wartete schon auf mich, *also* konnte ich nicht länger bleiben. Ich verabschiedete mich von allen, *dann* verließ ich das Haus.	My taxi was already waiting for me, *so* I could not stay any longer. I said goodbye to everybody, *then* I left the house.

4e   *The order of words and phrases: syntax*

German syntax is a flexible system in which some elements are fixed and others movable. The main clause of any German statement consists of three *blocks* of information. (The German names are given here in case you come across them.)

• The *'opening block'* (**das Vorfeld**) contains just one item of information – this may be a single word, a phrase or a subordinate clause.
• The *'central block'* (**das Mittelfeld**) contains most of the information and always starts with the main verb. Hence the often quoted rule 'main verb second'.
• The *'final block'* (**das Nachfeld**) contains elements that complete the meaning of the main verb – verbal particles, or the infinitive or past participle of other verbs.

Opening block	*Central block*	*Final block*
Mein Sohn	*schläft* immer wie ein Bär.	
Wenn er Ferien hat,	*steht* er morgens selten vor elf Uhr	auf.
Dann	*will* er immer gleich	frühstücken.

Paragraphs (i) to (iii) below look at main clause statements in greater detail. Paragraph (iv) deals with the differences in subordinate clauses. Paragraph (v) lists things which may come before the opening block or after the final block.

Note 1) Questions have the same word order as statements except that they start either with the main verb (Yes/No questions [➤6b]) or with a question word [➤6d].

2) Commands have the same word order as statements except that they start with the main verb [➤ch.13].

(i)   The opening block in main clauses

The opening block does not usually convey the main point of the statement. It often picks up and perhaps emphasizes something already mentioned or assumed to be known. The block may contain:

(A) the subject [➤4b]. This is naturally very common but, unlike in English or French, the subject has no more right to this position than any other element.

Ich	**habe 1981 einen Feinmechanikbetrieb**	**gegründet.**

In 1981 *I* founded a precision engineering firm.

(B) an adverb or adverbial phrase [➤28a]. Time phrases and short unemphatic adverbs like **da** or **also** often start the sentence, but almost any adverbial may do so, especially if it refers back in some way.

Damals	**hatten wir immer noch Hochkonjunktur.**	
In unserem Städtchen	**herrschte Mangel an Arbeitskräften.**	

In those days we were still in a boom.
In our small town there was a shortage of labo(u)r.

(C) a subordinate clause [➤4d(ii)]. These usually answer the same questions as adverbs.

Weil alles gut ging,	**habe ich eine erfahrene Betriebsleitererin**	**angestellt.**

Because it was all going well, I appointed an experienced plant manager.

(D) an object of the verb. This could be direct (accusative) [➤8d(i)], indirect (dative) [➤8d(ii), 8e] or prepositional [➤8g]. [A genitive object would also be possible, but ➤8d(iii)].

| *Ihr* | **vertraute ich die tägliche Organisation** | **an.** |
| *Auf sie* | **konnte ich mich ohne Bedenken** | **verlassen.** |

I entrusted the day-to-day organization *to her*. I could rely *on her* without hesitation.

(E) an infinitive or past participle [➤10a, 10b(iii)].

| *Bereut* | **habe ich es nie.** | |

I have never *regretted* it.

(F) a participle clause [➤10b(v)]. Apart from set phrases, this is uncommon in colloquial German.

| *Von ihr geleitet,* | **lief alles wie geölt.** | |

Managed by her, everything ran like clockwork.

(ii)   The central block in main clauses

The central block contains the main information of the statement, starting with the main verb. In general, information is given in increasing order of importance, so that elements which:

• give new information
• are emphasized or longer
• are closely linked to the verb

tend to come later than other elements.
This produces the following normal order after the verb, but remember that a particular emphasis or linking together of ideas may well change the order.

(A) Personal pronouns, if any, in the order subject – direct object – indirect object.

| Schließlich | **habe *ich es ihr* fast völlig** | **überlassen.** |

In the end *I* left *it* almost entirely *to her*.

(B) Other subjects (nouns or other pronouns such as **das, etwas, niemand**). If neither the subject nor the direct object

shows the case, then the subject must come before even pronoun objects.

| Ab 1989 | hat uns *die Rezession* immer mehr | geschadet. |

From 1989 on *the recession* affected us more and more.

(C) Indirect (dative) noun objects.

| Ich | habe *dem Personal* die Situation | erklärt. |

I explained the situation *to the staff*.

(D) Most adverbial expressions (but see F, G and H below), in
the order:

• Short adverbs expressing the speaker's attitude [➤29c(iii)];
• Time (**Wann?**);
• Reason and cause (**Warum?**);
• Place (**Wo?**).

(In the following example the * sign shows where each adverbial starts.)

| Wir | hatten *zwar *zu der Zeit *aus verschiedenen Gründen *in der Region wenig Konkurrenz. | |

For various reasons we had *at that time admittedly* little competition *in the region*.

(E) Direct (accusative) noun objects.

| Trotzdem | mußten wir von Zeit zu Zeit *Arbeiter* | entlassen. |

All the same we had to lay off *workers* from time to time.

(F) Negatives which refer to the whole statement. If **nicht** refers
only to one specific element, then it goes before that element.

| Die Firma | konnte bei sinkender Nachfrage ihren Lohn *nicht* (mehr) | zahlen. |

With the declining demand the firm could *not* (no longer) pay their wages.

(G) Adverbials of manner (**Wie?**).

Das	haben wir immer *sehr ungern*	gemacht.

We always did it *very unwillingly.*

(H) Complements of linking verbs [➤8c] and prepositional phrases which are closely linked to the verb. The latter include prepositional objects [➤8g] and phrases answering the questions **Wo?** 'Where?' after verbs of position and **Wohin?** 'Where to?' after verbs of motion.

Wir	haben das Arbeitsamt umsonst *um Hilfe*	gebeten.
Es	wurden immer mehr Leute *arbeitslos.*	
Man	sah sie Tag für Tag *vor dem Arbeitsamt*	stehen.

We asked the employment office in vain *for help.* More and more people were becoming *unemployed.* You could see them standing day after day *in front of the employment office.*

(iii)   The final block in main clauses

The final block contains elements which are directly linked to the main verb, whose meaning they complete. These are:

• verbal particles;
• past participles;
• infinitives.

The more complex the verb construction is, the more elements there are in the final block. If we start with a simple sentence and make it more complex in various ways, both the process and the order of elements become clear.

(A) Sentence with full verb in a simple tense (here the present). Final block empty.

Mein Partner	*kommt* heute mit dem Schnellzug aus Berlin.	

My partner *is coming* today on the fast train from Berlin.

(B) Verbal particle **an** added in final block. Also relevant to: all other verbal particles [➤16e(ii)].

Mein Partner	*kommt* bald mit dem Schnellzug aus Berlin	*an.*

My partner *is arriving* soon on the fast train from Berlin.

> **(C)** Modal auxiliary **soll** introduced. Infinitive **kommen** moved to end. Also relevant to: other modal verbs [➤ch.9]; compound future with auxiliary **werden** [➤12c].

Mein Partner	*soll* bald mit dem Schnellzug aus Berlin	*ankommen.*

My partner *is due to arrive* soon on the fast train from Berlin.

> **(D)** Perfect tense with auxiliary **ist**. Past participle **gekommen** moved to end. Also relevant to: all perfect tenses with auxiliaries **haben** or **sein** [➤17c]; passive with auxiliary **werden** [➤ch.15].

Mein Partner	*ist* gerade mit dem Schnellzug aus Berlin	*angekommen.*

My partner *has* just *arrived* on the fast train from Berlin.

> **(E)** Past conditional of modal auxiliary **können**. Infinitive-past participle **können** moved to end. Also relevant to: all perfect tenses of modal verbs [➤9b(i)].

Mit dem IC-Zug	*hätte* er früher	ankommen können

He *could have* arrived earlier on the InterCity train.

> **(F)** Future perfect with auxiliary **wird** [➤12c]. Auxiliary infinitive **sein** moved to end. Also relevant to: modal verbs with perfect infinitives [➤9c(ii), (iv) and (v)].

Bis vier Uhr	*wird* er wohl trotzdem	angekommen *sein*.

All the same, he *will* no doubt *have* arrived by four o'clock.

(iv) *Word order in subordinate clauses*

Subordinate clause word order differs from main clauses in two important ways:

(A) The finite verb is moved from second position to the end of the final block. This is in effect simply an extension of the verb movements shown in paragraph (iii) above. [Position of **hätte** in second example below: ▶9b(iii)].

(B) The subject normally comes immediately after the conjunction. As in main clauses, a pronoun object (especially **sich**) may come before a noun subject. [Relative clauses: ▶5b].
The following examples, adapted from examples (iii) A, E and F above, show these changes in action.

Main clauses	Subordinate (centre)	Subordinate (final)
Ich hoffe,	*daß* mein Partner heute zu uns	*kommt.*
Ich glaube nicht,	*daß* er mit dem IC-Zug	*hätte* kommen können.
Ich weiß nicht,	*ob* er bis vier Uhr	angekommen sein *wird.*

I hope *that* my partner *comes* to see us today.
I do not think *that* he *could have* come by InterCity train.
I don't know *whether* he *will* have arrived by four o'clock.

(v) *Outside the blocks*

(A) The folowing elements may come before the opening block without affecting the word order. They are separated off by a comma:

• the name of the person being spoken to;
• interjections [▶26b], including **ja, nein** and their equivalents;
• clauses starting with 'whoever', 'however', 'whenever' etc. [▶5a(ii)F];
• certain words and phrases put in as an aside, for example:

Das heißt (d.h.), ...	That is (i.e.), ...
Im Gegenteil, ...	On the contrary, ...
Kurz, ...	In short, ...
Nun/Na, ...	Well, ...
Offen gestanden, ...	To be frank, ...
So, ...	Well now/Right, ...
Sehen Sie/Siehst du, ...	Well, you see, ...
Wie gesagt, ...	As I said, ...
Wissen Sie/Weißt du, ...	You know, ...

(B) The following elements normally go after the final block:

• subordinate clauses, including relative clauses if possible, separated off by a comma. (Subordinate clauses may of course also fill the opening block.)
• **zu** + infinitive clauses;
• (usually) comparative phrases after **als** and **wie;**
• over-long phrases, and afterthoughts. The latter are naturally common in speech and in informal writing.

Wir haben gestern Siegfried gesehen, *der von Dir gesprochen hat.* **Er ist noch dicker geworden** *als sein Bruder.* **Wir haben vor, Dich bald zu besuchen,** *vielleicht nach Ostern.*	We saw Siegfried yesterday, *who spoke of you.* He has grown even fatter *than his brother.* We plan to visit you soon, *perhaps after Easter.*

Linking clauses together

5a   Clauses with conjunctions

'Conjunction' means 'joining'. There are two sorts of conjunction: 'coordinating' and 'subordinating'. Their names reflect their function in the sentence.

(i)   Joining equals: coordinating conjunctions

Coordinating conjunctions link clauses of equal status: main with main [➤4d(i)], subordinate with subordinate [➤4d(ii)]. They tell us something about how the clauses relate to each other (reinforcing, contrasting, etc.), but they do not affect the word order of the following clause. Almost all of them can also link words, phrases and parts of clauses.

(A) und 'and'.
Alternatives which link phrases but not clauses are **sowie** and **sowohl ... als/wie (auch) ...** 'both ... and ...'. These are more used in writing – in speech 'both X and Y' is normally rendered as **X und auch Y**.

Mein Geschäft wächst, *und* ich brauche dringend ein Darlehen.	My business is growing, *and* I urgently need a loan.

(B) oder 'or', **Entweder ... oder ...** 'either ... or ...', **beziehungsweise** 'or alternatively'/'... respectively'.
oder cannot be used for English 'not ... or ...' [➤(C) below].

***Entweder* die Bank leiht mir das Geld, *oder* ich kann nicht expandieren. Ich brauche eine halbe Million sofort, *bzw.* 1,5 Millionen über vier Jahre.**	*Either* the bank lends me the money, *or* I can't expand. I need half a million immediately, *or alternatively,* 1.5 million over four years.

(C) weder ... noch ... 'neither ... nor ...'
Note that **weder** does not usually start its clause, but comes after the verb. **noch** starts the second clause, but the verb comes immediately after it. In speech **und auch nicht/kein ...** is a common alternative; this is also used for 'not ... or ...' and for 'nor' without a preceding 'neither'.

| Ich habe *weder* selber das Geld, *noch* kenne ich jemand, der es mir leihen will. | I *neither* have the money myself, *nor* do I know anyone who will lend it to me. |

(D) aber, allein, jedoch 'but, however'.
Of these **aber** is by far the most common. The others are mainly literary alternatives. Unlike English 'but', **aber** and **jedoch** can be used not just at the start of a sentence or clause but also within it.

| Mein Onkel ist reich, *aber* ich kann ihn nicht darum bitten. Er ist zwar Millionär, will *aber/ jedoch* sein Geld nicht riskieren. | My uncle is rich, *but* I can't ask him for it. He may be a millionaire, *but* he doesn't want to risk his money. |

(E) nicht (nur) ... sondern (auch) ... 'not (only) ... but (also) ...'
sondern, not **aber**, must always be used when 'but' contrasts with an earlier 'not'. Thus **sie ist nicht groß**, *aber* **stark** means 'she is not big *but (she is)* strong'.

| Er ist *nicht nur* alt, *sondern auch* sehr vorsichtig. | He is *not only* old *but also* very cautious. |

(F) denn 'for, as, because'.
Now little used in speech. A useful alternative is to use the adverb **nämlich** 'you see' after the verb in the second main clause.

| Er vertraut mir nicht, *denn* er erinnert sich noch an meine Jugend! | He doesn't trust me, *for* he still remembers my youth! |
| Er vertraut mir nicht, er erinnert sich *nämlich* noch an meine Jugend! | He doesn't trust me – *you see*, he still remembers my youth! |

(ii) *Clauses dependent on other clauses: subordinating conjunctions*

Subordinating conjunctions link subordinate clauses [➤4d(ii)] to the rest of the sentence. Remember that the finite verb goes at the end. Usually these subordinate clauses are adverbial expressions [➤ch.28], and many of them answer one of the questions listed in paragraphs 6d(v) to (ix). Only the more common conjunctions are listed here.

(A) daß 'that'.
This is a pure linking word, with no meaning of its own. It is common after verbs of speech, thought, etc. [e.g. in reported speech, ➤14c(ii)]; here it is often left out, in which case the following clause has main clause word order. Do not use **daß** for other English uses of 'that', especially as in 'the person/thing *that* I saw' [➤25j] or *'that's* wrong' [➤25g].

Ich glaube wirklich, *daß* der Fritz mich meidet. (Ich glaube, der Fritz meidet mich.)	I really believe *(that)* Fritz is avoiding me.

(B) Time.

als	when	**sobald**	as soon as
bevor	before	**solange**	so long as
bis	until	**während**	while
nachdem	after	**wenn**	when(ever)
seit(dem)	since	**wie**	as

Note 1) **als** 'when' is used only for single events in the past. In all other cases use **wenn**.

2) **sobald** and **solange** are spelled as one word and are not followed by **wie**.

Wenn er mich sieht, haut er ab. *Als* ich neulich Einkäufe machte, bin ich ihm begegnet. *Sobald* er mich gesehen hat, ist er weggerannt!	*When(ever)* he sees me he clears off. Recently *when* I was doing some shopping I ran into him. *As soon as* he caught sight of me he ran off!

(C) Reasons and causes.

da	as, since	**weil**	because
nun da	now that, seeing that	**zumal**	especially as

Da ich ihn dringend sprechen wollte, bin ich ihm nachgelaufen, habe ihn aber aus den Augen verloren, *weil* er mir zu schnell war.	*As* I urgently wanted to speak to him I ran after him, but I lost sight of him *because* he was too quick for me.

(D) Purpose and result.
Be careful to distinguish the two meanings of the English 'so that', as shown in the examples.

damit	so that, in order that	**so daß**	so that, with the result that

> **Ich habe Tempo zugelegt, *damit* er mir nicht entwischen sollte. Es wurde dunkel, *so daß* ich nicht gut sehen konnte.**
>
> I got moving, *so that* he couldn't give me the slip. It was getting dark, *so that* I couldn't see well.

(E) Manner and degree.
After **als ob** the conditional is normal. In formal writing the **ob** in **als ob** may be left out; the verb then comes immediately after **als**. [**(an)statt/außer/ohne daß:** ▶27c]

als ob	as if, as though	**sofern**	provided that
dadurch daß	by ...ing	**soweit**	as, so far as
indem	by ...ing	**wie**	as, like

> **Ich habe ihn endlich eingeholt, *indem* ich mich durch den Verkehr schlängelte. Er tat, *als ob* er froh wäre, /*als* wäre er froh, mich zu sehen.**
>
> I finally caught up with him *by* dodg*ing* through the traffic. He pretended to be (made *as though* he was) glad to see me.

(F) Conditions and concessions
falls is sometimes used for 'if' where **wenn** could mean 'when(ever)' [▶(B) above]. **trotzdem** is not strictly correct here, but it is increasingly used.

es sei denn, (daß)	unless	**obwohl**	although
falls	if	**trotzdem**	even though
		wenn	if [▶14d]

> **Obwohl ich ziemlich böse war, habe ich nichts gesagt. Wenn ich nur wüßte, was mit ihm los ist – *es sei denn*, er schuldet meinem Vater Geld!**
>
> *Although* I was pretty annoyed I said nothing. *If* only I knew what was the matter with him – *unless* he owes my father money!

Note   Any of the question words **wer, wie, wo** etc. [➤6d] can be used with
auch (immer) to mean 'who*ever*', 'how*ever*', 'wher*ever*', etc. 'How*ever*'
+ adjective or adverb is **so … auch**. Notice that these clauses do not
usually affect the word order in the following sentence.

Was er *auch immer* gemacht hat, er braucht mir nicht aus dem Weg zu gehen. *So* seltsam er *auch* sein mag/ist, ich mag ihn gern.	*Whatever* he has done, he doesn't have to avoid me. *However* strange he may be, I like him.

5b   *Relative clauses*

Relative clauses are introduced by relative pronouns [➤25j for
fuller treatment]. They describe or define a noun and thus do
much the same job as an adjective [➤ch.24]. The relative
clause comes very soon (usually immediately) after the noun
it refers to. For this reason the noun is known as the
antecedent. [Avoiding relative clauses: ➤25j(viii).]

Es gibt ebensoviel Leute, *die* das Unglaubliche glauben, wie Leute, *die* das Unzweifelhafte bezweifeln.	There are just as many people *who* believe the incredible as people *who* doubt the indubitable.
Mein Vetter Alfons, *der* Philosoph ist, hat einen Goldfisch gekauft, *der* nicht schwimmen kann. Zum Glück hat er ein Goldfischglas, *das* sehr flach ist.	My cousin Alfons, *who* is a philosopher, has bought a goldfish *which* can't swim. Fortunately, he has a goldfish bowl *which* is very shallow.

 'The firm (*that*) I work *for* makes bottles': German cannot leave out
the relative pronoun or place a preposition at the end of the relative
clause in this way [➤25j(i)].

5c   *Indirect speech*

There are two ways of reporting what people have said (or perhaps thought). Both are introduced by verbs like **sagen** 'say',
antworten 'answer', **fragen** 'ask', **denken/glauben** 'think'.

(i)   *Repetition of direct speech*

The first way is simply to repeat what was said or thought, the *direct speech*. In writing we would then use quotation marks.

„Ich gehe um halb zehn zu einer Konferenz," sagte er.	"I am going to a meeting at half past nine," he said.
Ich dachte: „Sie werden zu spät kommen."	I thought, "You'll be late."
Ich fragte ihn: „Wie weit ist es?"	I asked him: "How far is it?"

(ii)   Indirect speech

The second way is known as *indirect speech* or *reported speech*. You rephrase what was said in a clause, which may start with the conjunction **daß** 'that' [➤5a] or a question-word [➤5d]. [Omission of **daß**: ➤5a(ii).]

Er sagte, er gehe um halb zehn zu einer Konferenz.	He said that he was going to a meeting at half past nine.
Ich dachte, *daß* er zu spät kommen würde.	I thought that he would be late.
Ich fragte ihn, *wie* weit es wäre.	I asked him how far it was.

(iii)   The effects of using indirect speech

As you can see, direct speech is changed in several ways when it is reported in the second way:

(A) Pronouns are changed if necessary so that they still refer to the right person. If a pronoun is the subject, the main verb is changed to match it.

(B) The changes in verb tenses are dealt with in paragraph 14c(i).

(C) If the reported speech starts with **daß** or a question-word, then subordinate clause word order is used [➤4e(iv)]. Otherwise, normal main clause order applies.

5d   Indirect questions

Indirect questions are a form of indirect speech [➤5c]. They are introduced by the same types of verb, followed by the relevant question-word [➤6d]. Indirect Yes/No questions [➤6b] and tag questions [➤6c], which have no question-word, are introduced by **ob** 'whether'. Indirect questions are used for various purposes:

(i) *Reporting*

To report that a direct question [➤6a] has been or is going to be asked:

Ich fragte ihn, *ob* er beschäftigt sei/wäre.	I asked him *whether* he was busy.

(ii) *Politeness*

To ask more courteously:

Könnten Sie mir sagen, *wann* die Konferenz anfängt?	Could you tell me *when* the meeting starts?

(iii) *Answering*

To say whether we know the answer:

Ich weiß nicht, *wer* den Vorsitz führt.	I don't know *who* is chairing it.

5e *Indirect requests and commands [➤ch.13]*

These are usually reported using **sollte(n)** + the infinitive [➤8h(ii)]. **müßte(n)/dürfte(n)** indicate a more forceful command.

Der Chef sagte mir, ich *sollte* die Tagesordnung vorbereiten. Ich *dürfte* auf keinen Fall den Kaffee wieder vergessen.	The boss told me I *should* prepare the agenda. On no account *was* I to forget the coffee again.

Asking for information: direct questions

6a What is a direct question?

A *direct question* is a form of direct speech. It tells us word for word what the person said or thought. The questions in the examples below are all direct questions – these are the actual words used, expecting a direct answer. But we often also talk about questions which have been or are going to be asked. These are indirect questions [➤5d].

6b True or false: Yes/No questions

In this type of question we are asking whether something is true or not, so it is always possible to answer 'Yes' or 'No'. A German Yes/No question normally starts with the main verb, followed immediately by the subject.

Fahren Sie in die Stadt? – Ja.	Are you going into town? – Yes.
Können Sie mich mitnehmen? – Nein!	Can you give me a lift? – No!

6c Checking up: tag questions

Tag questions are statements with a questioning 'tag' added to the end which asks for confirmation of the statement. English uses an enormous number of tags. German has one standard tag, **nicht wahr?** 'not true?'. Particularly in speech, people often just say **nicht?** or use some colloquial expression like the South German **gelt?**

Sie haben einen Viersitzer, *nicht wahr?* – Ja.	Your car is a four-seater, *isn't it?* – Yes.

6d Asking for details: question-word questions

We use these questions when we want to find out more about something we already know. They always start with a question-word such as those listed below and then continue like a

Yes/No question. As you can see, German question-words always begin with the letter **w**.

 Many of these question-words are the same as or closely related to relative pronouns [➤25j] or conjunctions [➤5a]. Do not confuse them!

➤ The questions in paragraphs 6d(i) to 6d(iv) are answered by a noun phrase [➤19b].

(i) *People:* ***Wer? Wen? Wem? Wessen?*** *'Who(m)? Whose?'*

***Wer** fährt mit Ihnen? – Niemand.* ***Wessen** Gepäck ist denn das? –* **Meins.**	*Who* is going with you? – Nobody. *Whose* luggage is that then? – Mine.

(ii) *Things:* ***Was?*** *'What'?*

***Was** wollen Sie in der Stadt* **machen? – Nichts Besonderes.**	*What* are you going to do in town? – Nothing much.

(iii) *Selection:* ***Welcher? Welche? Welches?*** *'Which ...? (What ...?)'*

***Welche** Straße nehmen Sie? –* **Die Autobahn.**	*Which* road are you taking? – The highway/motorway.

(iv) *Definition:* ***Was für (ein) ...?*** *'What sort of ...?'*

***Was für einen** Wagen haben* **Sie? – Einen sehr alten!**	*What kind of* car do you have? – A very old one!

➤ The questions in paragraphs 6d(v) to 6d(ix) are answered by adverbial expressions [➤ch.28].

(v) *Time:* ***Wann?*** *'When?'*

***Wann** fahren Sie los? – In einer* **halben Stunde.**	*When* are you leaving? – In half an hour.

(vi) Place: **Wo? Wohin? Woher?** *'Where? Where to? Where from?'*

Wo haben Sie Ihren Wagen stehen? – Das weiß ich nicht mehr.	*Where* have you left your car? – I've forgotten.

(vii) Manner (methods and means): **Wie?** *'How?'*

Wie wollen Sie ihn denn finden? – Ich werde es schon schaffen.	*How* are you going to find it then? – I'll manage.

(viii) Quantity, quality and degree: **Wieviel? Wie ...?** *'How much? How many? How ...?'*

Wieviel Gepäck haben Sie denn? – Sehr wenig. – *Wie* groß ist Ihr Wagen? – Ziemlich groß.	*How much* luggage do you have then? – Very little. – *How* big is your car? – Fairly big.

(ix) Reasons: **Warum?** *'Why?'*

Warum können Sie mich denn nicht mitnehmen? – Sie wiegen ja eine Tonne ... es ist ja ein sehr alter Wagen!	*Why* can't you take me then? – You weigh a ton ... it is a very old car after all!

C
ACTIONS AND STATES: VERBS AND THEIR USES

What verbs do

7a   Full verbs

The very great majority of verbs tell us about the actions, state of mind or situation of the subject of the sentence. These we call *full* verbs.

Dieses Jahr *fahren* wir mit meinen Eltern in Urlaub. Sie *wohnen* weit von uns, und wir *sehen* uns nicht oft.	This year we *are going* on vacation with my parents. They *live* a long way from us and we *don*'t *see* each other often.

7b   Auxiliary verbs

A much smaller group of verbs is used in combination with full verbs. For example, they may make a compound tense or give a certain slant to an action. These are called *auxiliary* (i.e. helping) verbs. Note that most German auxiliaries also have a full meaning.

The main auxiliary verbs are:

(A) haben, **sein**.
These form the compound past tenses [➤17c].

(B) werden.
This forms the compound future [➤12c] and the passive [➤ch.15].

(C) dürfen, können, mögen, müssen, sollen, wollen.
These are the modal verbs, which show the subject's attitude to an action [➤ch.9].

(D) lassen.
This means 'to have something done' [➤9c(vii)].

Ich *habe* eine Pauschalreise nach Thailand gebucht. Meine Eltern *werden* zuerst zu uns kommen. Wir *sind* nie in Thailand gewesen. Wir *wollten* letztes Jahr dorthin gehen, aber wir *konnten* keinen Flug finden.	I *have* booked a package vacation to Thailand. My parents *will* come to our house first. We *have* never been to Thailand. *We wanted* to go there last year, but we *could* not get a flight.

What verbs govern: their role in the sentence

8a What does a verb govern?

A sentence can contain many items of information besides that given by the subject and main verb. Some of these are optional extras, but others depend directly on the main verb and cannot be removed without leaving the sentence incomplete. These are said to be 'governed' by the verb.

Note   The groupings used in the following paragraphs are not the only possible ones, but differences of classification really do not matter. What is important is to know how a particular verb functions in a particular context.

8b Self–sufficient verbs

Any verb which does not govern a direct (accusative) object is *intransitive* [➤8d(i)]. Some of these verbs do not take any object at all.

Wir *schliefen* **(immer noch) (fest), als meine Eltern (mit dem Taxi)** *angekommen sind.*	We *were* (still) *sleeping* (soundly) when my parents *arrived* (by taxi).

8c Verbs linking equals: the complement

A small number of verbs simply act as a link between the subject and another word or phrase, which is called the *complement* of the verb. Because it refers to the same person or thing as the subject, the complement is always in the nominative case [➤22c].

Meine Eltern *sind* **beide ausgezeichnete Musiker. Mein Vater ist Amateur** *geblieben,* **aber meine Mutter ist Konzertpianistin** *geworden.*	Both my parents *are* excellent musicians. My father has *remained* an enthusiastic amateur, but my mother has *become* a concert pianist.

8d   *Verbs with one object*

A very large number of verbs normally govern a noun phrase [➤19b] which is affected by the action of the verb. This noun phrase is the object of the verb. In German it may be in one of three cases.

(i)   *Verbs with an object in the accusative [➤22d]*

These verbs are *transitive*, and the noun phrase is the direct object. Any verb which does not govern a direct object is *intransitive*.

Ich *höre* gern Musik, aber ich *spiele* kein Instrument. Statt dessen *besitze* ich einen Computer.	I like *listening* to music but I *don't play* any instrument. I *own* a computer instead.

Note   German cannot use the same verb both transitively and intransitively as easily as English can. Very often, some other construction is used to distinguish between the two usages:

(A) When the English intransitive is really an action done to the subject, German is likely to use the transitive verb with a reflexive pronoun as its object [➤8f].

In aller Eile haben wir *uns gewaschen* und angezogen.	We *washed* and *dressed* very hurriedly.

(B) Sometimes two different verbs are used, which may well be related to each other.

Die Kinder waren schon um halb sieben *aufgewacht,* aber sie hatten uns nicht *geweckt.*	The children had *woken* up at half past six, but they had not *woken* us.

Other examples of similar pairs are:

Ich besteige ihn.	I climb it (a mountain).	**Ich steige.**	I climb.
Ich betrete es.	I enter it (a room).	**Ich trete ... ein.**	I enter.
Ich ertränke ihn.	I drown him.	**Er ertrinkt.**	He drowns.
Ich lege mich ... hin.	I lie down.	**Ich liege.**	I am lying (there).
Ich setze mich.	I sit down.	**Ich sitze.**	I am sitting.

Ich stelle es ...	I stand it (somewhere).	**Es steht.**	It stands.
Ich verlasse es.	I leave it (a place).	**Ich gehe weg.**	I leave (go away).
Ich versenke es.	I sink it (a ship)	**Es sinkt.**	It sinks.

(C) Sometimes **lassen** 'let' [➤9c(vii)] + an intransitive verb may express a transitive meaning.

Mein Sohn hat das Fenster aufgemacht und seine Wollmütze *fallen lassen*.	My son opened the window and *dropped* his woolly hat.

(D) Conversely, **sich lassen** 'can be done' [➤15f(v)] + a transitive verb can translate an intransitive verb in English.

Sie ist auf die Straße gefallen – das Fenster *läßt sich* wirklich zu leicht *aufmachen*.	It dropped into the road – the window really *opens* too easily.

(ii) *Verbs with an object in the dative [➤22f]*

Though smaller, this group is still large, and some very common verbs belong to it. As many of these verbs take a direct object in other languages (e.g. in French or English), it is important to learn them with an object in the dative, as shown in the following examples. Some of these examples are given in the perfect tense, to show the use of **sein**.

(A) Some common verbs.

Ich habe ihnen ... geantwortet.	I answered them.
Ich bin ihnen ... begegnet.	I met them (by chance).
Ich werde ihnen ... danken.	I shall thank them.
Ich habe ihnen ... gedient.	I served them (as a servant).
Ich habe ihnen ... gedroht.	I threatened them.
Ich bin ihnen ... gefolgt.	I followed them.
Ich gehorchte ihnen nicht.	I did not obey them.
Gilt das mir?	Does that go for me? Are you referring to me?
Das gehört mir.	That belongs to me/That's mine.
Die kleine Wohnung genügt uns nicht mehr.	This little apartment is no longer big enough for us.
Die Kinder gleichen mir.	The children resemble/are like me.
Ich habe ihnen ... gratuliert.	I congratulated them.

Ich habe ihnen ... geholfen.	I helped them.
Das paßt mir nicht.	That doesn't suit/fit me.
Was ist Ihnen passiert/geschehen?	What has happened to you?
Mein Knie tut mir weh.	My knee is hurting (me).

➤   *I was followed* by two men: dative verbs used in the passive ➤15d.

(B) Verbs with the separable particles **bei-, entgegen-, nach-** and **zu-**, and with the prefixes **ent-** meaning 'escaping' and **wider-** meaning 'opposition'.

Ich bin meinem Partner *entgegengefahren.* **Normalerweise** *steht* **er mir** *bei,* **aber diesmal hat er mir** *widersprochen.* **Er hat mir** *zugenickt* **und ist weggegangen. Ich bin ihm** *nachgelaufen* **– er sollte mir nicht** *entkommen.*	I *drove to meet* my partner. Normally he *supports* me, but this time he *contradicted* me. He *nodded to* me and left. I *ran after* him – he wasn't going to *get away from* me.

(C) A number of verbs which are often used impersonally [feelings and sensations: ➤8j].

Es ist mir ... aufgefallen/eingefallen.	It struck/occurred to me.
Was fehlt Ihnen?	What's the matter with you?
Das hat mir nicht ... gefallen.	I didn't like it (it didn't please me).
Es ist ihnen ... gelungen (etwas zu tun).	They succeeded (in doing something).
Hat's (Ihnen) geschmeckt?	Did you like it (food)?
Es tut mir sehr leid (, daß ...)	I am very sorry (that ...).

(iii)   Verbs with an object in the genitive [➤22e]

Only a few verbs take a genitive object. They are only used in elevated written style. Many of them are reflexive. The first German text shows two of them. Their more usual alternatives appear in the second text.

H. *gedachte* nie der Leiden anderer Leute. Er *bedurfte* ihres Wohlwollens nicht. H. *dachte* nie an die Leiden anderer Leute. Er *brauchte* ihr Wohlwollen nicht.	H. never *thought* of the sufferings of other people. He did not *need* their goodwill.

Genitive objects are also used in a few set phrases, though these too have a very literary ring.

Die Hitze des Brandes *spottete jeder Beschreibung,* **aber der Feuermann** *achtete nicht der Gefahr.* **Erst im letzten Augenblick** *besann er sich eines Besseren* **und zog sich etwas zurück.**	The heat of the fire *beggared description,* but the fireman *paid no heed to the danger.* Only at the last moment did he *think better of it* and draw back a little.

8e   *Verbs with two objects: direct and indirect objects*

Some transitive verbs have not only a direct object in the accusative but also an indirect object in the dative case. (For the order in which these objects come in the sentence ➤4e.) The indirect object refers to a person (or a thing) involved in some way in the action of the verb.

(i)   *Indirect objects: to whom, from whom*

Indirect objects refer to people to whom something is said, given, sent, shown, etc., or from whom it is taken.

Mein Sohn hat *meinem Mann* **ein neues Program** *gegeben.* **Er hat** *mir gesagt,* **es wäre leicht zu verstehen, aber er mußte** *ihm zeigen,* **wie es funktionierte!**	My son *gave my husband* a new program. He *told me* that it was easy to understand, but he had to *show him* how it worked!

Other examples include:

Ich beschreibe es ihnen.	I describe it to them.
Ich erkläre es ihnen.	I explain it to them.
Ich erzähle es ihnen.	I tell them about it.
Ich rate es ihnen ... ab.	I advise them against it.
Ich teile es ihnen ... mit.	I inform them of it.
Ich bringe es ihnen.	I bring it to them.
Ich bringe es ihnen ... bei.	I teach it to them.
Ich schicke es ihnen.	I send it to them.
Ich leihe es ihnen.	I lend it to them.
Ich nehme es ihnen.	I take it from them.

Note also:

Es nutzt mir nichts.	It is of no benefit to me.
Es schadet mir nichts.	It does me no harm.

Note   **bitten** 'ask, request', **fragen** 'ask, enquire' and **sprechen** 'speak to' take a direct (i.e. accusative) object.

Ich habe *ihn gefragt,* wie es funktionierte, aber er hat *mich gebeten, ihn* später darüber zu sprechen.	I *asked him* how it worked, but he *asked me* to *speak to him* about it later.

➤   *She was given* a dictionary: indirect objects with passive verbs ➤15a, 15f(ii).

(ii)   Indirect objects: for whom

Sometimes indirect objects refer to people for whom something is done.

Ich *kaufe dir* ein Bier, wenn du *mir* einen Sitzplatz *findest.*	I'll *buy you* a beer if you *find me* a seat.

(iii)   Possessive dative

When referring to parts of the body and articles of clothing, German often uses the definite article **der** etc. 'the' where English uses 'my', 'your' etc. [➤23h(iii)]. An indirect object (known as a *possessive dative*) is sometimes added to emphasize the event, or for clarification if you would not otherwise know whose body or clothing it is. It *must* be added if the direct object does not belong to the subject of the sentence.

Kannst du *mir* die Brieftasche herausholen? Ich habe (*mir*) das linke Handgelenk verstaucht.	Can you get *my* wallet out (for me)? I have sprained *my* left wrist.

Note   A very few verbs take two objects in the accusative, the commonest being **kosten** 'cost', **lehren** 'teach', **angehen** 'concern', **nennen/heißen** 'call/name'.

Dein verflixtes Spezialbier hat *mich ein Heidengeld* gekostet! – *Was* geht *mich* das an?	Your blasted special beer cost *me a fortune*! – *What*'s that got to do with *me*?

8f   *Objects which refer to the subject: reflexive verbs*

In a reflexive verb the action is turned back on the subject. The object is a *reflexive pronoun* [➤25c], which refers to the same person or thing as the subject. The rules for reflexive verbs are exactly the same as for any other verb, for example, in the order of objects [➤4e] or in the use of **haben** to form compound past tenses [➤17c(i)].
There are various types of reflexive verb.

(i)   A limited number of verbs can only be used with a reflexive pronoun, which often has little independent meaning. For example:

Am Ende des Abends *bedankten* wir *uns* alle bei der Gastgeberin und *verabschiedeten uns.* Stefan *benahm sich* sehr schlecht, weil er *sich* in sie *verliebt* hatte. Meine Wohnung *befindet sich* außerhalb der Stadt. Ich *beeilte mich*, ein Taxi zu finden.	At the end of the evening we all *said thank you* to the hostess and *said goodbye*. Stefan *behaved* very badly, because he had *fallen in love* with her. My apartment *is (situated)* outside the town. I *hurried* to find a taxi.

(ii)   There are some verbs which do not have to be used with a reflexive pronoun but which alter their meaning, sometimes entirely, when they are. For example:

Leider *verlief* ich *mich* sofort. Ich hatte *mich* auf mein Gedächtnis *verlassen*, aber ich konnte *mir* nicht *vorstellen*, wo ich war. Endlich *stellte* es *sich heraus*, daß ich nicht weit von zu Hause war. Es *lohnte sich* nicht mehr, ein Taxi zu nehmen.	Unfortunately I *lost my way* immediately. I had *relied* on my memory, but I could not *imagine* where I was. Finally it *turned out* that I was not far from home. It *was* no longer *worth* taking a taxi.

(iii)   Finally, so long as it makes sense, any verb with an object in
the accusative [➤8d(i)] or dative [➤8d(ii), 8e] can have a
reflexive pronoun as an object, showing that in this case the
action relates back to the subject.

Erschöpft *goß* ich *mir* einen kleinen Schlummertrunk *ein*, *zog mich* schnell *aus* und *warf mich* ungewaschen ins Bett.	Exhausted, I *poured myself* a small nightcap, *got undressed* quickly and *threw myself* unwashed into bed.

8g   *Verbs + preposition + noun phrase: prepositional objects*

Very many German verbs can be linked to a noun phrase by a
preposition. These verb–preposition combinations are fixed:
you could not use a different preposition without at least
changing the meaning and probably making nonsense. Some
are similar to English but many are not. It is important to learn
each combination as you come to it.

Most German prepositions can be associated with a verb in
this way. The following paragraphs list some of the more common combinations. [For the basic meanings of prepositions,
and the cases that follow them, ➤ch.27.]

Note   When the preposition is followed by a pronoun referring to a thing or
things, the two combine to form a compound consisting of **da(r)-** +
the preposition. (The **-r-** is used before a vowel.) [➤25b(iv)A]

Sind das Ihre Papiere? – Ja, ich arbeite heute *daran*. Aber wo ist mein Rotstift? Ich habe eben *damit* geschrieben.	Are these your papers? – Yes, I'm working *on them* today. But where's my red pencil? I have just been writing *with it.*

➤   I am relying on (your) seeing him today: use of **da(r)–** + preposition
to introduce a clause ➤8h(ii)D, 8i.

(i)   *+ an*

Almost always + a dative noun phrase, which very often has
the sense of 'main cause or focus of the action'. For example:

Ich arbeite an ...	I work at ...
Ich erkenne sie an ...	I recognize her by ...
Ich freue mich an ...	I get pleasure from ...

Ich hindere ihn an ...	I prevent him from ...
Ich leide an ...	I suffer from ...
Ich nehme an ... teil.	I take part in ...
Ich rieche an ...	I sniff at ...
Er ist an ... gestorben.	He died of ...
Es fehlt mir an ...	I have no ...
Es liegt mir viel an ...	... is important to me.

There are a few common verbs with **an** + an accusative noun phrase, mostly referring to mental processes. For example:

Ich denke an ...	I think about ...
Ich erinnere dich an ...	I remind you of ...
Ich erinnere mich an ...	I remember ...
Ich glaube an ...	I believe in ...
Ich gewöhne mich an ...	I get used to ...

(ii)   *+ auf*

Almost always + an accusative noun phrase. This is the most common linking preposition, with a wide range of meanings, especially 'aim or direction of the action'. For example:

Ich achte auf ...	I pay attention to ...
Ich antworte auf	I reply to ...
Das bezieht sich auf ..	That refers to ...
Das folgt auf ...	That follows (on from) ...
Ich freue mich auf ...	I look forward to ...
Ich hoffe auf ...	I hope for ...
Es kommt auf ... an.	It depends on ...
Ich passe auf ... auf.	I keep an eye on ...
Ich schimpfe auf ...	I curse at ...
Ich verlasse mich auf ...	I rely on ...
Ich verzichte auf ...	I do/go without ...
Ich warte auf ...	I wait for ...
Ich zähle auf ...	I count/rely on ...
Ich zeige auf ...	I point at ...
Ich ziele/schieße auf ...	I aim/shoot at ...

There are very few verbs with **auf** plus a dative noun phrase. They mostly have the sense of 'based on, resting on'. For example:

Ich bestehe auf ...	I insist on ...
Das beruht auf ...	That is based on ...

[but **das gründet sich auf** + accusative]

(iii) + aus

Always + a dative noun phrase, mostly with the sense of '(out) of, from'. For example:

Es besteht aus ...	It consists of ...
Ich stelle es aus ... her.	I make it out of ...

(iv) + für

Always + an accusative noun phrase, mostly with the sense of 'for, concerning'. For example:

Ich bedanke mich bei ihnen für ...	I thank them (formally) for ...
Ich danke dir für ...	I thank you for ...
Ich halte ihn für ...	I think he is ...
Ich interessiere mich für ...	I am interested in ...

(v) + in

Usually + an accusative noun phrase, mostly with the sense of 'focus of the action'. For example:

Ich verliebe mich in ...	I fall in love with ...
Ich mische mich in ... ein	I stick my nose into ...

There are very few verbs with **in** + a dative noun phrase, the most common being:

Es besteht in ...	It consists in ...

(vi) + mit

Always + a dative noun phrase, mostly with the sense of 'matter in hand' or 'person concerned'. For example:

Ich befasse mich mit ...	I deal with ...
Ich beschäftige mich mit ...	I occupy myself with ...
Ich fange mit ... an.	I make a start on ...
Ich höre mit ... auf.	I stop doing ...
Ich finde mich mit ... ab.	I come to accept ...
Ich rechne mit ...	I count on (doing) ...
Ich telefoniere mit ...	I talk to ... on the phone.
Ich stimme mit ... überein.	I agree with ...
Ich unterhalte mich mit ...	I talk to ...
Ich versehe ihn mit ...	I provide him with ...

(vii) + nach

Always + a dative noun phrase, usually meaning 'thing desired or sought'. For example :

Ich frage nach ...	I ask/inquire about ...
Ich greife nach ...	I grab at ...
Ich rufe nach ...	I call (out) for ...
Ich sehne mich nach ...	I long for ...
Ich strebe nach ...	I strive for ...
Ich suche nach ...	I search for ...

After verbs of the senses, **nach** + the noun phrase refers to the thing sensed. For example:

Es duftet/riecht/stinkt nach ...	It smells of ... (in increasing order of unpleasantness!)
Es schmeckt nach ...	It tastes of ...
Es sieht nach ... aus.	It looks like ... (weather)

(viii) + über

Always + an accusative noun phrase, used with a large number of verbs, almost always in the sense of 'about, concerning'. For example :

Ich ärgere mich über ...	I am/get annoyed at ...
Ich denke über ... nach.	I think ... over.
Ich täusche mich über ...	I am wrong about ...
Ich freue mich über ...	I am pleased about ...
Ich spotte über ...	I make fun of ...

Verbs of 'talking, reading, writing, knowing' can often be used with either **über** + accusative or **von** + dative. **über** normally implies a longer, more thorough process than **von**. For example:

Sie weiß viel _über_ Eheberatung.	She knows a lot *about* marriage counselling.
Er wußte nicht _von_ meiner Heirat.	He did not *know* about my marriage.

(ix) + um

Always + an accusative noun phrase, mostly in the sense of 'concerning'. For example :

Ich bitte sie um ...	I ask her for ...
Ich bringe ihn um ...	I take ... away from him.

Es geht um ...	It is a matter of ...
Es handelt sich um ...	We are talking about ...
Ich kämpfe um ...	I fight for ...
Ich komme um ...	I lose ...
Ich kümmere mich um ...	I take care of ...

(x)   + von

Always + a dative noun phrase, mostly in the sense of 'away from' or 'about'. For example:

Ich erhole mich von ...	I recover from ...
Es hängt von ... ab.	It depends on ...
Ich rate ihm von ... ab.	I advise him against ...
Ich träume von ...	I dream of ...

(xi)   + vor

Always + a dative noun phrase, mostly in the sense of 'danger, risk'. For example:

Ich (be)schütze ihn vor ...	I protect him from ...
Ich fürchte mich vor ...	I am afraid of ...
Ich habe Angst vor ...	I am afraid of ...
Ich scheue mich vor ...	I am frightened of ...
Ich rette ihn vor ...	I save him from ...
Ich verberge ihn vor ...	I hide him from ...
Ich warne ihn vor ...	I warn him against ...

(xii)   + zu

Always + a dative noun phrase, mostly conveying 'belonging together' or 'inviting, persuading, forcing'. For example :

Das dient zu ...	That is used for ...
Das eignet sich zu ...	That is suitable for ...
Ich gehöre zu ...	I am one of ...
Ich lade Sie zu ... ein.	I invite you to ...
Das paßt zu ...	That matches ...
Ich trage zu ... bei.	I contribute to ...
Ich überrede sie zu ...	I talk her/them into ...
Ich zwinge ihn zu ...	I force him into ...

8h   Verbs + infinitives of other verbs

There are only two ways in which a German verb can be linked to the infinitive of another verb. With the exceptions noted below, the person performing the action must be the same for both verbs.

➤ Notes on forms of the infinitive and cross–references to its uses: ➤10a.

(i) The bare infinitive

A *bare* infinitive is one which is not introduced by **zu** 'to' [➤8h(ii)], as in English 'I must go'. Only certain groups of verbs govern bare infinitives, but many of them are very common. Some have alternative constructions which are indicated below.

Note   These are the main points to remember about the use of the bare infinitive. See A to G below for examples.

1) The infinitive is part of the same clause as the verb governing it and is therefore not separated from it by a comma.

2) In a main clause, the infinitive usually goes at the end, but especially with modals or **tun** it can be put at or very near the beginning for emphasis. [Infinitives in subordinate clauses: ➤4e(iv).]

The main groups of verbs which govern bare infinitives are:

(A) The modal verbs (**dürfen, können, mögen, müssen, sollen, wollen**) and **lassen**. As these are by far the most important verbs of this type they are discussed separately in Chapter 9.

(B) Certain verbs of motion: **fahren** 'go (in a vehicle)', **gehen** 'go (on foot or generally)', **kommen** 'come', **schicken** 'send'. With **schicken** the direct object carries out the action of the infinitive. If the reason is emphasized or the clause is long, the infinitive may be introduced by **um ... zu** 'in order to'. [**spazierengehen/ spazierenfahren** 'go for a walk/drive': ➤16e(ii)].

***Kommst** du heute schwimmen?*	Are you *coming swimming* today?
– Hast du denn vergessen?	– Have you forgotten then?
Ich bin extra *gekommen, um*	I *came* specially *to discuss* our
unser Projekt *zu besprechen!*	project!

(C) A few verbs of the senses: **fühlen** 'feel', **hören** 'hear', **sehen** 'see', **spüren** 'sense'. The direct object of these verbs carries out the action of the infinitive. With longer sentences, a clause with **wie** is often preferred. Notice how English often uses the '-ing' form of the verb instead of the infinitive.

| Ich *sah* den Dieb durchs Fenster *steigen* und *hörte, wie* er alle Schubladen *aufmachte.* | I *saw* the thief *climb(ing)* through the window and *heard* him *opening* all the drawers. |

(D) bleiben 'remain', **finden** 'find', **haben** 'have', when followed by a verb of position. With **finden** and **haben** the direct object carries out the action of the infinitive. Here English always uses the '-ing' form. [**stehenbleiben** 'stop', **sitzenbleiben** 'stay down (in school)' : ➤16e(ii)].

| Ich *blieb* voller Angst auf dem Bett *sitzen* – ich *hatte* ja einen Revolver in einer der Schubladen *liegen!* | I *stayed sitting* on the bed, very frightened – after all, I *had* a revolver *lying* in one of the drawers! |

(E) brauchen 'need', **heißen** 'command', **helfen** 'help', **lehren** 'teach', **lernen** 'learn'. These verbs may also be used with **zu** + infinitive, especially if the clause is complex. Except with **brauchen**, there is then a comma before the **zu** + infinitive clause. With **heißen**, **helfen** and **lehren**, the object carries out the action of the infinitive. [**heißen** 'mean': ➤(G) below. **kennenlernen** 'meet': ➤16e(ii).]

| Mein Onkel *lehrt* mich *kochen* – ich *lerne* alles *machen.* Dafür *helfe* ich ihm, seine Kochbücher in Ordnung *zu bringen*, aber er *heißt* mich immer wieder von vorne *anfangen.* Das *brauche* ich wirklich nicht (zu) *machen.* | My uncle is *teaching* me to *cook* – I am *learning* to *do* everything. In exchange, I am *helping* him (to) *tidy up* his cook books, but he keeps *telling* me to *start* again. I really don't *have/need* to *do* that. |

(F) tun (do) – often used in colloquial German to emphasize the action of the infinitive [➤8h(i)Note 2].

| Arbeitet er gerne? – Und wie! Er *tut* doch nichts als *arbeiten.* Sogar *schlafen tut* er wenig! | Does he like working? – And how! He *does* nothing but *work (and work)*. He *doesn't* even *sleep* much! |

(G) A few other verbs in certain idiomatic expressions only. For example:

Mein Onkel *hat gut reden,* er *macht* mich nie *glauben,* daß ich neu anfangen sollte. Das *heißt* Zeit *verschwenden.*	It's *all very well* for my uncle to *talk;* he'll never *convince* me that I should start again. That *means wasting* time.

(ii) *zu + infinitive*

A large number of verbs can be followed by a clause with **zu** + infinitive. The English equivalent is 'I refuse to go'.

Note   1) The **zu** + infinitive clause is normally separated from the main clause by a comma.

2) **zu** + infinitive is always placed at the end of the infinitive clause. [Other uses of **zu** + infinitive: ➤10a(iv).]

3) There are three cases when no comma is used before **zu** + infinitive.

• Often, when the main clause consists only of a verb and its subject:

Wir hofften (,) am Nachmittag ein Picknick zu machen, ...	*We hoped* to have a picnic in the afternoon, ...

• When the infinitive clause consists only of **zu** + infinitive:

... aber gegen halb zwei hat es angefangen *zu regnen.*	... but at about half past one it began *to rain.*

• When the main verb is one of those in group (A) below.

Verbs which may be followed by a clause with **zu** + infinitive can be grouped into loose categories:

(A) Verbs with a close link to the infinitive, whose meaning they modify in some way. (Note: no comma.) For example:

In der Reparaturwerkstatt *haben* wir/*gibt es* viel zu tun. Es *scheint* uns immer an Personal zu fehlen.	In the repair shop we *have*/there *is* a lot to do. We always *seem* to be short of staff.

Ich *bekomme* die schwierigen Apparate zu reparieren, weil sonst keiner es zu machen *weiß*. Darum *brauche* ich eine andere Stelle zu kriegen.

I *get* the difficult equipment to repair, because no one else *knows* how to do it. That is why I *need* to get another job.

(B) A fairly small number of verbs with an object (usually dative) which carries out the action of the infinitive. For example:

Erlauben Sie mir, Ihnen einen Rat zu geben. Ich *bitte* Sie, mich ruhig anzuhören. Ich kann Ihnen nicht *verbieten*, uns zu verlassen, aber ich *rate/empfehle* Ihnen, bei uns zu bleiben. Es *täte* mir *leid*, Sie zu verlieren.

Allow me to give you some advice. Please (I *ask* you to) listen to me calmly. I cannot *forbid* you to leave us, but I *advise/recommend* you to stay with us. I should *be sorry* to lose you.

(C) Other verbs include **anfangen** 'begin', **aufhören** 'stop, cease', **beschließen** 'decide', **fürchten** 'fear', **hoffen** 'hope', **vergessen** 'forget', **versprechen** 'promise', **versuchen** 'try', **vorhaben** 'plan', **wagen** 'dare', **zögern** 'hesitate'.

Bei meiner Arbeitslast *zögere* ich, hier zu bleiben. Ich habe *beschlossen,*/Ich *habe* vor, eine leichtere Arbeit zu suchen. Ich werde nicht *vergessen*, Sie auf dem laufenden zu halten.

With my work load I *hesitate* to stay here. I have *decided*/I *plan* to look for easier work. I shall not *forget* to keep you informed.

(D) Verbs with prepositional objects [►8g]. With these verbs, the infinitive clause is normally introduced by an adverb formed from **da(r)-** plus the preposition, though this may be left out with some verbs. For example:

Ich *erinnere mich* (daran), dieses Thema schon mal besprochen zu haben. Ich *freue mich* darauf, Sie noch eine Weile bei uns zu haben!

I *remember* discussing this subject before. I *look forward* to having you with us a little while yet!

8i Wanting someone else to do it: verbs + subordinate clauses

English frequently uses an object with following infinitive in constructions such as 'they told/wanted *me to leave.*' As noted above, some German verbs can also govern this construction, but usually the other person's action is put into a subordinate clause [➤4d(ii)].

Ich will, *daß Sie* mich fair behandeln. Ich habe nicht vergessen, *wie/daß Sie* mich letztes Jahr heruntergestuft haben. Sie erwarten immer, *daß ich* zu viel für zu wenig mache.	I want *you to* treat me fairly. I have not forgotten *your* downgrading me last year. You always expect *me to* do too much for too little.
Ich erinnere mich (daran), *daß wir* auch davon gesprochen haben. Ich bestehe darauf, *daß Sie* sich doch endlich entschließen!	I remember *our* talking about that as well. I insist on *your* finally making up your mind!

8j Impersonal verbs

Impersonal verbs have the general pronoun **es** 'it' as their subject. [For full details ➤25e.]

8k Feelings and sensations: idioms with haben and sein

German has two sets of idioms which are different from English. Some have alternatives which are more like English.

(i) ich habe etc. + noun

Ich habe Hunger/Durst (bin hungrig/durstig).	I am hungry/thirsty.
Ich habe Angst (fürchte mich) vor ...	I am afraid of ...
Ich habe Sorgen (bin besorgt).	I am worried.
Ich habe Fieber.	I have a temperature.

(ii) mir ist etc., alone or + adjective

Note that **ich bin kalt** means 'I am a cold person', and **es ist kalt** refers to the weather.

Mir ist, als hätte ich ihn schon einmal gesehen.

I have a feeling that I have seen him before.

Mir ist kalt/warm.

I am cold/hot.

Mir ist schlecht/übel.

I feel ill.

Attitudes to action: modal verbs

9a   The function of modal verbs

The verbs listed in paragraphs 9c(i) to (vii) are known as *modal auxiliaries* or *modals* for short. (**lassen** is not generally classed as a modal, but it shares many of their characteristics.) These verbs can occasionally carry a full meaning, as in **Kaffee mag ich nicht** 'I don't like coffee', but usually they are used with the infinitive of another verb [without **zu**, ➤8h(i)]. This chapter deals with the way modals are used in main and subordinate clauses. [For details on the formation of the tenses ➤16c(ii).]

9b   Modal verbs in action

Unlike their English equivalents ('can', 'must' etc.) German modals have a full range of tenses, though they avoid the longer forms. The tenses of **müssen** (taken as an example) are listed overleaf [➤9b(v)].

These are the main points to remember about modals and (unless specifically excluded below) **lassen.**

(i)   When any of the perfect tenses is used with an infinitive placed at the end of the clause (as is normal), the infinitive of the modal is used instead of the past participle. This creates a very characteristic rhythm of **-en -en**, which is the best way to remember this construction.

Warum habt ihr meinen Wagen nicht gleich reparieren *lassen?* **– Wir haben keinen Mechaniker finden** *können.*	Why didn't you *have* my car repaired at once? – We *could*n't find a mechanic.

(ii)   The simple conditionals **könnte**, **möchte**, etc. are always used rather than the compound conditional with **würde**. With **lassen**, the simple conditional **ließe** is used more in **wenn** clauses and the compound conditional **würde ... lassen** more in the main clause [➤14d(ii)Note].

| **Wenn ich einen Mechaniker finden *könnte, würde* ich den Wagen sofort reparieren *lassen.*** | If I *could* find a mechanic, I *would have* the car repaired immediately. |

(iii) When the perfect tenses are used in subordinate clauses, the auxiliary **haben** comes first in the final block [➤4e(iii), (iv)], not at the very end.

| **Es tut mir leid, daß ich nicht zu deiner Abschiedsparty *habe kommen können.*** | I'm sorry that I *could*n't *come* to your farewell party. |

(iv) In certain cases the following infinitive may be 'understood', that is, left out because it is obvious what it is. The modal then takes over any associated verbal particle [e.g. **zurück**, ➤16e(ii)], and perfect tenses use the past participles in **ge-**, not the infinitive. Apart from some set phrases, this happens mainly when the verb in question:

• has just been mentioned;
• is **tun/machen** 'do' or a verb of motion. [➤also 9c(ii).]

| **Warum bist du nicht gekommen? — Ich *konnte* (es) nicht. Ich *mußte* zur Garage zurück, um deinen Wagen zu holen.** | Why didn't you come? — I *could*n't. I *had to go* back to the garage to get your car. |

(v) In the following list the terms 'simple' and 'compound' refer to the forms of **müssen**, not to the whole construction.

Present/simple future	**Es muß ... warten.**	It must/has to wait.
Simple past	**Es mußte ... warten.**	It had to wait.
Perfect	**Es hat ... warten müssen.**	It (has) had to wait.
Pluperfect	**Es hatte ... warten müssen.**	It had had to wait.
Compound future	**Es wird ... warten müssen.**	It will have to wait.
Conditional	**Es müßte ... warten.**	It would have to wait.
Past conditional	**Es hätte warten müssen.**	It would have had to wait.
Konjunktiv I simple	**Es müsse warten.**	(They said that) it had to wait.
Konjunktiv I perfect	**Es habe ... warten müssen.**	(They said that) it had had to wait.

9c *The parts and meanings of modal verbs*

The headings for each verb give the infinitive, the **er/sie/es** form of the present and of the simple past, and finally the past participle.

(i) *dürfen, darf, durfte, gedurft: 'may, am allowed to; must not; might'*

(A) Permission (the basic meaning).
As in English, **kann** 'can' is often felt to be less formal than **darf** 'may', but the latter is not at all uncommon, even in colloquial speech.

Darf/**Kann ich ohne weiteres ein Buch aus der Stadtbücherei entleihen?**	*May*/Can I take a book out of the public library just like that?

(B) Prohibition (in the negative).
This is often equivalent to the English 'must not' and thus both the opposite of A above and one of the opposites of **muß**. The conditional **dürfte** can also express a strong 'should not'.

Leider nicht. Ohne Leserkarte *darf*/**kann man keine Bücher entleihen – das heißt, man** *dürfte* **es bestimmt nicht.**	I'm afraid not. Without a reader's card you *may* not/cannot take any books out – that is, you certainly *should* not.

(C) Polite suggestions or requests.

Darf/Dürfte **ich fragen, ob Sie hier in der Stadt wohnen oder arbeiten?**	*May/Might* I ask whether you live or work here in the town?

(D) Likelihood (in the conditional).

Sie arbeiten hier? Gut, dann *dürfte* **es keine Probleme geben.**	You work here? Good, then there *should*n't be any problems.

(ii) *können, kann, konnte, gekonnt: 'can, am able to; could'*

(A) Ability or opportunity.

Können **Sie mir sagen, was dieser schwedische Text bedeutet? –** *Könnten* **Sie Montag wiederkommen? Ich** *kann* **Ihnen leider nicht helfen.**

Can you tell me what this Swedish text means? – *Could* you come back on Monday? I'm afraid I *can't* help you.

Note Unlike English, German does not normally use **kann** with verbs of the senses:

Ich *höre* **jemanden kommen, aber ich** *sehe* **ihn noch nicht.**

I *can hear* someone coming, but I *can't see* him yet.

(B) Possibility, especially with **könnte.**
To avoid confusion with meaning (A) above an adverb such as **vielleicht** 'perhaps' or **möglicherweise** 'possibly' can be used.

Ich *kann* **mich irren, aber ich glaube, Montag** *kann* **ein Kollege von der Universitätsbibliothek da sein.**

I *may* be wrong, but I think that a colleague from the university library *may* be here on Monday.

(C) Knowledge of something learned.
Here **kann** is often used without any other verb, that is, the thing learned is its direct object.

Der *kann* **Schwedisch – ich** *kann* **es leider nicht.**

He *can speak* Swedish – I'm afraid I *can't*.

(D) Permission.

Sie *können* **aber gerne die schwedisch–deutschen Wörterbücher benutzen.**

But you're welcome to (*can* by all means) use the Swedish–German dictionaries.

1) Do not confuse the two meanings of the English 'could':

• **Ich konnte ihn sprechen/ habe ihn sprechen können** means 'I *was able* to speak to him'.
• **Ich könnte ihn sprechen** means 'I *would be able* to speak to him'.

2) Do not confuse the two meanings of the English 'They *could have spoken* to him yesterday', which correspond to (A) and (B) above:

• **Sie** *hätten* **ihn gestern** *sprechen* **können**. (missed opportunity (A): '... but they didn't').
• *Sie* **könnten** *ihn* **gestern** *gesprochen* **haben**. (possibility (B): '...and perhaps they did').

(iii)   *mögen, mag, mochte, gemocht*: '(would) like; may'.

(A) Likes and dislikes.
The present/past tenses **mag/mochte** and the conditional **möchte** correspond fairly closely to English 'like(d)' and 'would like':

• **mag** and **mochte** are most often used without any other verb, that is, the person or thing (dis)liked is their direct object. The English 'I like swimming' etc. is usually best expressed by **ich schwimme gern** (literally 'I swim willingly'). Note also the use of **gefallen** 'please', as in **Bremen gefällt mir sehr** 'I like Bremen very much'.

Möchten **Sie eine Zigarre?** – **Danke! Zigaretten** *mag* **ich auch nicht.**	*Would* you *like* a cigar? – No thank you! I *don't like* cigarettes either.

• **möchte**, on the other hand, *is* used with an infinitive or, if there is a change of subject, with a **daß** clause [➤8i]. **gern** is often used as well; the comparative **lieber** means 'would prefer'.

Ich *möchte gern/lieber* **ein bißchen frische Luft schnappen.**	I *should like/prefer* to get a bit of fresh air.

Note   **möchte** cannot be used for the English 'I *would have liked/preferred* to do it'. The German for this is **ich** *hätte* **es** *gern/lieber* **gemacht**.

Ich *wäre* **viel** *lieber* **zu Hause geblieben, aber ich wollte nicht unhöflich sein.**	I *would* much *rather have* stayed at home, but I didn't want to be rude.

(B) Possibility.
Apart from some set phrases, **mag/mochte** are little used in this sense in colloquial German. [**mag** after 'however, whatever, whoever' etc. : ➤5a(ii).]

| Das *mag* meinen Freunden seltsam erscheinen. – Ja, das *mag* wohl sein. | That *may* seem strange to my friends. – Yes, that *may* well be. |

(iv) ***müssen, muß, mußte, gemußt****: 'must, have to, need to; ought'*

(A) Necessity, obligation, compulsion.
Note that the negative **Sie *müssen* es nicht machen** means 'you don't *have to/need to* do it'. In fact, the alternative **Sie *brauchen* es nicht (zu) machen** is probably more common. The English phrase 'you *must* not do that' is **Sie *dürfen* das nicht machen** [➤9c(i)B].

| Dieses Buch ist überfällig – Sie *müssen* 1,80 Mark Gebühr zahlen. Die anderen Bücher *müssen/brauchen* Sie noch nicht zurückbringen. | This book is overdue – you'll *have to* pay a fine of 1.80 marks. You don't *have/need to* return the other books yet. |

(B) Logical deduction, supposition.

| Entschuldigung, ich *muß* es vergessen haben. – Na ja, Sie *müssen* ja viel zu tun haben. | Sorry, I *must* have forgotten it. – Well, you *must* have a lot to do. |

(C) The conditional **müßte**.
This adds the idea of 'ought to' or 'possibly' to (A) and (B) above [➤**sollte** overleaf].

| Stimmt, aber mein Gedächtnis ist doch nicht so gut, wie es sein *müßte*. | True, but still, my memory is not as good as it *ought to* be. |

 Do not confuse the two meanings of the English 'They *ought to/should have spoken* to him yesterday', which correspond to (A) and (B) above:

• **Sie *hätten* ihn gestern *sprechen müssen*** (obligation (A): '... but they didn't', with the added implication that it is now too late [➤9c(v)C Note].)

• Sie *müßten* ihn gestern *gesprochen haben* (supposition (B): '... and no doubt they did').

(v)   ***sollen, soll, sollte, gesollt***: *'am meant to, supposed to; should, ought to'*

(A) (In the present and past tenses) Somebody else's intention or requirement.
Soll ich **das machen?** is often the neatest way of saying '*Do you want me* to do that?'

Ich kann nicht mitkommen, ich ***soll*** **hier auf Monika warten. –** ***Soll*** **ich Ihnen etwas kaufen?**	I can't come with you, I *am (meant)* to wait for Monika here. – *Do you want me* to buy anything for you?

(B) (In the conditional) Obligation, duty.

Zigaretten bitte. Ja, ich weiß, ich ***sollte*** **nicht so viel rauchen.**	Cigarettes, please. Yes, I know *I should*n't smoke so much.

(C) (In the present and past tenses) Report, hearsay, rumor.

'Nikostopp' ***soll*** **einem das Rauchen abgewöhnen. Monika** ***soll*** **aber jetzt Nikostopp- süchtig sein!**	'Nikostopp' *is supposed to* cure you of smoking, but Monica *is said to* be a Nikostopp addict now!

(D) Commands, especially in indirect speech [➤5e].

Der Arzt hat mir auch gesagt, ich ***soll(te)*** **Pralinen aufgeben. Na! „Du** ***sollst*** **nicht ertappt werden!" lautet das elfte Gebot.**	The doctor also told me to give up (I *should* give up) chocolates. Hm! "Thou *shalt* not be found out!" says the eleventh commandment.

 When talking about the past, be careful to distinguish between 'They *ought* to have spoken to him yesterday' ((B) above) and 'They are said to have spoken to him yesterday' ((C) above):

• Sie *hätten* ihn gestern *sprechen sollen* (duty (B): '.. but they didn't' [➤9c(iv)B Note])
• Sie *sollen* ihn gestern *gesprochen haben* (hearsay (C): '... I don't know whether they did'.)

(vi) *wollen, will, wollte, gewollt*: 'want to, will'

(A) Wish, desire.
In this meaning **wollen** can be used without another verb.

Ich *will* dich nicht hetzen, aber wir *wollen* bald losfahren. – Moment mal, ich *will* nur diesen Artikel lesen. Oder *willst* du die Zeitung?	I don't *want to* rush you, but we *want to* leave soon. – One moment, I just *want to* read this article. Or do you *want* the paper?

(B) Willingness, intention.
Note the use of **will nicht** 'refuses to' even with things.

Willst du mir wenigstens mit diesem Koffer helfen? Das Ding *will* nicht zugehen. – Na, du *willst* nicht einsehen, daß er einfach zu voll ist.	*Will* you at least help me with this suitcase? The thing *will* not shut. – Well, you *refuse to* recognize that it is simply too full.

(C) Claim, assertion (often false).
Usually followed by a perfect infinitive (past participle + **haben/sein**).

Papa *will* letztes Jahr noch mehr hineingekriegt haben. – So? Na gut, ich *will* nichts gesagt haben.	Dad *says* that he got/*claims* to have got even more in last year. – Really? OK, *pretend* I didn't say anything.

(vii) *lassen, lasse/läßt, ließ, gelassen*: 'let, allow to; have/get ... done; can be done'

(A) Allowing something to happen.

Vorsicht! Du *läßt* noch den ganzen Koffer fallen. *Laß* mich versuchen! – Ach, *laß* mich in Ruhe!	Careful! You'll drop (*let* fall) the whole suitcase. *Let* me try! – Oh, *leave* me in peace!

➤ **fallenlassen** 'drop (a plan)', **stehenlassen/liegenlassen** 'leave behind': infinitives as particles ➤16e(ii).

(B) Causing something to happen.

Gut, ich *lasse* es deinen Vater machen – der wiegt ja genug! Ich *lasse* ihn gleich holen.	OK, I'll *get* your father to do it – he weighs enough! I'll *get* them to fetch him.

(C) Possibility (**sich lassen**).
This is a useful replacement for 'can be done' [➤15f(v)].

Solche Koffer *lassen sich* nicht ohne Gewalt zumachen.	Suitcases like this *cannot be* shut without brute force.

10 Verb forms not related to time: non-finite forms

The *non-finite* verb forms are so called because they do not by themselves define when the activity referred to happens. The three non-finite forms in German are the infinitive and the two participles.

10a   The infinitive

The *infinitive* is the part of the verb most commonly listed in dictionaries. It 'names' a certain activity or state without saying when it happens, and it usually completes the meaning of the main verb.

(i)   Formation of the infinitive

(A) All infinitives end in **-(e)n**; the **-e-** is dropped in **sein** 'be', **tun** 'do' and any verb ending in **-eln** or **-ern**.

(B) With the single exception of **sein** (which has **wir/sie *sind*** 'we/they *are*'), the infinitive of all German verbs is identical to the **wir/sie** forms (first/third person plural) of the present tense.

Wir fahren jedes Wochenende ins Grüne. Heute wollen wir nach Beck *fahren. Fahren Sie* mit?	*We drive* to the country every weekend. Today we are going to *drive* to Beck. *Are you coming* too?

(B) Verbal particles (e.g. **auf, beiseite, zurück** [➤16e(ii)]) and infinitives are written as one word, in the order particle **(+zu)** + infinitive.

Ich würde gerne *mitfahren*, aber ich habe versprochen, mit Andrea nach Frön *mitzufahren*.	I should like to *come with you*, but I have promised to *go with* Andrea to Frön.

(ii)   Uses of the infinitive

Paragraph 10a(iii) discusses infinitive-nouns and paragraph 10a(iv) infinitive clauses. Many of the equivalents for English '-ing' listed in paragraph 10b(ii) use the infinitive in German. Other usages involving the infinitive are described in the following paragraphs:

➤ I heard him *shout:* verbs + bare infinitives ➤8h.
He started *to run:* verbs + **zu** + infinitive ➤8h(ii).
I could not *help* him: modal verbs + infinitive ➤9b.
His *efforts to find* his car were in vain: nouns + **zu** + infinitive ➤19h.
I was *ready to call* the police: adjectives + **zu** + infinitive ➤24g(ii).
Without hesitating he jumped into the river: prepositions + **zu** + infinitive ➤27c.

(iii) *Infinitive-nouns*

Because they are 'names', German infinitives are frequently made into nouns which refer to the activity in question. The English equivalent often uses the '-ing' form of the verb. German *infinitive-nouns* are neuter, they are spelled with a capital and they function just like any other noun. In fact, some nouns have lost most of their active verbal sense, e.g.: **das Andenken** 'souvenir', **das Essen** 'meal', **das Verbrechen** 'crime', **das Vergnügen** 'pleasure'. In most instances, however, the basic verbal meaning is strongly preserved.

Ach, die ländliche Ruhe! Das *Bellen* **der Hunde, das** *Zwitschern* **der Vögel, das** *Blöken* **der Schafe – nur das** *Schlafen* **ist schwierig!**	Ah, rural peace! The *barking* of the dogs, the *twittering* of the birds, the *bleating* of the sheep – only *sleeping* is difficult!

(A) Infinitive-nouns are used after some prepositions to form useful constructions:

• **beim** + noun meaning 'while/on doing something';
• **zum** + noun expressing purpose, 'for doing something';
• **geraten/kommen** + **ins** + noun, indicating the start of an action.

Das mittlere Pedal dient *zum* **Bremsen.** **Vorsicht aber** *beim* *Fahren* **–** *bei zu starkem* *Bremsen* **gerät/kommt man leicht** *ins Schleudern.*	The middle pedal is *for braking.* Take care though *when driving – if you brake too hard* you'll easily get *into a skid.*

(B) Especially in written German, the object of the verb or other parts of the sentence may be included in the noun. Long compounds can be very clumsy, and it is often better to use a clause [➤10a(iv)].

> Das ständige
> *Miteinanderplaudern* ist beim
> Fahren nicht zu empfehlen, das
> *Zeitunglesen* noch weniger.
>
> Constant *chatting among*
> *yourselves* while driving is not to
> be recommended, still less
> *reading the newspaper.*

(iv) Infinitive clauses

These are normally governed by **zu** + infinitive, which comes at the end. The English equivalent may use either 'to' + infinitive or the '-ing' form of the verb. Paragraph 8h(ii) deals with verbs with **zu** + infinitive. Infinitive clauses may also be the subject of the sentence. If the clause comes first there is no comma between it and the verb:

> Ein guter Gebrauchtwagen mit
> niedrigem Kilometerstand *zu*
> *finden* ist nicht leicht.
>
> *Finding/To find* a good used car
> with low mileage is not easy.

Note 1) If the infinitive clause is short the **zu** may be left out, especially when the main verb is a part of **sein**.

> Hier Auto *(zu) fahren* ist kein
> Vergnügen.
>
> *Driving* here is no pleasure.

2) If the clause comes after the main verb it is often anticipated by the *caretaker* subject **es**.

> *Es* macht viel mehr Spaß, von
> anderen *gefahren zu werden.*
>
> *It* is much more fun *being driven*
> by others.

10b The present and past participles

Despite their traditional names, the two participles do not by themselves refer to any particular time.

(i) The formation and use of present participles: *-end*

(A) All *present participles* are formed in the same way, by adding **-d** to the infinitive, e.g. **wartend** 'waiting', **wandernd** 'hiking', **studierend** 'studying', **laufend**. 'running'. The verbs **sein** and **tun** insert **-e-** before the **-n** to form **seiend** 'being' and **tuend** 'doing'.

(B) Verbal particles (e.g. **auf, beiseite, zurück** [➤16e(ii)]) and present participles are written as one word, in the order particle + participle, e.g. **anstehend, weiterwandernd, zurücklaufend** [➤also 10b(iv); note that compounds of **sein** use -**wesend**].

(ii) *German equivalents for English '-ing'*

Apart from the usages listed in 10b(iv) and (v), the present participle cannot be used in German in the same way as it is in English. German equivalents of English '-ing' are described in the following paragraphs:

➤ *After seeing* her I caught the train home: conjunction + subordinate clause ➤5a(ii).
Stop doing that!: verb + **zu** + infinitive ➤8h(ii).
He *insisted on coming* too: verb + preposition + **zu** + infinitive ➤8h(ii).
Hang-gliding is marvellous: infinitive-nouns ➤10a(iii).
Hanging upside down by your heels is good for the brain: infinitive clauses as subjects ➤10a(iv).
I *am writing* a letter: present continuous tense ➤12a(i).
Instead of mailing it I phoned home: prepositions + **zu** + infinitive ➤27c.

(iii) *The formation and use of past participles: (ge)-t or (ge)-en*

With minor exceptions (for example their use as sharp commands [➤13c(ii)]) German *past participles* are used in the same ways as in English, mainly as part of the compound past tenses [➤12b] and of the passive [➤ch.15].

(A) Regular weak participles are formed by adding -**(e)t** to the verb stem (the infinitive minus -**en**). English equivalents are 'walk-walked' and 'burn-burnt'. The -**e**- is used after **t** and **d**, and after **m** or **n** preceded by any consonant apart from **l** or **r**. For example, **gemacht** 'did', **gelächelt** 'smiled', **gewarnt** 'warned' but **gerettet** 'saved', **gebadet** 'bathed', **geatmet** 'breathed', **geregnet** 'rained'. [Irregular weak verbs: ➤16c(ii)].

(B) Strong past participles have the same -**en** ending as the infinitive. Very often the stem vowel changes; in some irregular strong verbs there are also consonant changes, mainly minor. English equivalents here are 'give-given' and 'break-broken'. For example, **gebissen** 'bitten', **geflogen** 'flown', **gesungen** 'sung', **vergessen** 'forgotten', **getragen** 'carried'. [Summary of strong verb classes: ➤16d(v). List of strong verbs: ➤18e.]

(C) Both weak and strong past participles have the prefix **ge**- before the verb stem unless the verb:

• already starts with a fixed prefix (e.g. **be-, ent-, er-, ge-, ver-, -zer** [➤16e(i)]). For example, **ge**stört 'disturbed' but **zer**stört 'destroyed', **ge**standen 'stood' but **ver**standen 'understood'.
• is a weak verb ending in **-ieren**. For example, **ge**paßt 'suited' but **pass**iert 'happened', **ge**badet 'bathed' but **stud**iert 'studied'). Note also **interviewt** 'interviewed' and **miaut** 'meowed'.

(D) Verbal particles (e.g. **auf, beiseite, zurück** [➤16e(ii)]) and past participles are written as one word, in the order particle (+**ge–**) + participle. For example, **an**gestanden 'queued', **auf**gepaßt 'paid attention', **bei**behalten 'retained', **aus**verkauft 'sold out' [➤also 10b(iv)].

The following paragraphs deal with constructions involving the past participle:

➤   They *have invited* us to dinner: compound past tenses formed with **haben** ➤17c(i).

We *have been* there once before: compound past tenses formed with **sein** ➤17c(i).

The stairs to their apartment *had* just *been repaired*: the passive (formed with **werden**) ➤ch.15.

Look out!: abrupt commands ➤13c.

(iv)   Participles as adjectives

Provided it makes sense, any present or past participle can be used as an adjective. *Participle adjectives* obey the same rules as all other adjectives [➤ch.24], that is:

• they take normal adjective endings when they are part of a noun phrase [➤24b(ii)]:

Mit *zunehmendem* Interesse gingen wir zum *vereinbarten* Treffpunkt.	With *increasing* interest we went to the *agreed* rendez-vous.

• they can be used as nouns [➤24d]:

Der *Vorsitzende* war ein alter *Bekannter* von mir.	The *chairman* was an old *acquaintance* of mine.

• they can be used as adverbs [➤28b(i)]:

Er redete *erregt*, aber *treffend*.	He spoke *agitatedly* but *to the point*.

Many participles have developed distinct meanings of their own and are thought of as adjectives in their own right rather than as parts of the verb. For example:

(A) Present participles:

abwesend	absent	**empörend**	outrageous
ansteckend	infectious	**reizend**	charming
anwesend	present	**rührend**	touching
aufregend	exciting	**spannend**	exciting
bedeutend	important	**umfassend**	extensive
dringend	urgent	**wütend**	furious

(B) Past participles:

angesehen	respected	**erfahren**	experienced
aufgebracht	indignant	**geschickt**	skilled
aufgeregt	excited	**verliebt**	in love
ausgezeichnet	excellent	**verrückt**	crazy, insane
bekannt	famous		

(v)   *Participle clauses*

Both present and past participles can be used to make free-standing clauses.

• The participle normally comes last within its own clause, which is separated by commas.
• A few past participle clauses have become frequently used set phrases, for example, **offen gestanden** 'frankly speaking' or **nebenbei gesagt** 'incidentally'.
• Otherwise, participle clauses tend to be used only in very formal German; this is especially true of those with present participles, which are nowhere near as common as their English equivalents.

(A) Present participle clauses:

Dem Vorsitzenden in die Augen *sehend*, sagte ich: „Sie irren sich."	*Looking* the chairman in the eye I said, "You're wrong."

(B) Past participle clauses:

Vom Beistand der anderen *ermutigt*, **fuhr ich fort: „Das wissen Sie wohl selber.“**	*Encouraged* by the support of the others I continued, "No doubt you know that yourself."

The passage of time: the use of tenses

11a   What do tenses tell us?

'Tense' is not the same thing as 'time', though the same words are often used to refer to both. Time is a fact of life, in which there are only three time zones (past, present and future). Tenses, on the other hand, are grammatical structures which often reflect a way of looking at an event as well as just record-ing when it happened. Both the number of tenses, the names given to them and their uses vary greatly from one language to another.

11b   One word or two? Simple and compound tenses

In the language of grammar a *simple* tense is a one-word form, while a *compound* tense uses two or more words (an auxiliary verb + one or more non-finite forms). German has four simple tenses: the present, the simple past, the present subjunctive and the simple conditional. For the compound tenses it uses these auxiliary verbs [➤7b]:

• **haben** 'have' or **sein** 'be' + past participle forms the com-pound past tenses [➤17c(i)];
• **werden** 'become' + infinitive forms the compound future [➤17c(ii)] and conditional [➤17c(iii)];
• **werden** 'become' + past participle forms the passive [➤ch.15].

11c   Doing or done to? The active and the passive

The majority of statements are about something done or to be done *by* the subject of the sentence: the verb is then said to be *active*. However, some statements relate what is being done *to* the subject: here the verb is in the *passive*. Chapters 12 to 14 discuss the active tenses, and Chapter 15 deals with the passive.

11d   The active tenses

Chapter 17 deals with the formation of tenses. The following list of active tenses is given for reference, using **warten** as an

example of a *weak* verb and **bleiben** for the *strong* verbs
[➤16b]. (The tenses of **Konjunktiv** I and the conditional
[**Konjunktiv** II] are listed in paragraph 14b.) **Warten** uses
haben in compound past tenses and **bleiben** uses **sein**, but
this has nothing to do with being weak or strong.

Present/simple future	**Es wartet/bleibt.**	It waits/stays, is waiting/staying.
Simple past	**Es wartete/blieb.**	It waited/stayed, was waiting/staying.
Perfect	**Es hat ... gewartet/ ist ... geblieben.**	It has waited/stayed.
Pluperfect	**Es hatte ... gewartet / war ... geblieben.**	It had waited/stayed.
Compound future	**Es wird ... warten / bleiben.**	It will wait/stay.
Future perfect	**Es wird ... gewartet haben/geblieben sein.**	It will have waited/ stayed.

12 Statements of fact: past, present and future

The most used tenses are those which indicate that something is true or at least probable. For this reason they are known as the *indicative* tenses. This chapter discusses how they are used in German.

➤   Formation (conjugation) of tenses: ➤ch.17.
Word order in questions and commands: ➤4e Note.
Adding emphasis (I do/did do it): ➤29c(iii).

12a   *The present tense*

German verbs have only one present tense. It is a simple tense whose main functions span several English constructions. Normally it is clear which meaning is intended but any ambiguity can always be cured by adding an adverb such as **jetzt** 'now', **gewöhnlich** 'usually', **bald** 'soon'. More explicit constructions can also be used, but normally only for emphasis [➤(i) to (iii) below].

(i)   *What is happening now*

Was *machst* du nur da oben? – Ich *rasiere* mich.	What *are* you *doing* up there? – I *am shaving*.

A more emphatic alternative is **ich bin** *eben dabei, etwas zu machen* 'I'm just doing something' [➤also10a(iii) **beim** + infinitive-noun].

(ii)   *What happens sometimes, usually or always*

Bei dir *dauert's* immer so lange! – Du weißt, am Wochenende *stehe* ich später *auf*.	You always *take* so long! – You know I *get up* later on weekends.

The habitual nature of the activity can be stressed using **ich pflege, es** *zu machen* 'I am in the habit of doing it', though this sounds rather stilted.

(iii) *What is going to happen, often fairly soon*

This is the normal way of talking about the future, without any particular emphasis, and is used in German even in contexts where English would normally say 'I'*ll do* it' or 'I *am going to do* it'.

Wir *fahren* in zehn Minuten los! – Schon gut, ich *komme* gleich.	We *are leaving/are going to leave* in ten minutes! – All right, I'*m coming right now*.

The compound future with **werden** + infinitive either strengthens the assertion or adds some other emphasis [➤12c(i) and (ii)].

(iv) *What has been happening up to now and may be going to continue*

This is a different way of looking at it from English. German sees the action as still going on (therefore present tense) and asks **Wie lange?** 'How long?' or **Seit wann?** 'Since when?'. However, German, like English, uses the *perfect* tense to refer to single events which either did not happen or came in a series [➤12b(vi)].

Ich *warte* schon eine Ewigkeit auf dich! – Ich war müde. Seitdem wir hier *wohnen,*/Seit dem Umzug *schlafe* ich nicht mehr gut.	I'*ve been waiting* for you for ages already! – I was tired. Since we *have been living* here/Since the move I *have* not *been sleeping* well.

(v) *What happened in the (usually recent) past and is still fresh in the memory*

This usage, the so-called *narrative present*, is much more common in educated German, especially in speech, than in English. It may be used to stress the personal involvement of the narrator or simply to add a vivid or emphatic touch to the narration.

Ich *komme* ins Zimmer, und was *sehe* ich? Du *bist* immer noch im Bett!	I *come* (came) into the room and what *do* (did) I see? You *are* (were) still in bed!

12b   *The past tenses*

German has three active tenses which make statements about the past: one *simple* tense, **ich *machte* es** 'I *did* it' and two compound tenses: the *perfect* , **ich** *habe* **es** *gemacht* '*I have done* it' and the *past perfect* (or *pluperfect*), **ich** *hatte* **es** *gemacht* '*I had done it*'.

Note 1) Naturally, many past tense usages mirror those of the present tense, but transferred back in time.

2) The German distinguishes between the simple past and the perfect in ways which are often very different from English and a good deal less clear-cut. Two important features are:

• the simple past is virtually unknown in colloquial speech in South Germany;

• throughout Germany the simple past is much less common in speech than in writing, where it is more concise and avoids relagating of the full verb (i.e. the past participle) to the end of the sentence. However, the simple past of **haben** (**hatte** 'had', **sein** (**war** 'was') and the modals [➤ch.9] is common in both speech and writing.

In all cases, at least in speech and personal writing, the foreign learner should get used to using the perfect.

3) The German use of the pluperfect (the 'past in the past') is generally similar to English, though it is also used colloquially instead of the perfect.

(i) *Past events which are over and done with*

Use perfect or simple past, as indicated in 2) above.

Vor zwei Jahren *haben* **wir meine Eltern auf dem Land** *besucht.* **Unsere älteste Tochter** *ist* **nicht** *mitgekommen.*	Two years ago we *visited* my parents in the country. Our eldest daughter *didn't come.*

(ii) *Past events accompanying the main narrative*

The simple past is normal, at least in writing, but the perfect is possible. This is the parallel in the past to the present tense usage in paragraph 12a(i).

Während wir eine kleinere Landstraße entlang *fuhren (gefahren sind),* **sind wir plötzlich auf eine Herde schwarzer Schafe gestoßen.**	While we *were driving* along a small country road, we suddenly came on a flock of black sheep.

(iii)   *Past habits, generally assumed to be finished with*

Use perfect or simple past, as indicated in 2) above. This is the parallel of the present usage in paragraph 12a(ii); similarly, **ich pflegte es zu machen** 'I used to do it' is sometimes used to stress the habitual nature of the action.

In meiner Jugend *arbeitete* **ich oft auf dem Bauernhof und** *kannte* **jede Schafsorte.**	In my youth I often *used to work* on the farm and *knew* every breed of sheep.

(iv)   *A state or activity which began before the events being narrated and continued right up to them*

The simple past is normal. This is an exact parallel to the present tense usage described in paragraph 12a(iv). Similarly, German, like English, uses the pluperfect tense to refer to a series of separate actions or states [➤12b(ix)].

Inzwischen *wohnte* **ich aber schon seit zwanzig Jahren in der Stadt, und ich wußte ihren Namen nicht mehr.**	By that time, though, I *had been living* in the town for twenty years and I no longer knew their names.

(v)   *Events, especially recent ones, whose effects can still be felt in the present*

Use the perfect.

Letzte Woche *hat* **meine Frau mich an diesen Vorfall** *erinnert.*	Last week my wife *reminded* me of this incident.

(vi)   *A series of separate events leading up to the present (including events which did **not** happen)*

Use the perfect. Contrast this with the present tense in paragraph 12a(iv).

Seitdem *habe* **ich mehrmals von den Schafen** *geträumt* **und** *bin* **immer voller Angst** *aufgewacht.*	Since then I *have dreamed* about the sheep several times and *have* always *woken up* full of fear.

(vii)   *The completion of a future activity*

Even in main clauses the perfect is often used instead of the
future perfect [➤12c(iii)]. In subordinate clauses the perfect is
always used.

Ich werde froh sein, wenn ich ihren Namen *entdeckt habe.* Bis dann *habe* ich aber bestimmt viel Schlaf *verloren.*	I shall be glad when I *have discovered* their names. By then, though, I *shall* certainly *have lost* a lot of sleep.

(viii)   *A way of defining the nature of the subject of the sentence*

This use of the perfect has no exact English equivalent but is
common in, for example, games instructions.

„Ein Mensch mit gutem Gewissen *hat* keine bösen Träume *gehabt,"* sagt meine Frau.	"A person with a clear conscience *doesn't have* bad dreams," says my wife.

(ix)   *Events even further in the past than the main narrative*

Use the pluperfect. These may be single events or a whole
series. The uses of the pluperfect correspond to the uses of
the perfect listed in paragraphs 12b(i), (v) and (vi), shifted one
stage further into the past.

Mag sein, aber bis letzte Woche *hatte* ich immer sehr gut *geschlafen.* Ich *hatte* nicht einmal Schafe *gezählt!*	Maybe, but up to last week I *had* always *slept* very well. I *had* not even *counted* sheep!

12c   *The future tense*

The normal way to refer to future action in German is to use
the present tense [➤12a(iii)]. There are also two compound
tenses: the *future*, **ich *werde* es *machen*** 'I *shall do* it', and the
future perfect, **ich *werde* es *gemacht haben*** 'I *shall have
done* it'. The compound future is used in the first three usages
that follow; the future perfect is used in the fourth.

(i) *To avoid ambiguity, where the present tense could mean either 'now' or 'soon'*

„Als Abgeordneter für diesen Wahlkreis *werde* ich immer in eurem Interesse *handeln!*" rief der Kandidat.	"As member for this electoral district I *shall* always *act* in your interests!" cried the candidate.

(ii) *To emphasize that you really are going to do the thing in question*

„Ich verspreche euch, ich *werde sicherstellen,* daß neue Arbeitsplätze hier geschaffen werden."	"I promise you, I *shall ensure* that new jobs are created here."

(iii) *To make a prediction or estimate the reason for something*

Wohl 'no doubt, probably' [➤29c(iii)] is often added (**dürfte** + infinitive has a similar meaning [➤9c(i)]).

Das *wird* wohl unser Herr Schwätzle *sein.* Später *wird* er sicherlich sein Versprechen *bereuen.*	That*'ll be* our Mr. Schwätzle. Later he *will* certainly *regret* his promise.

(iv) *To refer to events completed before the future time being talked about (the 'past in the future')*

Like English, German uses the future perfect for this in main clauses [but ➤12b(vii)] and the perfect tenses in subordinate clauses, for example after **bis** 'by the time that', **wenn** 'when' or **nachdem** 'after'.

Glaubst du? Bis er ins Parlament *gekommen ist, wird* er jedes Wort *vergessen haben.*	Do you think so? By the time he *has got* into parliament he *will have forgotten* every word.

13 Requests and commands: the imperative

13a What does the imperative express?

The *imperative* is used for a variety of purposes including requests, commands, warnings, instructions, invitations and advice.

13b What you are to do: second person imperatives

➤ Uses of second person forms: ➤25b(ii). Formation of the imperative: ➤17d. Reported commands: ➤5e, 9c(v).

(i) The three second person imperatives (for **du, ihr** and **Sie**) come *first* in the sentence, apart of course from names or exclamations. The pronoun **Sie** is always included, after the verb; **du** and **ihr** are not usually included, but they may be added for emphasis or when different people are being asked to do different things.

Hänschen, *bring(e)* **(du) das Geschirr in die Küche! Inge und Martin, *räumt* (ihr) eure Sachen weg! Frau Körner, *reichen Sie* mir bitte das Salz!**	Hänschen, (you) *take* the dishes into the kitchen. Inge and Martin, (you) *clear* away your things. Mrs Körner, please *pass* me the salt.

(ii) Because straight imperatives are felt to be somewhat brusque, questions are often used instead. Auxiliaries like **würden Sie ...?** or **willst du/wollen Sie ...?** and **könnten Sie?** are also frequently introduced.

Hänschen, *bringst du* das Geschirr in die Küche? Inge und Martin, *wollt ihr* eure Sachen wegräumen? Frau Körner, *würden Sie* mir bitte das Salz reichen?	Hänschen, *(could you)* *take* the dishes into the kitchen? Inge and Martin, *will (would) you clear* away your things? Mrs Körner, *would you* please *pass* me the salt?

13c   *Instructions and firm commands*

(i)   *Imperative usage of the infinitive*

The infinitive is often used in official warnings and directions and in instructions for games, recipes etc. It is also used in colloquial speech for urgent warnings.

Endstation! Alle *umsteigen*!	End of the line/Terminus! All *change*!
Bei Kurzschluß gleich *abschalten*!	In case of a short *switch off* immediately.
Äpfel *schälen*, in Scheiben *schneiden*, mit Zucker *bestreuen* und mit etwas Rum *übergießen*.	*Peel* the apples, *cut* in slices, *sprinkle* with sugar and *pour* a little rum *over*.
Aufpassen! Links *gucken*!	*Look out! Look* left!

(ii)   *Imperative usage of the past participle*

The past participle can be used as a very sharp command, for example in military language. In colloquial speech it is restricted to a few set phrases, including expletives, which are after all a sort of sharp command!

Verdammt noch mal!	*Damn!*
Abgemacht!	*Done!/Agreed!*
Stillgestanden!	*Attention!* (military)

13d   *Wishes and suggestions*

(i)   *What we are to do*

The German equivalents of 'let's go' include **gehen wir jetzt** (now felt to be rather stilted), **laß uns jetzt gehen** and (perhaps most commonly) **wollen wir jetzt gehen?**

Laß uns heute abend *ausgehen*.	*Let's go out* tonight.
Wollen wir ins Kino *gehen*?	*Let's (shall we) go* to the cinema.

(ii)   *If only ...*

Free-standing **wenn** clauses with the verb in the conditional [➤14b] express a heartfelt wish that something had or had not happened.

Wenn ich *doch nur* wüßte,   *If only* I knew what movies were
welche Filme gezeigt werden!   on! *If only* you hadn't thrown away
Wenn du *bloß* die Zeitung nicht   the newspaper!
weggeschmissen hättest!

(iii)   Expressing a wish for the future

The third person forms of **Konjunktiv** I [➤14b] can express a
wish for the future, but nowadays only in some set phrases.

Gott *sei Dank!* **Verhüte** Gott!   *Thank* God! God *forbid*!

14 Areas of uncertainty: das Konjunktiv

14a   Konjunktiv or subjunctive?

Konjunktiv is a term used in modern German grammars to refer to a series of tenses parallel to the indicative [►ch. 12]. It is also called the *subjunctive*, but this is misleading as it has almost none of the usages which the subjunctive has in other languages. We shall therefore use the German term, with references to other terms where helpful.

14b   The tenses of the Konjunktiv

► Formation of Konjunktiv: ►17a.

(i) The **Konjunktiv** has two series of tenses, referred to in German simply as **Konjunktiv** I and **Konjunktiv** II. Each has one simple tense and two compound tenses. Older grammars call the two simple tenses *present subjunctive* and *past subjunctive*, but in fact the first refers mainly to the past and the second often to the future.

(ii) With some additions, **Konjunktiv** II is used like the conditional in, for example, English and French, and it is sensible to think of it in this way in German and to call it the *conditional*.

(iii) In the following lists the tenses are given in the **es** form because this is a good marker for **Konjunktiv** I.

Konjunktiv I		Konjunktiv II	
Simple	es warte/ komme	Simple Conditional	es wartete /käme
Future	es werde warten/ kommen	Compound Conditional	es würde warten/ kommen
Perfect	es habe gewartet/ sei gekommen	Past Conditional	es hätte gewartet/ wäre gekommen

Konjunktiv tenses have two main uses.

(A) Indirect/Reported speech [►14c.]

(B) Conditional clauses [➤14d.]

14c   *What did they say? Indirect speech*

In *indirect* or *reported* speech, what was actually said is not repeated word for word but rephrased in a clause introduced by a suitable verb [➤5c for the syntax of the construction]. Usage on indirect speech has changed considerably over the years, and even educated Germans now find it hard to say what is 'correct' in every instance. The following guidelines take account of the differences between reporting in speech and in writing, but it is impossible in a book of this size to cover all possibilities.

(i)   Rules for indirect speech

The traditional rule for indirect speech in written German has two stages. (See examples in the next paragraph.)

(A) As a first principle, the actual tense used is changed into the **Konjunktiv I** tense which best indicates the time zone spoken of. This is the only function of **Konjunktiv I**.

(B) If, however, the resulting **Konjunktiv I** form is the same as the corresponding indicative form, then the conditional **(Konjunktiv II)** is used.

The basis of this rule is that indirect speech should if possible be indicated by a distinct **Konjunktiv** form. As **sie seien** (from **sein** 'be') is the only **sie** (third person plural) form in **Konjunktiv I** which is different from the indicative, the effect is to put all other plural verbs into the conditional.

(ii)   Changes to the verb

The resultant verb changes may be summarized as follows. The introductory verbs could be in any past tense. The reported speech clause may start:

• with **daß**, with the verb at the end, as in the last three examples shown below;
• simply with a comma, as in the first three examples, in which case normal main clause word order is used.

Words actually used	*Indirect speech*
Present	
„**Ich *komme* aus Lübeck.**"	**Paul sagte, er *komme* aus Lübeck.**
"I *come* from Lübeck."	He said he *came* from Lübeck.

Words actually used	*Indirect speech*
„Wir *sind* vier in der Familie." "There *are* four of us in the family."	Er sagte, sie *seien* vier in der Familie. He said there *were* four of them in the family.
„Wir *haben* dort eine Wohnung." "We *have* an apartment there."	Er sagte, sie *hätten* dort eine Wohnung. He said they *had* an apartment there.

Future

„Wir *ziehen* morgen nach Köln." „Wir *werden* morgen nach Köln *ziehen*." "We *are/shall be moving* to Cologne tomorrow."	Er sagte, daß sie tags darauf nach Köln *ziehen würden*. He said that they *were/would be moving* to Cologne the next day.

Past

„Ich *wohnte* als Junge dort." „Ich *habe* als Junge dort *gewohnt*." "I *lived/used to live* there as a boy."	Er erzählte uns, daß er als Junge dort *gewohnt habe/hätte*. He told us that he *had lived* there as a boy.
„Meine Mutter *hatte* früher im Osten *gelebt*." "My mother *had* earlier *lived* in the east."	Er behauptete, daß seine Mutter früher im Osten *gelebt habe/hätte*. He claimed that his mother *had* earlier *lived* in the east.

(iii)   Variations to the rules

In any sort of non-personal writing these rules are generally adhered to, so that both **Konjunktiv I** and the conditional often appear in the same sentence. Newspapers use the construction frequently — reporting is after all their job. There are, however, important factors which often alter the indirect speech verb forms shown above.

(A) Apart from in a few set phrases, **Konjunktiv I** is virtually never used in everyday speech and seldom in personal writing.

• In speaking, indirect speech normally uses the same indicative tenses as were used by the speaker.

Paul sagt, er *kommt* aus Lübeck.	Paul says he *comes* from Lübeck.

• In writing, use of the same indicative tense is increasingly common when the subordinate clause begins with **daß** (which replaces the **Konjunktiv** as a marker of indirect speech).

Er hat uns erzählt, daß er als Junge in Köln *gewohnt hat*.	He told us that he *lived* in Cologne when he was a boy.

• Alternatively, and especially if what was said may not be true, the conditional may be used in both speech and writing.

Er behauptet, seine Mutter *hätte* im Osten *gelebt*.	He claims that his mother *had lived* in the east.

(B) In speech, and increasingly even in formal writing, there is now a strong tendency to use the compound conditional (e.g. **er würde kommen**) instead of the simple conditional (**er käme**) [➤14d(iv) Note]. The compound conditional is:

• *less* used with auxiliary verbs (**haben**, **sein** and the modals);
• *more* used when the simple conditional is either the same as the simple past (e.g. **machte**) or felt to be archaic (e.g. **stünde** from **stehen** 'stand').

Paul hat gesagt, er *würde* gleich *umziehen*, wenn er das Geld *hätte*. Vor allem *müßte* er in Köln eine Stelle finden.	Paul said he *would move* at once if he *had* the money. Above all he *had to/would have to* get a job in Cologne.

14d   *What if? Conditional statements (Konjunktiv II)*

A *conditional statement* deals not with what is so but with what *would* be so *if* something else happened. Sentences therefore generally have the form:

Wenn ich zu viel denke, bekomme ich Kopfschmerzen.	If I think too much I get a headache.

Which tenses are used depends on how likely the event is and the time zone referred to. A very important difference between German and (for example) French and English is that the same type of tense is used both in the **wenn** 'if' clause and in the main clause.

Wenn ich den Grund dafür wüßte, würde ich es dir sagen.	If I *knew* (*would know*) the reason for it I *would* tell you.

(i) Likely future events

Some future events are very likely to happen. The verb in the **wenn** clause is then in the normal present tense and the main verb is either also present, referring to the future [➤12a(iii)] or compound future (**werden** + infinitive) [➤12c].

Wenn es so *weitergeht, bitte* ich den Arzt um Rat/*werde* ich den Arzt um Rat *bitten*.	If it *goes on* like this, I *shall ask* the doctor for advice.

(ii) Giving advice

As an extension of this, the conditional can be used in the main clause to give advice about something which is known to be happening. Here the **wenn** clause may well be replaced by a phrase such as **an Ihrer/deiner Stelle** 'if I were you', **in dem Fall** 'in that case' etc.

An Ihrer Stelle *würde* ich mir keine Sorgen *machen*.	If I were you I *should*n't *worry*.

(iii) Possible events

Other future possibilities depend on events which may or may not happen. Here both the **wenn** clause verb and the main verb are in the conditional. The use of the compound conditional with **würde** in the **wenn** clause is more colloquial.

Wenn es ein gutes Mittel dagegen *gäbe* (*geben würde*), *würde* ich es nehmen.	If there *was/were* a good remedy for it I *would* take it.

(iv) Dependent events in the past

Some past events only happened (or did not happen) because of something else. In such cases, the verbs in both clauses are in the past conditional. If we are talking about the effects now, then the main verb is in the normal conditional.

Wenn du meinem Rat nur *gefolgt wärst, hättest* **du diese Probleme nicht** *gehabt/würdest* **du dich jetzt viel wohler** *fühlen.*	If you *had* only *taken* my advice you *would*n't *have had* these problems/you *would feel* much better now.

Note German use of the simple conditional (e.g. **käme**) as against the compound conditional (e.g. **würde kommen**) varies very greatly, making it difficult to make hard-and-fast rules for this usage [➤14c(iii)].

(A) In general the simple conditional is more likely to be used:

• in the **wenn** clause;
• with auxiliaries (**haben, sein** and the modals) and other common verbs;
• in non-personal writing.

(B) Conversely, the compound conditional is more used:

• in all cases in colloquial speech;
• in the main clause;
• with weak verbs [➤16c] with no distinct simple conditional form (e.g. **wartete**);
• with strong verbs [➤16d] whose simple conditional is felt to be archaic or stilted (e.g. **begönne** 'begin', **hülfe** 'help').

(C) Almost all weak and a good many strong verbs are in the last two categories, which reinforces the tendency to use the compound conditional. It is considered clumsy to use **würde** + infinitive in both halves of the sentence, though this does not prevent its happening, even in writing.

Things done to you: the passive

15a   What does the passive express?

In the *passive*, the subject does not perform the action of the verb but is the thing or person primarily affected by it. This is just what the direct object of a transitive verb describes, and only transitive verbs can be used in the passive [➤8d(i)]. All the same, the passive is not just another way of saying the same thing as the active form – it emphasizes different things, especially what happens to the subject. Who the doer of the action is usually matters less and may well not be stated.

Unser Haus *wird* im Augenblick *ausgebaut*. Das Dach *wird* auch neu *gedeckt*.	Our house *is being extended* at the moment. It *is* also *being re-roofed*.

15b   The tenses of the passive

The passive has the same range of tenses as the active, but they are all compound, formed with the relevant tense of the auxiliary **werden** + past participle. (The English equivalent is 'be' + past participle.) The more complex tenses are rare in the passive – other tenses tend to be substituted for them.

In the following list the terms *simple* and *compound* refer to the forms of **werden**, not to the whole tense; this helps to show how the passive and active tenses are parallel. Note that in the compound past tenses the past participle of **werden** loses its **ge-** and becomes **worden**.

Present/		
Simple future:	**Es wird gemacht.**	It is being/will be done.
Simple past:	**Es wurde gemacht.**	It was being done.
Perfect:	**Es ist gemacht worden.**	It has been done.
Pluperfect:	**Es war gemacht worden.**	It had been done.
Compound		
future:	**Es wird gemacht werden.**	It will be done (*rare*).
Conditional:	**Es würde gemacht.**	It would be done.
Past conditional:	**Es wäre gemacht worden.**	It would have been done.

Konjunktiv I simple:	**Es werde gemacht.**	(They said that) it was being done.
Konjunktiv I perfect:	**Es sei gemacht worden.**	(They said that) it had been done.

15c By whom? How? With what? The agent, the means and the instrument

Three German prepositions translate the English 'by' with a passive.

(i) **von** + dative noun phrase describes the person who (or possibly thing which) did the action.

Zunächst ist das alte Dach *von den Bauarbeitern* entfernt worden.	First the old roof was removed *by the construction workers*.

(ii) **durch** + accusative noun phrase describes the means by which the action was done.

Es war *durch die letzten Winterstürme* schwer beschädigt worden.	It had been badly damaged *by the last winter storms*.

(iii) **mit** + dative noun phrase describes the instrument with which the action was done. (**durch** + accusative can also be used).

Dann sind die neuen Ziegel *mit langen Nägeln* an den Dachlatten befestigt worden.	Then the new tiles were secured *by/with long nails* to the roof battens.

15d The passive with intransitive verbs

(i) In German, unlike English, only the direct (accusative) object of an active verb can become the (nominative) subject of a passive verb. Dative objects [▶8d(ii), 8e] can be used with passive verbs but:

• they remain in the dative case;
• the main verb is in the third person singular;

• main clauses must start with the dummy subject **es** if no other word or phrase is occupying first position.

***Uns** ist empfohlen worden, einen Architekten einzustellen. **Es** ist **mir** geraten worden, es nicht alleine zu unternehmen.*	*We* were recommended to hire an architect. *I* was advised not to undertake it alone.

(ii)   Prepositional objects [➤8g] can similarly be used with passives.

***Für alle möglichen Fälle** ist gesorgt worden.*	*Every possible eventuality* was taken care *of*.

Note   In both cases alternative constructions are often preferable [➤15f].

15e   *What is going on? Passive verbs with no subject*

Unlike English, German can use a passive verb to refer generally to an activity. Such constructions have no subject, but main clauses must start with the dummy subject **es** if no other word or phrase is occupying first position. Even intransitive verbs are sometimes used in this way.

Beim Richtfest *wird getrunken.* **Am Abend *wird* wohl *gesungen* und *getanzt.***	At the topping-out (roof completion) ceremony *there are drinks*. In the evening *there is* probably *singing* and *dancing*.

15f   *Alternatives to the passive*

The passive is not uncommon in German, and it is certainly not to be avoided if it is the most suitable way of saying something. Indeed, it has uses like those in paragraph 15e which have no English equivalent. All the same, German does have a range of alternatives to the passive.

(i)   In English we may use the passive in order to stress something other than the doer of the action. In German this can easily be done by placing (say) the accusative or dative object at the start of the sentence.

> *Unseren Anbau* hat eine
> **Fachzeitschrift ausführlich
> beschrieben.** *Dem Architekten*
> **hat der Verfasser insbesondere
> gratuliert.**

> *Our extension* was extensively
> written up by a trade journal. *The
> architect* was especially
> congratulated by the writer.

(ii) Where in English we describe the process using the passive, German may well use an active verb describing the outcome. This is especially useful as a way of avoiding passive verbs with indirect objects [➤8e].

> **Ich** *habe erfahren,* **daß der
> Architekt einen Preis** *erhalten
> hat.*

> I *was told* that the architect *was
> given* a prize.

(iii) *The indefinite pronoun:* **man**

If the doer of an action is 'they' (people in general), the indefinite pronoun **man** 'one' is often used as the subject.

> **Solche Preise** *verleiht man* **nicht
> ohne guten Grund.**

> Such prizes *are* not *awarded*
> without good reason.

Note **man** cannot be used to narrate a chance event for which nobody is held responsible, so:

Ein Bauarbeiter wurde verletzt. A building worker was injured.

or **Ein Bauarbeiter hat sich verletzt.** A building worker injured himself.

(but not **Man hat einen Bauarbeiter verletzt.** They injured a building worker.)

(iv) *Passive usage of reflexive verbs*

A reflexive verb often replaces an English passive. Similarly, many German reflexive verbs translate the English construction 'be' + past participle, for example, **ich ärgere/freue/schäme mich** 'I am annoyed/pleased/ashamed'.

Ich *wundere mich* nur (darüber), daß der Artikel mich gar nicht erwähnt hat. Das *erklärt sich* wohl dadurch, daß ich kein Architekt bin!	I *am* only *surprised* that the article did not mention me at all. That *is* no doubt *explained* by the fact that I am not an architect!

(v) *'Can be done' can be expressed using:*

(A) das läßt sich ... machen [➤8d(i)] and **das ist ... zu machen**. The latter can also mean 'must be done'. Notice that the normal infinitive is used (here **machen**), rather than the passive infinitive (**gemacht werden**).

(B) sein + an adjective formed from the verb stem + **-bar** or **-lich** (equivalent to the English ending '-able').

Solche Arbeit *läßt sich* leicht *machen*, wenn man Architekt ist. Sonst *ist* sie aber kaum *zu machen*/kaum *machbar*. Ein Fachmann *ist* immer *einzustellen*.	That sort of work *can* easily *be done* if you are an architect, but otherwise it *is* hardly *to be done* (*is* hardly *doable*). An expert *must* always *be hired*.

(vi) **bekommen** or the colloquial **kriegen** are sometimes used with a past participle.

Dadurch *bekommt/kriegt* man alle technischen Probleme *gelöst*.	That way you *get* all the technical problems *solved*.

15g Action or description? The descriptive passive

The true passive always describes a process, but when it is over the same past participle can describe the result. For this, German uses **sein** + past participle. This construction is often called the *descriptive passive,* but it must not be used instead of the true passive with **werden**.

The first example below describes a process which is still going on, the second a recently completed process and the third the result of a process which may have happened years before. In this last case, the participle could well be replaced by an adjective.

Die Mauern *werden* gerade verputzt.	The walls *are* just *being* plastered.
Die Mauern *sind* verputzt *worden*.	The walls *have been* plastered.
Die Mauern *sind* verputzt (weiß/sehr hoch).	The walls *are* plastered (white/very high).

Types of German verb

➤ Tense stems and endings: ➤ch.17. Verb tables: ➤ch.18.

16a   Predictability: regular or irregular?

(i)   Conjugation

The whole set of a verb's stems and endings is called its *conjugation*.

• *Regular* verbs are verbs in which you can predict any part of any tense from the spelling of the infinitive – plus of course a knowledge of the rules!
• Verbs in which some parts cannot be predicted in this way are known as *irregular* verbs. Some of the most common German verbs are irregular, but there are not very many of them, and the irregularities are often quite small.

(ii)   Predicting the conjugation

The conjugation of German verbs is very systematic. In all but a handful of verbs you can predict any part just by knowing four basic forms:

• the *infinitive;*
• the **er/sie/es** (third person singular) form of the present tense and of the simple past;
• the past participle.
In fact, in the great majority the other forms can be predicted from the infinitive alone.

(iii)   Compound verbs

Compound verbs [➤16e] always conjugate in the same way as their base verb. Apparent exceptions are in fact verbs made from nouns related to the base verb.

Sie trägt es/trug es/hat es ... getragen.	She carries/(has) carried it.
Sie erträgt es/ertrug es/hat es ... ertragen.	She endures/(has) endured it.
Sie trägt es ... ein/trug es ... ein/hat es ... eingetragen.	She enters/(has) entered it (on a list).

but:

Sie beantragt es/beantragte es/hat es ... beantragt.	She applies/(has) applied for it.

This last example is in fact formed from **der Antrag** 'application'.

16b *Weak and strong verbs*

Like other Germanic languages (including English), German has two main categories of verb, traditionally known as *weak* and *strong*. They have very different ways of forming their simple past tense and past participle.

Note 'Weak' and 'strong' are not the same as 'regular' and 'irregular'. In both categories most verbs are regular, that is, they follow the rules for their category.

16c *Weak verbs*

If any new verb is coined (from another language, for example), it always follows the weak pattern.

(i) *Regular weak verbs*

Weak verbs add endings to the stem of the infinitive (the infinitive minus **-(e)n**), as in the English 'walk, walked' or 'learn, learned(t)'. German weak verbs add:

• **-(e)te** to the stem to form the base of the simple past (that is, the basic form to which the endings are added [➤17a]);
• **-(e)t** to the stem to form the past participle.

For example, **lachen** 'laugh': **ich lache, ich lachte, ich habe, ... gelacht.**
The **-e-** is used if the stem ends in **d** or **t**, or in **m** or **n** preceded by any consonant other than **l** or **r**.

For example, **regnen** 'rain': **es regnet, es regnete, es hat ... geregnet.**

(ii) *Irregular weak verbs*

There are only sixteen irregular weak verbs.

• They all add the normal weak endings in the simple past and past participle, but they have minor variations in the stem. The verbs can be grouped together according to these variations.

• Only **haben** and the modals/**wissen** group are also irregular in the present tense.

The parts of the verb shown in the examples below are the infinitive, and the present (only if irregular), simple past and perfect tenses.

(A) haben loses its **-b-** in the **du** and **er/sie/es** forms of the present tense and in the whole of the simple past (where the **-t-** of the ending doubles). The past participle is regular.

haben, hast/hat, hatte, hat ... gehabt	have

(B) The six modal verbs [➤ch.9] and **wissen** form the largest group of irregular weak verbs.

• The present tense singular looks like the simple past of a strong verb, that is, the **ich** and **er/sie/es** forms (first and third persons) are the same, and neither has any ending. All but **sollen** change the stem vowel. The plural is regular.
• The four modals with **ö** or **ü** in the stem drop the Umlaut in the simple past and past participle; the **i** in **wissen** changes to **u**. [Infinitive-past participle: ➤9b(i).]

dürfen, darf, durfte, hat ... gedurft	allowed to (may)
können, kann, konnte, hat ... gekonnt	able to (can)
mögen, mag, mochte, hat ... gemocht	like (to)
müssen, muß, mußte, hat ... gemußt	have to (must)
sollen, soll, sollte, hat ... gesollt	supposed to, ought to
wollen, will, wollte, hat ... gewollt	want to
wissen, weiß, wußte, hat ... gewußt	know (a fact)

(C) Four verbs change **-enn-** in the stem to **-ann-**. You will notice that they all rhyme.

brennen, brannte, hat ... gebrannt	burn
kennen, kannte, hat ... gekannt	know (a person, place, etc.)
nennen, nannte, hat ... genannt	name
rennen, rannte, ist ... gerannt	race, scamper

(D) Two verbs change **-end-** in the stem to **-and-**. **senden** 'broadcast' and **wenden** '(turn) (a car) round, meat over' are regular (**sendete, wendete**), as are the compounds **entwenden** 'purloin' and **verwenden** 'use'.

senden, sandte, hat ... gesandt	send
wenden, wandte, hat ... gewandt	turn

(E) Two verbs change the last three letters of the stem to **-ach-**. Like their English counterparts, they therefore rhyme in the simple past and past participle but not in the infinitive or present tense.

bringen, brachte, hat ... gebracht　　　bring (brought)
denken, dachte, hat ... gedacht　　　think (thought)

16d *Strong verbs*

(i) *Formation of strong verbs*

Strong verbs change the stem vowel of the infinitive, as in the English 'bite, bit, bitten', 'give, gave, given' or 'sing, sang, sung'.

• In the **du** and **er/sie/es** forms of the present tense, the stem vowels **e**, **a** and **o** often change to **i(e)**, **ä** and **ö**.
• In all strong verbs the stem vowel changes in the simple past.
• In all strong verbs except **tun** (**getan**) the past participle ends in **-en**, and in four of the seven classes the stem vowel changes.

(ii) *Vowel changes*

Strong verbs fall into seven major classes. Each class has a distinctive pattern of vowel changes, and the verbs within it often rhyme. You can predict the forms of most strong verbs by knowing which class they fall into. [For examples of verbs in each class ➤(v) below.] You will see that there is a clear progression both in the stem vowels of the infinitive (**ei → ie → i → e/i → e → a → a**) and in other ways, and this can be a great help when learning the parts of the verbs.

(iii) *Irregular strong verbs*

Irregular strong verbs are of three kinds.

• Verbs with minor variations in the stem consonants. These are noted as they occur in each class.
• Verbs in which the simple past and past participle follow a regular pattern but the infinitive and present tense do not. The most common of these are listed below by class.
• Two verbs which do not fit into any class. These are:

stehen, steht, stand, hat ... gestanden　　　stand
tun, tut, tat, hat ... getan　　　do, pour

(iv) *Verbs with both weak and strong forms*

Some verbs have both weak and strong forms, sometimes with different meanings. The most common of these are noted below.

(v) *The seven strong verb classes*

In the following listings these parts of the verb are given:

• the infinitive
• the **er/sie/es** (third person singular) form of the present tense, the simple past and the perfect.

(The **du** form has the same stem vowel as the **er/sie/es** form.)

● *Class I*

-ei- in infinitive and present tense, changing to -ie- (before a single consonant) or -i- (before a double, including **ß**) in both simple past and past participle.

• -f- and -t- are doubled, changing -eif- to -iff- and -eit- to -itt-.
• -eid- also usually becomes -itt- (but **meiden, m*ied***).

beißen, beißt, biß, hat ... gebissen	bite
bleiben, bleibt, blieb, ist ... geblieben	remain
greifen, greift, griff, hat ... gegriffen	grab at
schneiden, schneidet, schnitt, hat ... geschnitten	cut

● *Class II*

-ie- in infinitive and present tense, changing to -o- in both simple past and past participle.

• Note the -g- in **ziehen: zog**.

fliegen, fliegt, flog, ist ... geflogen	fly
gießen, gießt, goß, hat ... gegossen	pour

Irregular verbs. Class II has collected a number of verbs whose stem vowel is not -ie-.

bewegen, bewegt, bewog, hat ...bewogen	persuade
betrügen, betrügt, betrog, hat ... betrogen	deceive
erwägen, erwägt, erwog, hat ... erwogen	consider
gären, gärt, gor, hat/ist ... gegoren	ferment
glimmen, glimmt, glomm, hat ... geglommen	glow
heben, hebt, hob, hat ... gehoben	lift, raise
lügen, lügt, log, hat ... gelogen	(tell a) lie
melken, melkt, molk, hat ... gemolken	milk
scheren, schert, schor, hat ... geschoren	shear
schwören, schwört, schwor, hat ... geschworen	swear (an oath)

(**bewegen** 'move' and **gären** 'seethe (with rage, etc.)' are weak.)

• Some verbs change the vowel in the **du** and **er/sie/es** forms of the present tense, usually to -i-.

dreschen, drischt, drosch, hat ... gedroschen	thresh
erlöschen, erlischt, erlosch, ist ... erloschen	go out (of fire)
fechten, ficht, focht, hat ... gefochten	fence (fight)
flechten, flicht, flocht, hat ... geflochten	plait
quellen, quillt, quoll, ist ... gequollen	well up, stream

saufen, säuft, soff, hat ... gesoffen — drink (of animals), booze

schmelzen, schmilzt, schmolz, hat/ist ... geschmolzen — melt

schwellen, schwillt, schwoll, ist ... geschwollen — swell

(**löschen** 'extinguish' is weak.)

● *Class III*

-ind-, -ing- or -ink- in infinitive and present tense, changing to -a- in the simple past and to -u- in the past participle.

finden, findet, fand, hat ... gefunden — find
singen, singt, sang, hat ... gesungen — sing
sinken, sinkt, sank, ist ... gesunken — sink

● *Class IV*

-imm-, -inn-, or -e- + two consonants (except -ss-) in infinitive, changing -e- to -i- in the du and er/sie/es forms of the present tense, and -e-/-i- to -a- in the simple past and to -o- in the past participle.

erschrecken, erschrickt, erschrak, ist ... erschrocken — be frightened, startled
helfen, hilft, half, hat ... geholfen — help
sterben, stirbt, starb, ist ... gestorben — die
schwimmen, schwimmt, schwamm, ist/hat ... geschwommen — swim
beginnen, beginnt, begann, hat ... begonnen — begin

(**erschrecken** 'frighten' is weak.)

Irregular verbs. Note the single and double consonants.

kommen, kommt, kam, ist ... gekommen — come
nehmen, nimmt, nahm, hat ... genommen — take
treffen, trifft, traf, hat ... getroffen — meet, hit (target)
werden, wirst/wird, wurde, ist ... geworden — become

● *Class V*

-e- + single consonant or -ss- in infinitive, changing to -i- in the du and er/sie/es forms of the present tense and to -a- in the simple past, but retaining the stem of the infinitive in the past participle.

• Note that only **essen** inserts a -g- into the past participle.

geben, gibt, gab, hat ... gegeben — give
essen, ißt, aß, hat ... gegessen — eat

Irregular verbs.

liegen, liegt, lag, hat ... gelegen — lie (flat)
sitzen, sitzt, saß, hat ... gesessen — sit
sein, ist, war, ist ... gewesen — be

(**sein** is very irregular, especially in the present [➤18b]. It is a mixture of two verbs, one of which fits the pattern of Class V.)

● *Class VI*

-**a**- in infinitive, changing to -**ä**- in the **du** and **er/sie/es** forms of the present tense and to -**u**- in the simple past, but retaining the stem of the infinitive in the past participle.

fahren, fährt, fuhr, ist ... gefahren	go (in a vehicle), drive
graben,, gräbt, grub, hat ... gegraben	dig
laden, lädt, lud, hat ... geladen	load
schlagen, schlägt, schlug, hat ... geschlagen	hit, strike
wachsen, wächst, wuchs, ist ... gewachsen	grow
waschen, wäscht, wusch, hat ... gewaschen	was**h**

Irregular verbs. There are only two of these.

backen, backt, backte/(buk), hat ... gebacken	bake (**buk** is now archaic)
schaffen, schafft, schuf, hat ... geschaffen	create

(**schaffen** 'do, achieve' is weak)

● *Class VII*

-**a**- in infinitive, changing to -**ä**- in the **du** and **er/sie/es** forms of the present tense and to -**ie**- (after single consonant) or -**i**- (after a double) in the simple past, but retaining the stem of the infinitive in the past participle.

• Apart from the eight verbs in Class VI, all strong verbs with -**a**- in the infinitive stem belong to this class.

fangen, fängt, fing, hat ... gefangen	catch
schlafen, schläft, schlief, hat ... geschlafen	sleep

Irregular verbs. Class VII has collected some half dozen verbs whose stem vowel is not -**a**- but which follow this pattern in the past (participle) and sometimes in the present.

laufen, läuft, lief, ist ... gelaufen	run, walk
stoßen, stößt, stieß, hat ... gestoßen	push (sharply)
hängen, hängt, hing, hat ... gehangen	hang (*intransitive*)
gehen, geht, ging, ist ... geg*ang*en	go (on foot or generally), walk
hauen, haut, hieb/haute, hat ... gehauen/gehaut	hew, bash (weak forms are more colloquial)
heißen, heißt, hieß, hat ... geheißen	be called, command
rufen, ruft, rief, hat ... gerufen	call, shout

(**hängen** [*transitive*] is weak)

16e Compound verbs

German has a wide range of compound verbs, which greatly extend the meanings of the simple verbs on which they are based. There are two forms of compound verb:

(A) those formed with a *fixed prefix* [➤16e(i)] (often marked *insep. [inseparable]* in dictionaries).

(B) those combined with a *verbal particle* [➤16e(ii)] (marked *sep. [separable]* in dictionaries).
These are often called **(A)** *inseparable prefixes* and **(B)** *separable prefixes*. However, as all true prefixes are inseparable, making the second term confusing, we prefer to use the terms *(fixed) prefix* and *(verbal) particle* .

Note The major distinctions between the two affect both speech and writing.

1) Fixed prefixes are never detached from the verb stem.

• They are never stressed, that is, they never receive the main emphasis within the word. The stress remains on the verb stem.
• Verbs with a fixed prefix do not add **ge-** for the past participle.
• **zu** and the infinitive (including the prefix) are two separate words.

Ich hatte ihnen *erlaubt*, meinen Wagen *zu verkaufen*.	I had *allowed* them *to sell* my car.

2) Verbal particles are always in the final block [➤4e[iii]].

• They are stressed, even when they are attached to their verb.
• When the verb is also in the final block its particle is attached to it. Both **ge-** and **zu** (if present) are then 'sandwiched' between the two.

Sie hatten sich *angeboten*, mir den Wagen *abzukaufen*.	They had *offered to buy* the car *from* me.

(i) Fixed prefixes

Fixed prefixes usually make verbs from other verbs, but they can also make verbs from adjectives and occasionally from nouns. They almost always add a sense of completion — they carry the action of the verb further or to a conclusion (for better or worse). The general sense of each prefix is given below, but you will find many verbs with different meanings. Only a few examples are listed.

(A) be- makes transitive verbs from other verbs, nouns or adjectives (the latter usually ending in **-ig**), often applying the original meaning to something.

Ich begreife es.	I grasp, understand it.
Ich bespreche es.	I discuss it.
Ich betrete es.	I enter (a room etc.).
Ich bewässere es.	I water, irrigate it.
Ich berichtige es.	I correct it.
Ich beruhige mich.	I calm down.

(B) emp- is used with three verbs beginning in **f**. There is no longer any recognizable link to the meaning of their base verbs.

Ich empfange sie.	I receive them.
Ich empfehle es ihr.	I recommend it to her.
Ich empfinde.	I feel (emotions).

(C) ent- with verbs of motion takes a dative object, meaning 'getting away from'.

Ich entkomme ihnen.	I escape from them.
Ich entlaufe ihm.	I run away from him.

ent- with adjectives, nouns or other verbs often means 'removing'.

Ich entferne es/mich.	I remove it/move away.
Ich entziffere es.	I decipher it.
Ich entschuldige mich.	I say sorry.
Ich entwässere es.	I drain, dehydrate it.

(D) er- with verbs usually carries the action to a conclusion.

Ich ergreife es.	I seize, grasp, grip it.
Ich erhalte es.	I receive it.
Ich erlebe es.	I experience it.
Ich erreiche e.	I reach it (a place).
Ich erwarte es.	I await, wait for it.
Ich erzähle es.	I narrate, tell it.

er- with adjectives means 'making' or 'changing to'.

Es ermöglicht etwas.	It makes something possible.
Ich ermüde (ihn).	I tire (him).
Ich erröte.	I blush.

(E) ge- makes compounds which considerably alter the meaning of the base verb.

Ich gebrauche es.	I use it.
Das gefällt mir.	I like that.
Es gehört ihnen.	It is theirs, belongs to them.
Es gelingt mir.	I succeed.

(F) hinter- adds the meaning of 'behind' to verbs, usually in a metaphorical sense.

| Ich hintergehe ihnen. | I go behind their back. |
| Ich hinterlasse es ihr. | I leave her it (in my will). |

(G) miß- has the same meaning as English 'mis-'.
• Note the double prefix in **er mißversteht es** 'he misunderstands it' and the position of **-zu-** in **mißzuverstehen** 'to misunderstand'.

Es mißlingt.	It goes wrong.
Das mißfällt mir.	I don't like that.
Ich mißtraue ihnen.	I mistrust them.

(H) ver- is very common and has a range of meanings. With verbs it conveys the sense of 'finishing off' or 'wrongly, by mistake'. In a few cases it gives an opposite.

Ich verdiene es.	I earn, deserve it.
Ich verfahre mich.	I lose my way (driving).
Ich verlasse es.	I leave it (a place).
Ich verliere es.	I lose it.
Ich verlerne es.	I forget, 'unlearn' it.
Ich verschließe es.	I lock it (up).

ver- with adjectives means 'making' or 'becoming'. With nouns it conveys 'providing or applying'.

Sie vereinigen sich/es.	They unite (it).
Es verfärbt sich.	It discolours.
Sie verhaften ihn.	They arrest him.
Sie vergiften es.	They poison, pollute it.

(I) zer- with other verbs always adds the sense of 'in pieces'.

Ich zerlege es.	I dismantle it, take it apart.
Ich zerquetsche es.	I squash it.
Ich zerreiße es.	I tear it up.
Ich zerstöre es.	I destroy it.

(ii) *Verbal particles*

A *verbal particle* is a semi-independent word closely linked to a verb, whose meaning it modifies. Most are derived from prepositions, adverbs, other verbs, adjectives or nouns. There are far too many verbal particles to list. The following examples are grouped by their derivation or form.

(A) Particles from prepositions (**ein** is the particle for **in**).

Dreh das Licht *aus*, sperr die Katze *ein*, und mach alle Fenster *zu*. Kommt der Peter *mit*? Oder hat er *vor*, uns *nach*zufahren? Pünktlichkeit werden wir ihm nie *bei*bringen! Der Sechsuhrzug ist schon *ab*gefahren. Nun werden wir erst um Mitternacht in Berlin *an*kommen.	Turn the light out, shut the cat in and close all the windows. Is Peter coming with us? Or is he planning to follow later? We'll never teach him punctuality! The six o'clock train has already left. Now we shall not arrive in Berlin before midnight.

(B) Compound particles.

Ich ging eine enge Gasse *hinunter*, da kam mir ein Mann *entgegen*.Als er an mir *vorbei*ging, schob er mich *beiseite*. Ich ließ meine Papiere fallen, die ganz *durcheinander*kamen. „Passen Sie doch auf!" stieß ich *hervor* und fügte *hinzu*: „Sind Sie betrunken?" Ohne zu antworten lief er *davon*, ich ihm *hinterher*.	As I was walking down a narrow alley, a man came towards me. As he passed me, he pushed me aside. I dropped my papers, which got into a complete mess. "Look out!" I gasped, adding, "Are you drunk?" Without answering he ran off, with me behind him.

(C) Particles from other verbs (infinitives or past participles). These are usually linked to just one or two verbs.

Meinen Wagen hatte ich auf der Hauptstraße *stehen*(lassen). Kurz davor blieb er *stehen*. Ich wollte ihn wieder anreden, da erkannte ich ihn – ich hatte ihn vor ein paar Wochen *kennen*gelernt. Ich wußte, an ihm würden meine Worte *verloren*gehen, also ließ ich mein Vorhaben *fallen* und ging weiter *spazieren*.	I had parked my car on the main street. Just before it stopped. I was going to speak to him again, then I recognized him – I had met him a few weeks earlier. I knew that my words would be wasted on him, so I abandoned my plan and continued with my walk.

(D) Particles from adverbs, adjectives or nouns. These also are usually linked to just one or two verbs.

Ich nahm an Verhandlungen *teil*, die in einem großen Hotel *statt*fanden. Sie waren im allgemeinen *glatt*gegangen. Am Abend ging ich in die Bar, wo verschiedene Leute *fern*sahen. Plötzlich hielt mich jemand am Ärmel *fest*, und eine Stimme sagte: „Ich höre, Sie arbeiten die meiste Zeit *schwarz*!"	I was taking part in negotiations which were taking place in a big hotel. In general they had gone smoothly. In the evening I went into the bar, where various people were watching television. Suddenly someone caught me by the sleeve, and a voice said, "I hear you spend most of your time moonlighting!"

(iii)   Dual use as prefix and particle

A few words can be both fixed prefixes and particles. The particles (in italics in the following examples) usually have more literal meanings than the prefixes.

(A) durch-

Ich habe eben Ihren Bericht *durch*gelesen. Jetzt durchschaue ich die Lage besser.	I have just read through your report. Now I understand the situation better.

(B) über-

Wir gehen ja bald zu einem neuen Computersystem *über*. Ich bitte Sie, die Verantwortung dafür zu übernehmen.	Of course we are going over soon to a new computer system. I am asking you to take over responsibility for it.

(C) um-

Das Computernetz umspannt unser ganzes Unternehmen. Viele Angestellte müssen *um*geschult werden.	The computer network covers our whole operation. Many employees will have to be retrained.

(D) unter-

Wir müssen alles unternehmen, um konkurrenzfähig zu bleiben, sonst gehen wir *unter*.	We must do everything to remain competitive, otherwise we shall go under.

(E) voll- : used as prefix in a few verbs, meaning 'complete', but now stilted.

Um unseren Entwicklungsplan zu vollführen (auszuführen), müssen wir die Firma mit kompetenten Leuten *voll*füllen.	In order to fulfil our development plan we must fill the firm full of competent people.

(F) wider- : used as a particle with only two verbs, **widerhallen** 'echo' and **widerspiegeln** 'reflect'.

Das spiegelt unseren festen Entschluß *wider*, in diesem Bereich aller Konkurrenz zu widerstehen.	This reflects our strong resolve to stand firm against all the competition in this field.

(G) wieder- : used as a prefix with only one verb **wiederholen** 'repeat'.

Ich wiederhole es, wir sind entschlossen, unseren ehemaligen Marktanteil *wieder*zugewinnen.	I repeat, we are determined to regain our former market share.

(iv) *Particle or independent word?*

The same word may sometimes be used as a particle or as an independent word. In general, if the combination with the verb produces a new meaning, then the word is treated as a particle (again in italics below). If each part keeps its own original meaning, then the two are written separately, and stressed separately in speech.

Ich will lieber stehen bleiben.	I prefer to remain standing.
but	
Ich bin plötzlich *stehen*geblieben.	I suddenly stopped (came to a halt).
Wir haben die Platten fallen lassen.	We dropped the records.
but	
Wir haben den Plan *fallen*lassen.	We dropped the plan.
Das hat er sehr schön gemacht.	He did that very beautifully.
but	
Der hat sich aber *schön*gemacht!	He really has got dressed up!

17 The formation of tenses: how are verbs conjugated?

Any part of any simple tense is made up of the basic stem ('base') for that tense plus the ending which goes with the verb's subject.

➤   Compound tenses: ➤17c. Imperative: ➤17d. Passive: ➤Chapter 15.

17a   *The basic form (base) of simple tenses*

(i)   Tense bases are more complex than endings. For this reason they have been discussed fully in paragraphs 16c (weak verbs, especially irregular) and 16d (strong verbs). Once the base is known, the endings are added to it as shown in paragraph 17b.

(ii)   The bases of the four simple tenses are summarized below.

Present: = stem of infinitive (i.e. infinitive minus **-(e)n**)
e.g. **setz-, wart-, lächel-, wander-, hab-; bleib-, geb-, trag-, tu-**

Simple past
– weak: = infinitive stem + **-(e)te**
e.g. **setzte-, wartete-, lächelte-, wanderte-**
– strong: = infinitive stem with change of vowel
e.g. **blieb-, gab-, sang-, trug-**

Konjunktiv I:
= infinitive minus **-n**
e.g. **setze-, warte-, lächle-, wandere-, habe-; bleibe-, gebe-, trage-, sei-**. Note **tue-**.

Simple conditional:
(*a*) if the simple past is regular weak: = simple past
e.g. **setzte-, wartete-, lächelte-, wanderte-, sollte-**
(*b*) if strong or irregular weak: = simple past + Umlaut if stem vowel is **a**, **o** or **u**, + final **-e** if not already there
e.g. **bliebe-, gäbe-, trüge-, wäre-, würde-; hätte-, wüßte-, möchte-**

Note   The rules for the simple conditional are very consistently applied, except that:

1) there are some strong verbs which change their stem vowel again, for example, **half → hülfe, schwamm → schwömme, schwor → schwüre, stand → stünde**;
2) irregular weak verbs which change **-enn-/-end-** to **-ann-/-and-** in the simple past and past participle [➤16c(i)] return here to the infini-

tive stem, for example, **brannte → brennte, kannte → kennte, sandte → sendete, wandte → wendete**. (**ä** would of course be pronounced like **e** in any case.)

In both instances, the compound conditional (**würde** + infinitive) would usually be preferred [➤14d(ii)Note].

17b   Tense endings

(i)   German tense endings are very straightforward. Apart from in the **ich** and **er/sie/es** forms of the present tense, all tenses add the same set of endings to the base of the tense [➤17a]. With the fairly minor variations listed in (iii) below, this goes for almost all weak and strong verbs. The only major exceptions are in the present tenses of **sein** [➤18b], **wissen** and the modals [➤16c(ii)].

(ii)   In each tense there are three *persons* in both *singular* (one person) and *plural* (more than one):

First person: the speaker(s)   **ich** 'I', **wir** 'we'
Second person: the person(s) spoken to   **du, ihr** 'you' (familiar singular, plural)
  Sie 'you' (polite singular/plural)
Third person: the person(s) or thing(s) spoken about   **er/sie/es** 'he/she/it', **sie** 'they' or any noun phrase

Singular endings	*Examples*
First person **ich**:	
present tense = base + **-e**	**mache, warte, bleibe**
other tenses = base (no ending)	**machte, wartete, blieb, würde, käme**
Second person **du**:	
all tenses = base + **-(e)st**	**machst, wartest, bleibst, macht-est, würdest**
Third person **er/sie/es**:	
present = base + **-(e)t**	**macht, wartet, bleibt**
other tenses = base (no ending)	**machte, wartete, blieb, würde, käme**
Plural endings	
First person **wir**:	
all tenses = base + **-(e)n**	**machen, bleiben, warteten, blieben, würden**
Second person **ihr**:	
all tenses = base + **-(e)t**	**macht, wartet, bleibt, machtet, würdet**
Third person **sie/(Sie)**:	
all tenses = base + **-(e)n**	**machen, bleiben, warteten, blieben, würden**

(iii) *Variations in the pattern of endings*

Most of these variations simply make the word easier to pronounce.

(A) The linking **-e-** is included before **-st** and **-t** after bases ending in **t** or **d**, or in **m** or **n** preceded by any consonant except **l** or **r**, e.g. **wartest, findet, atmest, regnet** but **qualmt, wärmst, warnt.**

Note 1) In strong verbs, there is no **-e-** after a vowel change in the present tense or in the (little used) **du** form of the simple past, e.g. **trittst, tritt, lädst, lädt**; **fandst, tratst**.

2) In **werden**, note the dropping of the **d** in **du wirst** and of the **t** in **er/sie/es wird**.

(B) The linking **-e-** is always included before **-n** *unless* the base ends in **e, el** or **er**, e.g. **warten, finden, atmen** but **möchten, lächeln, wandern**. Note also **tun**.

(C) After present tense bases ending in **s, ß, x** or **z** the **du** ending **-st** reduces to **-t** e.g. **niest, heißt, boxt, sitzt** (replacing the older form **niesest,** etc.).

(D) Bases ending in **-el** lose the **e** of the base before the **ich** ending **-e**; particularly in speech, this also sometimes happens to bases ending in **-er**, e.g. **ich klingle, lächle, (wandre).**

(E) The **b** in **haben** is dropped in present tense **du hast** and **er/sie/es hat** (as also in the base of the simple past **hatte**).

17c *Compound tenses*

(i) *Compound past tenses*

These are formed with the auxiliaries **haben** or **sein** + past participle. (Paragraphs 18a/b list **haben** and **sein** in full.).

Note In German, it is the meaning of the verb that determines which auxiliary it takes. This is why some verbs can take either **sein** or **haben** [➤(C) below]. For example:

• To say that people have just gone into town you would always start „**Sie** *sind* **in die Stadt …**" whether you then finished with „ **… gegangen**", „ **… gefahren**" or whatever.
• However, if the verb had a direct object, you would always use **haben**, as in **er hat das Auto in die Garage gefahren**.

(A) The following groups of verbs take **sein**. Note that some take an object in the dative but none takes an object in the accusative.

• Intransitive verbs of motion:

Das Kind ist in den Garten *gegangen/gerannt/gekommen/ gekrochen.*	The child *went/ran/came/crawled* into the yard.
Es ist *hingefallen,* **ist aber gleich** *aufgestanden.*	He (It) *fell over* but *got up* again at once.
Es war früher auf die Bank *gestiegen* **und dann in den Sandkasten** *gesprungen.*	He had earlier *climbed* onto the bench, then he had *jumped* into the sandpit.
Es ist im Sandkasten der Katze *begegnet* **und ist ihr ins Haus** *gefolgt.*	He *met* the cat in the sandpit and *followed* it into the house.

• Intransitive verbs describing a change of state. This often includes the start or end of a process:

Es war wärmer *geworden.* **Die Eisblumen waren schon** *geschmolzen/getaut/ verschwunden.*	It had *become* warmer. The frost patterns had already *melted/thawed/disappeared.*
Bis das Feuer *erloschen* **war, war das Kind schon** *eingeschlafen.* **Erst zehn Stunden später ist es wieder** *aufgewacht.*	By the time the fire had *gone out,* the child had *gone to sleep.* He only *woke up* ten hours later.
Das Kind ist im Mai 1990 *geboren.* **Einen Monat später ist sein Großvater** *gestorben.*	The child was *born* in May 1990. One month later his grandfather *died.*

• Most verbs meaning 'happen', 'succeed' or 'fail':

Es ist mir nicht *gelungen,* **ins Parlament zu kommen. Das ist mir schon dreimal** *passiert/geschehen/zugestoßen.*	I have not *succeeded* in getting into Parliament. That has *happened* to me three times already.

• The verbs **sein** and **bleiben**:

Wo bist du gestern *gewesen?* **Ich bin den ganzen Tag allein** *geblieben.*	Where *were* you yesterday? I *remained* alone the whole day.

(B) All other verbs take **haben**. This includes:

• All transitive verbs except **ich *bin* es losgeworden** 'I got rid of it':

Der Feuerwehrmann hat das Haus *betreten*, eine Leiter *bestiegen* und das Feuer *gelöscht*. Dafür hat er viel Lob *bekommen*.	The fireman *entered* the house, *mounted* a ladder and *put out* the fire. For that he *received* a lot of praise.

• All reflexive verbs except for a few verbs with **sein** where **sich** means 'each other':

Ich habe *mich gewaschen*, *rasiert* und *angezogen*, dann habe ich *mich* zu Tisch *gesetzt*. but **Wir *sind uns* zufällig in Rom *begegnet*.**	I *washed, shaved* and *dressed (myself)*, then I *sat down* at the table. We *met (each other)* by chance in Rome.

• Intransitive verbs not included in (A) above:

Ich habe drei Stunden lang in einem Meeting *gesessen*, dann noch zwei Stunden bei einer Abschiedsparty *gestanden*. Kein Wunder, daß ich gut *geschlafen* habe.	I *sat* for three hours in a meeting, then *stood* for two more hours at a farewell party. No wonder I *slept* well.

• The modal auxiliaries, even used with verbs taking **sein** [Perfect of modals: ►9b(i) and (iii)]:

Wir haben nicht länger bleiben *können*, weil wir nach Hause haben zurückkehren *müssen*.	We *could* not stay longer because we *had to* return home.

(C) Two groups of verbs may take either **sein** or **haben**.

• Some verbs of motion or change of state may also be transitive, possibly with a different meaning.

Sie *sind* sehr langsam *gefahren.*	They *drove* very slowly.
but	
Sie *haben* mich zum Bahnhof *gefahren.*	They *drove* me to the station.
Ich *bin* auf meinen Freund Hans *gestoßen.*	I *bumped* into my friend Hans.
but	
Ich *habe* ihn in die Rippen *gestoßen.*	I *nudged* him in the ribs.

• A few verbs of motion also describe physical activities, with no sense of moving in a given direction. They then take **haben**.

Wir *haben* vier Stunden lang *geschwommen/gesegelt/ gerudert/geritten/getanzt.*	We *swam/sailed/rowed/rode/ danced* for four hours.

(ii) *The compound future*

This is formed from the present tense of **werden** + infinitive. [➤12c(i)-(iii)]. (Paragraph 18c lists **werden** in full.)

Keine Angst! Wir *werden* am Sonntag bestimmt da *sein.* Elisabeth *wird* wohl auch *mitkommen.*	Don't worry! We *shall* certainly *be* there on Sunday. Elisabeth *will* probably *come* too.

The future perfect uses the present tense of **werden** + the perfect infinitive (past participle + **haben** or **sein**) [➤12c(iii)].

Bis dann *wird* sie ihren Bericht *fertig geschrieben haben.*	By then she *will have finished writing* her report.

(iii) *The compound conditional*

This is formed with **würde** + infinitive [➤14d(ii)].

Sie hat gesagt, sie *würde* ihn spätestens Samstag *abschicken.*	She said she *would send* it *off* on Saturday at the latest.

The past conditional (conditional perfect) is formed with **hätte** or **wäre** + past participle [➤14d(iv)].

Wenn sie fleißiger _gewesen_ wäre, hätte sie ihn schon längst beendet.	If she _had (would have) been_ more industrious she _would have finished_ it long ago.

17d   Formation of the imperative

➤   Uses of imperative: ➤ch.13. First and third persons: ➤13d.

Each of the three second persons [➤25b(ii)] has its own imperative.

(i)   _du_ form (singular)

Infinitive stem + **-e**, but note:

(A) The **-e** is often dropped in speech (though not with verbs that use the linking **-e-** in the **du** form of the present tense [➤17b(iii)]).

Komm her! Mach schnell! Sag mal! Sei ruhig! Lächle nicht! but **Antworte doch! Lade sie ein! Atme langsam!**	Come here! Hurry up! Tell me! Be quiet! Don't smile! (Do) Answer! Invite them! Breathe slowly!

(B) Strong verbs which change **-e-** to **-i(e)-** in the present tense also change in the **du** imperative. These have no final **-e**.

Gib her! Nimm es! Lies das vor!	Give it to me! Take it! Read that out loud!

(ii)   _ihr_ form (plural)

This is the same as **ihr** form present tense:

Macht schnell! Seid ruhig! Lächelt nicht! **Antwortet doch! Ladet sie ein! Atmet langsam!** **Gebt her! Nehmt es! Lest das vor!**	Hurry up! Be quiet! Don't smile! (Do) Answer! Invite them! Breathe slowly! Give it to me! Take it! Read that out loud!

(iii) **Sie** *form (*singular and plural)

This is the same as the **Sie** form present tense inverted, except for **sein → seien Sie!** The pronoun **Sie** is always included.

Kommen Sie herein! Sagen Sie mal! Seien Sie bitte ruhig!	Come in! Tell me! Please be quiet!
Laden Sie sie ein! Atmen Sie langsam!	Invite them! Breathe calmly!
Nehmen Sie es! Lesen Sie das bitte vor!	Take it! Please read that out loud!

Verb tables

This chapter contains:

(A) The full conjugation of the three auxiliary verbs **haben, sein** and **werden** [➤18a/b/c]. These also show the use of **haben** and **sein** to form the compound past tenses and serve as general models for weak and strong verbs.

(B) The conjugation of the verb **warnen** 'warn' in the passive [➤18d].

(C) A list of about 150 strong verbs in current use, giving the infinitive and the present (if the vowel changes), simple past and perfect tenses [➤18e]. These are the verbs' *principal parts*, so called because all other parts can be formed from them.

➤ The following sections give further information which you should use in conjunction with these tables.

- conjugation of modal auxiliaries: ➤9b(v).
- formation of the present participle: ➤10b(i).
- formation of the past participle: ➤10b(iii).
- summary of active tenses: ➤11d.
- summary of **Konjunktiv** I and conditional (**Konjunktiv** II) tenses: ➤14b.
- choice of simple or compound conditional: ➤14d Note.
- summary of passive tenses: ➤15b.
- principal parts of irregular weak verbs: ➤16c(ii).
- summary of seven strong verb classes: ➤16d(v).
- tense bases and endings: ➤17a and b.
- choice of **haben** or **sein** for compound past tenses: ➤17c(i).
- formation of the compound future: ➤17c(ii).

18a   *haben* *to have*

[Weak irregular. Auxiliary verb. Example of verb making perfect tenses with **haben**.]

Present participle
habend

Past participle
gehabt

Imperative

(du) hab(e)! (ihr) habt! haben Sie!

Present		**Simple past**	
ich	habe	ich	hatte
du	hast	du	hattest
er/sie/es	hat	er/sie/es	hatte
wir	haben	wir	hatten
ihr	habt	ihr	hattet
sie/Sie	haben	sie/Sie	hatte

Konjunktiv I		**Simple conditional (Konjunktiv II)**	
ich	habe	ich	hätte
du	habest	du	hättest
er/sie/es	habe	er/sie/es	hätte
wir	haben	wir	hätten
ihr	habet	ihr	hättet
sie/Sie	haben	sie/Sie	hätten

Perfect		**Past perfect (Pluperfect)**	
ich habe	... gehabt	ich hatte	... gehabt
du hast	... gehabt	du hattest	... gehabt
er/sie/es hat	... gehabt	er/sie/es hatte	... gehabt
wir haben	... gehabt	wir hatten	... gehabt
ihr habt	... gehabt	ihr hattet	... gehabt
sie/Sie haben	... gehabt	sie/Sie hatten	... gehabt

Future		**Future perfect**	
ich werde	... haben	ich werde	... gehabt haben
du wirst	... haben	du wirst	... gehabt haben
er/sie/es wird	... haben	er/sie/es wird	... gehabt haben
wir werden	... haben	wir werden	... gehabt haben
ihr werdet	... haben	ihr werdet	... gehabt haben
sie/Sie werden	... haben	sie/Sie werden	... gehabt haben

Compound conditional		**Past conditional**	
ich würde	... haben	ich hätte	... gehabt
du würdest	... haben	du hättest	... gehabt
er/sie/es würde	... haben	er/sie/es hätte	... gehabt
wir würden	... haben	wir hätten	... gehabt
ihr würdet	... haben	ihr hättet	... gehabt
sie/Sie würden	... haben	sie/Sie hätten	... gehabt

Konjunktiv I perfect

ich habe	... gehabt
du habest	... gehabt
er/sie/es habe	... gehabt
wir haben	... gehabt
ihr habet	... gehabt
sie/Sie haben	... gehabt

Konjunktiv I future

ich werde	... haben
du werdest	... haben
er/sie/es werde	... haben
wir werden	... haben
ihr werdet	... haben
sie/Sie werden	... haben

18b sein *to be*

[Strong irregular. Auxiliary verb. Example of verb making perfect tenses with **sein**.]

Present participle
seiend

Past participle
gewesen

Imperative

(du) sei!   (ihr) seid!   seien Sie!

Present

ich	bin
du	bist
er/sie/es	ist
wir	sind
ihr	seid
sie/Sie	sind

Simple past

ich	war
du	warst
er/sie/es	war
wir	waren
ihr	wart
sie/Sie	waren

Konjunktiv I

ich	sei
du	sei(e)st
er/sie/es	sei
wir	seien
ihr	seiet
sie/Sie	seien

Simple conditional (Konjunktiv II)

ich	wäre
du	wärest
er/sie/es	wäre
wir	wären
ihr	wäret
sie/Sie	wären

Perfect

ich bin	... gewesen
du bist	... gewesen
er/sie/es ist	... gewesen
wir sind	... gewesen
ihr seid	... gewesen
sie/Sie sind	... gewesen

Past perfect (Pluperfect)

ich war	... gewesen
du warst	... gewesen
er/sie/es war	... gewesen
wir waren	... gewesen
ihr wart	... gewesen
sie/Sie waren	... gewesen

Future

ich werde	... sein
du wirst	... sein
er/sie/es wird	... sein
wir werden	... sein
ihr werdet	... sein
sie/Sie werden	... sein

Future perfect

ich werde	... gewesen sein
du wirst	... gewesen sein
er/sie/es wird	... gewesen sein
wir werden	... gewesen sein
ihr werdet	... gewesen sein
sie/Sie werden	... gewesen sein

Compound conditional

ich würde	... sein
du würdest	... sein
er/sie/es würde	... sein
wir würden	... sein
ihr würdet	... sein
sie/Sie würden	... sein

Past conditional

ich wäre	... gewesen
du wärst	... gewesen
er/sie/es wäre	... gewesen
wir wären	... gewesen
ihr wäret	... gewesen
sie/Sie wären	... gewesen

Konjunktiv I perfect

ich sei	... gewesen
du seiest	... gewesen
er/sie/es sei	... gewesen
wir seien	... gewesen
ihr seiet	... gewesen
sie/Sie seien	... gewesen

Konjunktiv I future

ich werde	... sein
du werdest	... sein
er/sie/es werde	... sein
wir werden	... sein
ihr werdet	... sein
sie/Sie werden	... sein

18c *werden* to become

[Strong irregular. Auxiliary verb. Example of verb making perfect tenses with **sein**.]

Present participle
werdend

Past participle
geworden

Imperative

(du)   werde!   (ihr)   werdet!   werden Sie!

Present

ich	werde
du	wirst
er/sie/es	wird
wir	werden
ihr	werdet
sie/Sie	werden

Simple past

ich	wurde
du	wurdest
er/sie/es	wurde
wir	wurden
ihr	wurdet
sie/Sie	wurden

Konjunktiv I

ich	werde
du	werdest
er/sie/es	werde
wir	werden
ihr	werdet
sie/Sie	werden

Simple conditional (Konjunktiv II)

ich	würde
du	würdest
er/sie/es	würde
wir	würden
ihr	würdet
sie/Sie	würden

Perfect

ich bin	... geworden
du bist	... geworden
er/sie/es ist	... geworden
wir sind	... geworden
ihr seid	... geworden
sie/Sie sind	... geworden

Past perfect (Pluperfect)

ich war	... geworden
du warst	... geworden
er/sie/es war	... geworden
wir waren	... geworden
ihr wart	... geworden
sie/Sie waren	... geworden

Future

ich werde	... werden
du wirst	... werden
er/sie/es wird	... werden
wir werden	... werden
ihr werdet	... werden
sie/Sie werden	... werden

Future perfect

ich werde	... geworden sein
du wirst	... geworden sein
er/sie/es wird	... geworden sein
wir werden	... geworden sein
ihr werdet	... geworden sein
sie/Sie werden	... geworden sein

Compound conditional

ich würde	... werden
du würdest	... werden
er/sie/es würde	... werden
wir würden	... werden
ihr würdet	... werden
sie/Sie würden	... werden

Past conditional

ich wäre	... geworden
du wärst	... geworden
er/sie/es wäre	... geworden
wir wären	... geworden
ihr wäret	... geworden
sie/Sie wären	... geworden

Konjunktiv I perfect

ich sei	... geworden
du seiest	... geworden
er/sie/es sei	... geworden
wir seien	... geworden
ihr seiet	... geworden
sie/Sie seien	... geworden

Konjunktiv I future

ich werde	... werden
du werdest	... werden
er/sie/es werde	... werden
wir werden	... werden
ihr werdet	... werden
sie/Sie werden	... werden

18d *gewarnt werden* to be warned

[Example of the passive.]

Present participle
–

Past participle
gewarnt worden

Imperative
(du) sei ... gewarnt! (ihr) seid ... gewarnt! seien Sie .. gewarnt!

Present		**Simple past**	
ich werde	... gewarnt	ich wurde	... gewarnt
du wirst	... gewarnt	du wurdest	... gewarnt
er/sie/es wird	... gewarnt	er/sie/es wurde	... gewarnt
wir werden	... gewarnt	wir wurden	... gewarnt
ihr werdet	... gewarnt	ihr wurdet	... gewarnt
sie/Sie werden	... gewarnt	sie/Sie wurden	... gewarnt

Konjunktiv I		**Simple conditional (Konjunktiv II)**	
ich werde	... gewarnt	ich würde	... gewarnt
du werdest	... gewarnt	du würdest	... gewarnt
er/sie/es werde	... gewarnt	er/sie/es würde	... gewarnt
wir werden	... gewarnt	wir würden	... gewarnt
ihr werdet	... gewarnt	ihr würdet	... gewarnt
sie/Sie werden	... gewarnt	sie/Sie würden	... gewarnt

Perfect		**Past perfect (Pluperfect)**	
ich bin	... gewarnt worden	ich war	... gewarnt worden
du bist	... gewarnt worden	du warst	... gewarnt worden
er/sie/es ist	... gewarnt worden	er/sie/es war	... gewarnt worden
wir sind	... gewarnt worden	wir waren	... gewarnt worden
ihr seid	... gewarnt worden	ihr wart	... gewarnt worden
sie/Sie sind	... gewarnt worden	sie/Sie waren	... gewarnt worden

Future		**Future perfect**	
ich werde	... gewarnt werden	ich werde	... gewarnt worden sein
du wirst	... gewarnt werden	du wirst	... gewarnt worden sein
er/sie/es wird	... gewarnt werden	er/sie/es wird	... gewarnt worden sein
wir werden	... gewarnt werden	wir werden	... gewarnt worden sein
ihr werdet	... gewarnt werden	ihr werdet	... gewarnt worden sein
sie/Sie werden	... gewarnt werden	sie/Sie werden	... gewarnt worden sein

Compound conditional (rare)

ich würde	... gewarnt (werden)
du würdest	... gewarnt (werden)
er/sie/es würde	... gewarnt (werden)
wir würden	... gewarnt (werden)
ihr würdet	... gewarnt (werden)
sie/Sie würden	... gewarnt (werden)

Past conditional

ich wäre	... gewarnt worden
du wärst	... gewarnt worden
er/sie/es wäre	... gewarnt worden
wir wären	... gewarnt worden
ihr wäret	... gewarnt worden
sie/Sie wären	... gewarnt worden

Konjunktiv I perfect

ich sei	... gewarnt worden
du seiest	... gewarnt worden
er/sie/es sei	... gewarnt worden
wir seien	... gewarnt worden
ihr seiet	... gewarnt worden
sie/Sie seien	... gewarnt worden

Konjunktiv I future (rare)

ich werde	... gewarnt (werden)
du werdest	... gewarnt (werden)
er/sie/es werde	... gewarnt (werden)
wir werden	... gewarnt (werden)
ihr werdet	... gewarnt (werden)
sie/Sie werden	... gewarnt (werden)

18e List of strong verbs

The following alphabetical list gives the principal parts of about 150 strong verbs, using the **er/sie/es** form. Weak or alternative strong/weak forms are given where they are in current usage. [I/II/III etc. after the infinitive refers to the strong verb class: ▶16d(v).]

Infinitive	English	Present (if vowel changes)	Simple past	Perfect
backen (VI)	*bake*		backte	hat ... gebacken
befehlen (IV)	*command*	befiehlt	befahl	hat ... befohlen
beginnen (IV)	*begin*		begann	hat ... begonnen
beißen (I)	*bite*		biß	hat ... gebissen
betrügen (II)	*deceive*		betrog	hat ... betrogen
bewegen (II)	*persuade*		bewog	hat ... bewogen
biegen (II)	*bend*		bog	hat/ist ... gebogen
bieten (II)	*offer*		bot	hat ... geboten
binden (III)	*tie*		band	hat ... gebunden
bitten (V)	*ask, request*		bat	hat ... gebeten
blasen (VII)	*blow*	bläst	blies	hat ... geblasen
bleiben (I)	*remain*		blieb	ist ... geblieben
braten (VII)	*roast, grill*	brät	briet	hat ... gebraten
brechen (IV)	*break*	bricht	brach	hat/ist ... gebrochen
dreschen (II)	*thresh*	drischt	drosch	hat ... gedroschen

dringen (III)	*penetrate*		drang	ist ... gedrungen
empfehlen (IV)	*recommend*	empfiehlt	empfahl	hat ... empfohlen
erlöschen (II)	*go out (fire)*	erlischt	erlosch	ist ... erloschen
[**löschen** *put out, extinguish* is weak]				
erschrecken (IV)	*start (fright)*	erschrickt	erschrak	ist ... erschrocken
[**schrecken** *frighten, scare* is weak]				
essen (V)	*eat*	ißt	aß	hat ... gegessen
fahren (VI)	*go, drive*	fährt	fuhr	ist/hat ... gefahren
fallen (VII)	*fall*	fällt	fiel	ist ... gefallen
fangen (VII)	*catch*	fängt	fing	hat ... gefangen
fechten (II)	*fight, fence*	ficht	focht	hat ... gefochten
finden (III)	*find*		fand	hat ... gefunden
fliegen (II)	*fly*		flog	ist/hat ... geflogen
fliehen (II)	*flee*		floh	ist ... geflohen
fließen (II)	*flow*		floß	ist ... geflossen
fressen (V)	*eat, gobble*	frißt	fraß	hat ... gefressen
gären (II)	*ferment*		gor/gärte	hat ... gegoren/gegärt
gebären (IV)	*bear (child)*	gebiert	gebar	hat ... geboren
geben (V)	*give*	gibt	gab	hat ... gegeben
gedeihen (I)	*prosper*		gedieh	ist ... gediehen
gehen (VII)	*go, walk*		ging	ist ... gegangen
gelingen (III)	*succeed*		gelang	ist ... gelungen
gelten (IV)	*be valid, true*	gilt	galt	hat ... gegolten
genesen (V)	*recover (health)*		genas	ist ... genesen
genießen (II)	*enjoy*		genoß	hat ... genossen
geschehen (V)	*happen*	geschieht	geschah	ist ... geschehen
gewinnen (IV)	*win*		gewann	hat ... gewonnen
gießen (II)	*pour*		goß	hat ... gegossen
gleichen (I)	*resemble*		glich	hat ... geglichen
gleiten (I)	*slide, glide*		glitt	ist ... geglitten
glimmen (II)	*glow, glimmer*		glomm	hat ... geglommen
graben (VI)	*dig*	gräbt	grub	hat ... gegraben
greifen (I)	*grab, grasp*		griff	hat ... gegriffen
halten (VII)	*hold, keep*	hält	hielt	hat ... gehalten
hängen (VII)	*hang (intr)*		hing	hat ... gehangen
hauen (VII)	*hew, bash*		haute/hieb	hat ... gehauen
heben (II)	*lift, raise*		hob	hat ... gehoben
heißen (VII)	*be called, command*		hieß	hat ... geheißen
helfen (IV)	*help*	hilft	half	hat ... geholfen

klimmen (II)	*clamber*		klomm/klimmte	
				ist ... geklimmt/geklommen
klingen (IV)	*sound*		klang	hat ... geklungen
kneifen (I)	*pinch*		kniff	hat ... gekniffen
kommen (IV)	*come, get (somewhere)*		kam	ist ... gekommen
kriechen (II)	*crawl*		kroch	ist ... gekrochen
laden (VI)	*load*	lädt	lud	hat ... geladen
lassen (VII)	*let*	läßt	ließ	hat ... gelassen
laufen (VII)	*run, walk*	läuft	lief	ist ... gelaufen
leiden (I)	*suffer*		litt	hat ... gelitten
leihen (I)	*lend*		lieh	hat ... geliehen
lesen (V)	*read*	liest	las	hat ... gelesen
liegen (V)	*lie (flat)*		lag	hat ... gelegen
lügen (II)	*(tell a) lie*		log	hat ... gelogen
mahlen (–)	*grind (grain)*		mahlte	hat ... gemahlen
melken (II)	*milk*		melkte/(molk)	
				hat ... gemolken/(gemelkt)
messen (V)	*measure*	mißt	maß	hat ... gemessen
nehmen (IV)	*take*	nimmt	nahm	hat ... genommen
pfeifen (I)	*whistle*		pfiff	hat ... gepfiffen
quellen (II)	*well, gush*	quillt	quoll	ist ... gequollen
raten (VII)	*advise*	rät	riet	hat ... geraten
reiben (I)	*rub*		rieb	hat ... gerieben
reißen (I)	*tear*		riß	hat ... gerissen
reiten (I)	*ride*		ritt	ist/hat ... geritten
riechen (II)	*smell*		roch	hat ... gerochen
ringen (III)	*wrestle*		rang	hat ... gerungen
rinnen (IV)	*trickle*		rann	ist ... geronnen
rufen (VII)	*call*		rief	hat ... gerufen
saufen (II)	*drink, booze*	säuft	soff	hat ... gesoffen
saugen (II)	*suck*		sog/saugte	hat ...
				gesogen/gesaugt
schaffen (VI)	*create*		schuf	hat ... geschaffen
[**schaffen** *do, achieve* is weak]				
scheiden (I)	*divorce; (depart)*		schied	hat/(ist) ...
				geschieden
scheinen (I)	*seem; shine*		schien	hat ... geschienen
scheißen (I)	*shit*		schiß	hat ... geschissen
schelten (II)	*scold*	schilt	scholt	hat ... gescholten
scheren (II)	*shear, clip*		schor	hat ... geschoren
schieben (II)	*push, shove*		schob	hat ... geschoben
schießen (II)	*shoot*		schoß	hat ... geschossen
schinden (III)	*maltreat, overwork*		schindete	hat ... geschunden

schlafen (VII)	*sleep*	schläft	schlief	hat ... geschlafen
schlagen (VI)	*strike, hit*	schlägt	schlug	hat ... geschlagen
schleichen (I)	*creep, slink*		schlich	ist ... geschlichen
schleifen (I)	*sharpen, whet*		schliff	hat ... geschliffen
[**schleifen** *drag* is weak]				
schließen (II)	*close, shut*		schloß	hat ... geschlossen
schmeißen (I)	*hurl, chuck*		schmiß	hat ... geschmissen
schmelzen (II)	*melt, smelt*	schmilzt	schmolz	hat/ist ... geschmolzen
schneiden (I)	*cut*		schnitt	hat ... geschnitten
schreiben (I)	*write*		schrieb	hat ... geschrieben
schreien (I)	*shout, cry out*		schrie	hat ... geschrie(e)n
schreiten (I)	*stride; proceed*		schritt	ist ... geschritten
schweigen (I)	*be(come) silent*		schwieg	ist ... geschwiegen
schwellen (II)	*swell*	schwillt	schwoll	ist ... geschwollen
schwimmen (IV)	*swim, float*		schwamm	ist/hat ... geschwommen
schwingen (III)	*swing*		schwang	hat ... geschwungen
schwören (II)	*swear (oath)*		schwor	hat ... geschworen
sehen (V)	*see, look*	sieht	sah	hat ... gesehen
sein (V)	*be*	ist	war	ist ... gewesen
singen (III)	*sing*		sang	hat ... gesungen
sinken (III)	*sink*		sank	ist ... gesunken
sinnen (IV)	*ponder*		sann	hat ... gesonnen
sitzen (V)	*sit*		saß	hat ... gesessen
speien (I)	*spew*		spie	hat ... gespie(e)n
spinnen (IV)	*spin*		spann	hat ... gesponnen
sprechen (IV)	*speak*	spricht	sprach	hat ... gesprochen
springen (III)	*jump, spring*		sprang	ist ... gesprungen
stechen (IV)	*sting, prick*	sticht	stach	hat ... gestochen
stehen (IV)	*stand*		stand	hat ... gestanden
stehlen (IV)	*steal*	stiehlt	stahl	hat ... gestohlen
steigen (I)	*rise, climb*		stieg	ist ... gestiegen
sterben (IV)	*die*	stirbt	starb	ist ... gestorben

stinken (III)	*stink*		stank	hat ... gestunken
stoßen (VII)	*push*	stößt	stieß	hat ... gestoßen
streichen (I)	*spread; move*		strich	hat/ist ... gestrichen
streiten (I)	*quarrel, argue*		stritt	hat ... gestritten
tragen (VI)	*carry*	trägt	trug	hat ... getragen
treffen (IV)	*meet, hit*	trifft	traf	hat ... getroffen
trinken (III)	*drink*		trank	hat ... getrunken
tun (–)	*do, pour*		tat	hat ... getan
verderben (IV)	*spoil*	verdirbt	verdarb	hat ... verdorben
verdrießen (II)	*annoy*		verdroß	hat ... verdrossen
vergessen (V)	*forget*	vergißt	vergaß	hat ... vergessen
verlieren (II)	*lose*		verlor	hat ... verloren
verschlingen (III)	*engulf, swallow*		verschlang	hat ... verschlungen
verschwinden (III)	*disappear*		verschwand	ist ... verschwunden
verzeihen (I)	*forgive*		verzieh	hat ... verziehen
wachsen (VI)	*grow*	wächst	wuchs	ist ... gewachsen
waschen (VI)	*wash*	wäscht	wusch	hat ... gewaschen
weichen (I)	*yield, give way*		wich	ist ... gewichen
[**weichen** *soak* is weak]				
weisen (I)	*point*		wies	hat ... gewiesen
werben (IV)	*advertise*	wirbt	warb	hat ... geworben
werden (IV)	*become*	wird	wurde	ist ... geworden
werfen (IV)	*throw*	wirft	warf	hat ... geworfen
wiegen (II)	*weigh*		wog	hat ... gewogen
winden (III)	*wind*		wand	hat ... gewunden
wringen (III)	*wring*		wrang	hat ... gewrungen
ziehen (II)	*pull; move*		zog	hat/ist ... gezogen
zwingen (III)	*force, compel*		zwang	hat ... gezwungen

D

PEOPLE, THINGS AND IDEAS: NOUNS AND NOUN PHRASES

Labelling the world: nouns

19a What does a noun do?

Nouns answer the questions **Wer ist das?** 'Who is that?' and **Was ist das?** 'What is that?'. They are the labels we attach to everything in the world around us or in our own minds: people, animals, things, events, processes, ideas.

Meine jüngste *Tochter* studiert *Physik* an der *Universität*.	My youngest *daughter* is studying *physics* at the *university*.

19b Adding details: the noun phrase

The noun phrase often consists of more than just a noun – it can be extended so as to provide more information, as in the phrase **meine jüngste Tochter** in the previous example. The additional words and phrases which supply this information are:

• determiners [➤ch.23];
• adjectives and adjectival phrases [➤ch.24];
• relative clauses [➤5b, 25j];
• following prepositional phrases [➤19h, ch.27].

To avoid repetition, noun phrases are often represented by pronouns [➤ch.25].

19c Individual names and general labels: proper and common nouns

A *proper noun* (or 'proper name') is the name of a particular individual person like **Willi Brandt, Steffi Graf**, of a place like **Innsbruck, Österreich, Europa** or of a thing (such as a commercial product). All other nouns are *common nouns*. In German all nouns are written with a capital (not just proper names, as in many other languages).

der Sohn, Löffel, Haß	son, spoon, hate
die Tochter, Gabel, Liebe	daughter, fork, love
das Kind, Messer, Mitleid	child, knife, pity

Note In recent years there has been a movement to abolish capital letters for nouns, but this is not yet generally regarded as correct. It can in fact be a real help to be able to pick out the nouns in a sentence.

19d Names of people

Personal names are treated in German very much as in English. The main points to note are:

(i) For the possessive, **-s** is added to both first names and surnames. There is no apostrophe.

Käthes Fahrrad ist kaputt, und Frau Kerners Rad ist zu groß für sie.	Käthe's bicycle is broken, and Mrs. Kerner's bike is too big for her.

• If the name ends in **-s, -ß, -x** or **-z** the possessive **-s** is usually replaced in writing by an apostrophe; with short names, the ending **-ens** is sometimes used. In speech a following phrase with **von** is usual; **von** is in fact much used colloquially with all names. For example **Max'/Maxens Familie – die Familie *von* Max** 'Max's family', **Moritz' Freund – der Freund *von* Moritz** 'Moritz's friend'.

• Titles and forms of address like **Frau** 'Mrs.' or **Dr.** 'Dr.' are generally treated as a whole with the following name. **Herr** always adds **-n**. For example, **Frau Dr. Stauffens Job** 'Dr. Stauffen's job), **Herrn Kerners Anschrift** 'Mr. Kerner's address', **Onkel Konrads Hörgerät** 'Uncle Konrad's hearing aid'.

• When not used with a name, any words used to address members of the family add **-s**. For example, **Omas Wagen** 'Grandma's car', **Vatis Regenschirm** 'Dad's umbrella'. **Tantes Haus** 'Aunt's house'.

(ii) A plural **-s** is added to surnames to refer to the whole family. Surnames ending in **-s, -ß, -x** or **-z** add **-ens**. The definite article **die** is often omitted, especially after prepositions or when the family name is the possessive.

(Die) Gaußens **sind nette Leute. Wir haben sie bei** *Brandts* **kennengelernt. Frau Gauß ist** *Brandts* **Tochter.**	*The Gauss's* are nice people. We met them at *the Brandts.* Mrs. Gauss is *the Brandts'* daughter.

(iii) The definite article **der, die** etc. is used when a name is preceded by an adjective, except at the start of a letter. This is also done:

• as a sign of familiarity (which may be either affectionate or disparaging);
• when referring to well-known people, especially performing artists, and to characters in plays.

Lieber Heiner!/*Sehr geehrte* **Frau Beck!**	Dear Harry/Dear Mrs. Beck
Der alte Konrad – das ist der Großonkel *der kleinen* Angelika – wollte gestern mit *der* Jenny ins Kino gehen. *Der* Konrad ist doch ein dummer Kerl! In unserem letzten Laienspiel wollte er *den* Romeo spielen! Bloß weil er *die* Garbo gekannt hat!	*Old* Konrad – that's *little* Angelika's great-uncle – wanted to go to the movies yesterday with *(our)* Jenny. *(That)* Konrad really is a stupid fellow! In our last amateur dramatics he wanted to play *(the part of)* Romeo! Just because he used to know Garbo!

19e Geographical names

(i) *Names of places*

• All continents and towns, and almost all countries and provinces, are neuter. The article **das** is used only when the name is defined or described in some way.
• The '-ia' ending on the English name of some countries and continents becomes **-ien** in German, but plain '-a' endings do not change, for example, **Asien** 'Asia' but **Afrika** 'Africa'.
• The prepositions of position and motion are **aus** 'originally from', **in** 'at, in', **nach** 'to' and **von** 'from (also of)'.

(nach) Österreich/Wien;	(to) Austria/Vienna;
(in) Amerika/Pittsburg;	(in) America/Pittsburg;
(von) Hessen/Frankfurt;	(from/of) Hessen/Frankfurt;
das mittelalterliche Venedig;	mediaeval Venice;
vom industriellen Wolfsburg;	from industrial Wolfsburg;
im ländlichen Skandinavien	in rural Scandinavia

However, some countries and provinces are masculine, feminine or plural. These are always used with the article **der** or **die**. **in** + dative is normally used for 'in', **in** + accusative for 'to', though **nach** + dative may also be used.

Masculine **der Irak, in den Iran, im Jemen, vom Libanon**	Iraq, to Iran, in the Yemen, from Lebanon
Feminine **(in) die Schweiz, in der Türkei, von der Pfalz**	(to) Switzerland, in Turkey, from the Palatinate
Plural **(in) die Niederlande, in den Vereinigten Staaten (in den USA)**	(to) the Netherlands, in the United States (in the USA)

(ii) *Names of oceans, seas, lakes, rivers and mountains*

These tend to follow the gender of the word which describes them: **der Ozean** 'ocean', **das Meer** 'sea (often warmer)' or **die See** 'sea (usually colder)', **der See** 'lake', **der Fluß** 'river', **der Berg** 'mountain'. The main exceptions are:

• all but half a dozen native German names of rivers, and almost all others which end in **-a** or **-e**, are feminine;

• mountains which end in an ordinary word have the same gender as that word. A few mountain ranges are feminine, while many are plural.

der Atlantik, der Stille Ozean (der Pazifik);	the Atlantic, the Pacific;
das Mittelmeer, das Sargassomeer, die Ostsee, die Tasmansee;	the Mediterranean, the Sargasso Sea, the Baltic, the Tasman Sea;
der Bodensee, der Genfer See, der Ontario-See;	Lake Constance, Lake Geneva, Lake Ontario;
der Inn, der Lech, der Neckar, der Main, der Regen, der Rhein + der Nil, der Shannon, der Hudson but **die Donau, die Oder, die Ruhr, die Weichsel + die Wolga, die Themse;**	the Inn, the Lech, the Neckar, the Main, the Regen, the Rhine + the Nile, the Shannon, the Hudson but the Danube, the Oder, the Ruhr, the Vistula + the Volga, the Thames;
der Brocken, der Montblanc, der Vesuv but **das Matterhorn, die Zugspitze;**	the Brocken, Mont Blanc, Vesuvius but the Matterhorn, the Zugspitze;
der Harz, der Himalaja, der Jura but **die Eifel** (*feminine*), **die Pyrenäen, die Ardennen, die Dolomiten** (*plural*)	the Harz, the Himalayas, the Jura but the Eifel, the Pyrenees, the Ardennes, the Dolomites

19f   *Nationalities and languages*

(i)   The precise forms of nouns of nationality and inhabitants of towns and regions are hard to predict and best looked up. Note that:

(A) the great majority end in **-er**, sometimes **-ier** or **-aner**, and form their feminine by adding **-in**, without Umlaut;

Europa ➜ die Europäer	Europe ➜ the Europeans
Amerika ➜ die Amerikaner	America ➜ the Americans
Australien ➜ die Australier	Australia ➜ the Australians

(B) about a dozen nationalities and some regional and ethnic names end in **-e**. These are weak masculine nouns [➤22g(i)], which drop the **-e** before adding **-in** for the feminine; only **der Franzose – die Französin** 'French' has an Umlaut on the feminine;

die Chinesen, die Dänen,	the Chinese, the Danes,
die Franzosen, die Iren, die Polen,	the French, the Irish, the Poles,
die Portugiesen, die Russen,	the Portuguese, the Russians,
die Schotten, die Schweden,	the Scots, the Swedes,
die Tschechen, die Sachsen,	the Czechs, the Saxons,
die Schwaben	the Swabians

(C) only one nationality is an adjective-noun [➤24d];

der Deutsche	the German (man)
ein Deutscher	a German (man)
die/eine Deutsche	the/a German (woman)
die Deutschen	the Germans
Deutsche	Germans

(ii)   The names of all languages are the same as the national adjectives. Apart from **Deutsch** most of the more widely spoken languages end in **-isch** and are normally spelled with a capital (though see **(A)** below). They have two forms, both neuter.

(A) The stem without any ending is the general name for the language. In certain idioms this form is spelled with a small letter, mainly after verbs of speaking and in the expression **auf** 'in'.

Meine Muttersprache ist Französisch.	My mother tongue is French.

Ich kann/spreche auch englisch, ungarisch und jiddisch, und ich lese ziemlich gut Deutsch. Ich träume immer auf ungarisch!	I also speak English, Hungarian and Yiddish, and I can read German quite well. I always dream in Hungarian!

(B) The stem with **-e/-en** adjective endings [➤24b(ii)] has a sense of 'the ~ version', 'the ~ way of putting it'.

Dieses Handbuch ist aus dem Englischen ins Französische übersetzt worden.	This handbook has been translated from English into French.

19g *Nouns formed from other parts of speech*

German nouns are formed from other words in a number of ways. The most common examples are listed below. The English equivalents given are only approximate.

➤ The great and the good: adjectives used as nouns ➤24d. Singing and dancing: infinitive-nouns ➤10a(iii).

(i) Other parts of speech used as nouns are neuter, except for numerals, which are feminine (**die Eins, eine Sechs, eine Million**).

das Wenn und Aber	ifs and buts
ein großes A	a big A
das Schwarz-Rot-Gold	black, red and gold (German national colo(u)rs)
das ewige Hin und Her	the continual to-ing and fro-ing
ein völliges Durcheinander	a complete mess

(ii) A series of masculine nouns are made from the stem of strong verbs [➤16d(v)].

Plurals add **-e**, often with Umlaut. No firm rules can be given for the choice of vowel, but it is useful to be aware of the series.

(A) with the vowel of the infinitive:

der Fall, Gewinn, Hang, Lauf, Rat, Ruf, Schlaf, Schlag, Schrei, Stoß, Streit	fall/case, profit, slope, run, piece of advice, call/reputation, sleep, blow, shout, push, quarrel

(B) with the vowel of the simple past:

der Griff, Klang, Pfiff, Riß, Ritt,	grip, sound, whistle, tear, ride,
Schnitt, Schritt, Trieb, Zwang	cut, step/stride, drive/urge, compulsion

(C) with a third vowel, often **u:**

der Bruch, Flug, Fluß, Gang,	break, flight, river, corridor/gait/walk,
Guß, Schluß, Schub,	gush/casting, conclusion, shove,
Spruch, Sprung, Tritt,	saying, leap/jump, (foot)step,
Wurf, Zug	throw, pull/train/draft (draught)

(iii) *Forming nouns with suffixes*

Some nouns are formed from other words by adding the following suffixes. Most of these nouns are feminine.

• **~chen, ~lein** '~kin, ~let, ~ling'. A small or young ~. Forms neuter nouns from other nouns, usually with Umlaut if possible (**-chen** is more common; **-lein** is mainly southern German).

das Häuschen, Hühnchen,	little house, pullet,
Kätzchen, Mädche	kitten, girl,
das Büchlein, Entlein, Fräulein	booklet, duckling, Miss (less used nowadays)

• **~e** Usually the result of ~ing, or a related object. Forms feminine nouns from verbs (by dropping the **-n** from the infinitive). Note **helfen – die Hilfe** 'help'.

die Anleihe, Binde, Bitte, Falle,	loan, bandage, request, trap,
Fliege, Fresse, Klinge, Lüge,	fly, gob (*slang*), blade, lie/untruth,
Pfeife, Quelle, Wende	pipe, source, turning point

~e The quality of being ~. Forms feminine nouns from adjectives, with Umlaut if possible. Only possible with some adjectives, often describing physical qualities. Note **heiß – die Hitze** 'hot – heat'

.die Breite, Ferne, Höhe,	breadth, distance (in general), height,
Kälte, Kürze, Länge,	cold, brevity, length,
Schwäche, Stärke	weakness, strength

• **~ei**. The workplace or activity of a ~. Forms feminine nouns from other nouns, without Umlaut.

die Brauerei, Metzgerei,	brewery/brewing, butcher's shop,
Schlosserei, Wäscherei	metalworking (shop), laundry

• **~er, ~ler** '~er'. A person or thing that ~s. Forms masculine nouns from verbs, verb phrases and a few nouns, sometimes with Umlaut. [Nouns of nationality: ➤19f(i).]

| der Arbeiter, Bäcker, Bohrer, | worker, baker, drill, |
| Briefträger, Sportler, Staubsauger | mailman, sportsman, vacuum cleaner |

- **~heit, ~(ig)keit** '~ness'. The quality of being ~. Forms feminine nouns from adjectives. **-keit** is used with adjectives which themselves end in a suffix [▶24f(i)] and a few others. **-igkeit** is used with adjectives in **-haft** and **-los** and a few others.

die Dummheit, Gleichheit,	stupidity, equality,
Schönheit, Weisheit,	beauty, wisdom,
die Bäurischkeit, Freundlichkeit,	boorishness, friendliness,
Haltbarkeit, die Geschwindigkeit,	long-lastingness, speed,
Hilflosigkeit, Lebhaftigkeit	helplessness, liveliness

- **~in** '~ess'. The female of most persons and many animals. Plural **-innen**. Persons usually with Umlaut, and some animals.

die Arbeiterin, Ärztin, Bäckerin,	female worker, doctor, baker,
Freundin, Heldin, Köchin, Müllerin,	friend, heroine, female cook, miller,
Professorin, Sportlerin,	professor, sportswoman,
die Füchsin, Löwin, Tigerin	vixen, lioness, tigress

- **~nis** '~ness, ~ion'. The effect of ~. Forms feminine and neuter nouns from verbs and adjectives. Plural **-nisse**.

die Erkenntis, Finsternis;	realization, darkness;
das Erlebnis, Gedächtnis,	experience, memory,
Geheimnis, Verhältnis	secret, relationship

- **~schaft** '~ship, ~hood'. A quality or organization associated with ~s. Forms feminine nouns from other nouns, usually referring to people, without Umlaut.

die Brüderschaft, Freundschaft,	brotherhood/'du' friendship, friendship,
Landschaft, Schwesternschaft,	landscape, sisterhood/nursing staff,
Studentenschaft	student body

- **~tum** '~dom'. An institution or feature associated with ~s. Forms neuter nouns from other nouns, usually referring to people. (Note however *der* **Irrtum** 'error' and *der* **Reichtum** 'wealth'.)

| das Beamtentum, | civil servants, |
| Bistum (from Bischof), Fürstentum | diocese, principality |

- **~ung** '~ing, ~ion'. The action or fact of ~ing. Forms feminine nouns from verbs, without Umlaut.

die Ahnung, Empfindung,	inkling/idea, feeling,
Erfahrung, Erwartung, Hoffnung,	experience, expectation, hope,
Kreuzung, Öffnung, Verbindung,	crossroads, opening, connection,
Verwirrung	confusion

(iv) *Forming nouns with prefixes*

Nouns can also be formed from other words by adding prefixes. Apart from **Haupt-**, **Mit-** and **Fehl-**, the only prefixes listed here are those which are not words in their own right. Only **Ge-** changes the gender of the original noun.

• **Erz~** 'arch~, complete ~'. Can be added to both nouns and adjectives, magnifying their position or qualities, whether good or bad. (Do not confuse these words with compounds of **das Erz** meaning 'ore'!)

der Erzengel, Erzbischof,	archangel, archbishop,
Erzfeind, Erzreaktionär	arch-enemy, ultra-reactionary

• **Fehl~** 'mis~, wrong ~'. Compared to **Miß-**, a fairly neutral negative.

der Fehldruck, Fehlschlag,	misprint, failure,
Fehlschluß, Fehlstoß;	false conclusion, miskick/miscue;
die Fehldiagnose,	wrong diagnosis,
Fehlgeburt	miscarriage

• **Ge~** 1) A collection of ~. Forms neuter nouns from other nouns, with Umlaut if possible. (**-e-** in the stem changes to **-i-**.)

das Gebirge, Gebiß,	mountain range, set of teeth/dentures,
Geflügel, Getriebe, Gewitter	poultry, gears, thunderstorm

• **Ge~** 2) Repeated, probably irritating ~ing. Forms usually neuter nouns from verbs.

das Gekreisch(e), Gelächter,	screeching, laughter,
Geschwätz, Getue	gossip/chatter, fuss

but

der Gebrauch, Gedanke, Gehalt,	custom, thought, content(s),
Geruch, Geschmack, Gewinn;	smell, taste, profit;
die Gebärde, Geduld, Gemeinde,	gesture, patience, community,
Gewalt	force

• **Haupt~** 'main ~'.

der Hauptbahnhof, Hauptmann;	main station, (army) captain;
die Hauptstadt, Hauptpost,	capital (city), main post office,
Hauptsache;	main thing;
das Hauptbüro, Hauptfach	headquarters, main subject

• **Miß~** 'mis~, wrong ~'. Usually gives a stronger emphasis than **Fehl-**.

der Mißbrauch, Mißerfolg, Mißmut;	abuse, failure/flop, sullenness/discontent;
die Mißgeburt, Mißhandlung;	deformed creature, maltreatment;
das Mißtrauen, Mißverständnis	mistrust, misunderstanding

- **Mit~** 'co-~, fellow ~'.

der (die) Mitarbeiter(in), Mitwisser(in);	colleague, accomplice/accessory;
die Mitarbeit, Mithilfe;	collaboration, assistance;
das Mitgefühl, Mitglied, Mitleid	sympathy, member, pity

- **Un~** 'un~, abnormal ~'.

der Unfall, Unfug, Unmensch, Unsinn;	accident, mischief, (human) monster, nonsense;
die Ungeduld, Unmenge, Unruhe, Unschuld;	impatience, vast number, disquiet, innocence;
das Ungeziefer, Unglück, Unkraut, Unrecht	vermin, misfortune, weeds, injustice

- **Ur~** 'original ~, ancient ~, typical ~'.

der Urbayer, Urgroßvater, Urwald;	typical Bavarian, great-grandfather, jungle;
die Uraufführung, Urenkelin, Ursache	première, great-granddaughter, cause/reason

19h *Nouns governing phrases and clauses*

As a rule, nouns govern the same type of clause or prepositional phrase as their corresponding verbs or adjectives, as shown below.

Verbs + prepositions: ➤*8g*

Ich arbeite/Meine Arbeit *an diesem Projekt* ...	I am working/My work *on this project* ...

Verbs + zu + infinitive: ➤*8h(ii)*

Er versprach, /Sein Versprechen, mir *zu helfen*, ...	He promised/His promise *to help* me ...

Verbs + **daß** *clauses:* ➤*8i*

Sie erwarten,/Ihre Erwartung, daß du mitkommst, ...	They expect/Their expectation *that you will come too* ...

Adjectives + prepositions: ➤*24g(ii)*

Sie war wütend/hatte eine Wut auf mich.	She was furious *at me*.

Adjectives + **zu** *+ infinitive/+* **daß** *clauses:* ➤*24g(ii)*

Sie sind bereit,/Ihre Bereitschaft, mitzuhelfen, ...	They are willing/Their willingness *to help* ...
Ich bin stolz darauf,/Mein Stolz darauf, daß es gelungen ist, ...	I am proud of the fact/My pride in the fact *that it was a success* ...

Note Nouns related to verbs or adjectives followed by the accusative or dative generally use the genitive or whatever preposition best conveys the meaning.

***Das Schiff* wurde versenkt.**	*The ship* was sunk.
Nach Versenkung *des Schiffs* ...	After the sinking *of the ship* ...
Wir haben *sie* gebeten, hier zu warten. Unsere Bitte *an sie* ...	We asked *them* to wait here. Our request *to them* ...
Alle gehorchen *ihm*. Ihr Gehorsam *ihm gegenüber* ...	They all obey *him*. Their obedience *of him* ...
Er ist *seiner Oma* sehr ähnlich.	He is very like *his grandmother*.
Seine Ähnlichkeit *mit ihr* ...	His resemblance *to her* ...

20 Classes of German noun: the three genders

20a What is meant by gender?

The word *gender* means 'kind' or 'type'. All German nouns belong to one of three genders: *masculine, feminine* or *neuter*. Each gender has its own set of case endings [➤ch.22]. The gender of a noun is not the same thing as the sex of the person or animal it may refer to.

• Nouns which refer to people and animals are normally masculine for males and feminine for females, but there are important exceptions [➤20b(iii) and (iv)].
• Other nouns can be of any of the three genders.
• There are some groupings of meanings which will help you [➤20b], but the best thing is to learn a noun with its definite article **der, die** or **das**, which always shows the gender.

Note There are some endings which indicate the gender of a noun but, apart from the suffixes listed in paragraph 19g, most of them either are too uncommon or have too many exceptions to be of much use.

20b What does it mean? Gender groupings by meaning

➤ Geographical names: ➤19e.

(i) These groups of nouns are normally masculine.

(A) Male persons and animals:

der Bock, Kater, Mann, Onkel, Neffe, Richter, Sohn, Stier, Vater	buck (deer), tom-cat, man, uncle, nephew, male judge, son, bull, father

(B) Rocks and minerals:

der Diamant, Felsen, Lehm, Kalk, Kies, Kiesel, Kristall, Schlamm, Stein, Ton	diamond, rock, loam, lime, gravel, pebble, crystal, mud, stone, clay
but	but
die Erde, Kohle, Kreide;	earth, coal, chalk;
das Erz, Mineral	ore, mineral

(C) Compass directions, kinds of weather:

der Norden, Süden, Osten, Westen,	North, South, East, West,

der Frost, Hagel, Nebel,	frost, hail, mist/fog,
Schnee, Sturm, Wind	snow, storm, wind
but	but
das Eis, Gewitter, Wetter	ice, thunderstorm, weather

(D) Days of the week, months, seasons [➤31b(i) on].

(E) Makes of car [compare (ii)(C) below]:

der BMW, Cadillac, Mercedes,	BMW, Cadillac, Mercedes,
Peugeot, Trabant	Peugeot, Trabant

(ii) These groups of nouns are normally feminine.

(A) Female persons and animals:

die Frau, Hündin, Kuh, Mutter,	woman, bitch, cow, mother,
Nichte, Richterin, Tante, Tochter	niece, female judge, aunt, daughter

(B) Names of numerals [➤30a(ii)].

(C) Names of ships, makes of airplanes and motorbikes:

die Bremen, Graf Spee,	the Bremen, Graf Spee,
Mayflower, Titanic	Mayflower, Titanic
die Boeing, Concorde, Dakota	Boeing, Concorde, Dakota
die BMW, Harley-Davidson,	BMW, Harley-Davidson,
Honda	Honda [compare (i)(E) above]

(iii) These groups of nouns are normally neuter.

(A) The young of persons and animals, and all nouns with the endings **-chen** and **-lein** [➤19g(iii)]. Note that **das Junge – ein Junges** 'young (of animals)' takes adjective endings [➤24d].

das Baby, Ferkel, Kalb, Kind,	baby, piglet, calf, child,
Küken, Lamm	chick, lamb

(B) Metals and chemical elements, except compounds (for example, of **der Stoff**); scientific units. (Note that in southern German **Liter** and **Meter** are masculine.)

das Aluminium, Blei, Eisen, Gold,	aluminum, lead, iron, gold,
Kupfer, Messing, Silber, Uran,	copper, brass, silver, uranium,
but	but
der Stahl, Schwefel	steel, sulphur
das Atom, Gramm, Liter, Meter,	atom, gram(me), liter, meter,
Neutron, Pfund, Volt	neutron, pound, volt

(C) Letters of the alphabet (note that these are masculine in Swiss German):

das ABC	the ABC/alphabet
z.B. – mit kleinem z und großem B	**z.B.** 'e.g.' – with a small z and a capital B
Er läßt sich kein X für ein U vormachen.	He's not easily fooled.

(D) Names of theaters (theatres), movie houses, hotels, cafés and restaurants.

(iv) Unexpected genders

The gender of some nouns is different from the sex of the person or animal they refer to. Sometimes, as in the neuter examples in (A) below, this is because they are compounds taking the gender of the final part.

(A) Many names of animals have no separate masculine and feminine forms. If necessary, **das ~männchen** 'male ~' and **das ~weibchen** 'female ~' can be used.

der Adler, Elefant, Frosch, Kuckuck;	eagle, elephant, frog, cuckoo;
die Eule, Giraffe, Kröte, Maus, Ratte;	owl, giraffe, toad, mouse, rat;
das Eichhörnchen, Nilpferd, Nashorn, Rotkehlchen	squirrel, hippopotamus, rhinoceros, robin

(B) Some nouns refer to both women and men.

der Mensch, Vormund;	human being/person, legal guardian;
die Geisel, Person, Wache, Waise;	hostage, person, sentry, orphan;
das Mitglied, Mündel	member, legal ward

20c Gender benders: nouns with double gender

Several dozen words have different genders for different meanings. These are some of the most common, with their plurals.

der Band – Bände	volume, book	**das Band – Bänder**	ribbon
(die Bande – Banden	gang, band)	**das Band – Bande**	fetter, bond
der Bund – Bünde	union, federation	**das Bund – Bunde**	bunch, bundle
der Erbe – Erben	heir	**das Erbe – Erbschaften**	inheritance
der Gefallen – Gefallen	favo(u)r	**das Gefallen** – *no plural*	pleasure
der Gehalt – Gehalte	content(s)	**das Gehalt – Gehälter**	salary

der Heide – Heiden	heathen	die Heide – Heiden	heath
der Junge – Jungen	boy	das Junge – *adj.-noun*	young (animal)
der Kiefer – Kiefer	jaw	die Kiefer – Kiefern	pine
der Laster – Laster	truck	das Laster – Laster	vice
der Leiter – Leiter	leader, chief	die Leiter – Leitern	ladder
der Mangel – Mängel	lack	die Mangel – Mangeln	mangle
die Mark – Mark	mark (coinage)	das Mark – *no plural*	bone marrow
der Messer – Messer	surveyor; gauge	das Messer – Messer	knife
der Moment – Momente	moment (time)	das Moment – Momente	factor
der Schild – Schilde	shield	das Schild – Schilder	sign, metal plate
der See – Seen	lake	die See – *no plural*	sea
die Steuer – Steuern	tax	das Steuer – Steuer	steering wheel

One or more?
Singular and plural

21a   Predicting the plural

(i)   In German the *plural* of a noun is not as easy to predict as in English. This is because German has kept the older Germanic endings and vowel changes which are still to be seen in the English 'one ox, two oxen' **ein Ochse, zwei Ochsen** and 'one mouse, two mice' **eine Maus, zwei Mäuse**. As with genders, there are some guidelines to help you, but you should always learn the plural of a noun together with its meaning and gender.

(ii)   German nouns fall into five groups according to the ending (if any) which they add to make their plural. In three of these groups the stem vowel may also take Umlaut when possible (that is, **a(u) ➜ ä(u), o ➜ ö, u ➜ ü**). You will see from the following paragraphs that feminine nouns have the fewest ways of making their plurals and are therefore easiest to predict. Neuters are fairly predictable, but masculines have a wide range of possibilities.

➤   Four *bottles* of wine and two *dozen* sausages, please!: plural measures ➤3d(ii).

21b   Plural groupings

(i)   *-(e)n group*

This group is never combined with Umlaut. The **-e-** is included when the noun ends in a consonant. All nouns ending in **-e** add **-n**, except **der Käse** and neuters starting with **Ge-**, which do not change. The group includes:

• a good number of masculine nouns, including the weak masculines [➤22g(i)] and the eight nouns like **der Name** [➤22g(ii)], but also foreign borrowings ending in unstressed **-or** (which shift their stress to the **-or** in the plural) and some two dozen others:

der Dorn – Dornen	thorn
der Muskel – Muskeln	muscle
der Schmerz – Schmerzen	pain

der See – Seen	lake
der Professor – Professoren	professor
der Staat – Staaten	state
der Stachel – Stacheln	barb, prickle
der Strahl – Strahlen	ray, beam
der Vetter – Vettern	male cousin

• the great majority (many thousands) of feminine nouns:

die Ecke – Ecken	corner
die Frau – Frauen	woman, wife
die Schulter – Schultern	shoulder
die Schüssel – Schüsseln	dish
die Schwester – Schwestern	sister
die Station – Stationen	(small) station

• about a dozen neuter nouns, the most common being:

das Auge – Augen	eye
das Bett – Betten	bed
das Ende – Enden	end
das Hemd – Hemden	shirt
das Herz – Herzen	heart
das Insekt – Insekten	insect
das Interesse – Interessen	interest
das Juwel – Juwelen	jewel
das Ohr – Ohren	ear
das Elektron – Elektronen	electron

(and other scientific terms ending in **-on**).

(ii)   No ending group

This group is sometimes combined with Umlaut. The group includes:

• all masculine nouns ending in **-el**, **-en** or **-er** except **der Bauer – Bauern** 'farmer' and **der Vetter – Vettern** 'cousin'. Most do not add Umlaut, but about 20 do:

der Löffel – Löffel	spoon
der Schlüssel – Schlüssel	key
der Reifen – Reifen	tire
der Wagen – Wagen	car, railroad carriage
der Fehler – Fehler	mistake
der Koffer – Koffer	suitcase
der Apfel – Äpfel	apple

der Nagel – Nägel	nail
der Garten – Gärten	yard, garden
der Laden – Läden	store, shop
der Acker – Äcker	(plowed/ploughed) field
der Bruder – Brüder	brother

• two feminine nouns, both with Umlaut:

| die (Groß)mutter – (Groß)mütter | (grand)mother |
| die Tochter – Töchter | daughter |

• all neuter nouns ending in **-el**, **-en** or **-er**, or in the diminutive endings **-chen** and **-lein** [➤19g(iii)]. The only ones with Umlaut are **das Kloster – Klöster** 'convent, monastery', and **das Abwasser – Abwässer** 'effluent' and other compounds of **-wasser**:

das Mittel – Mittel	means; medicine
das Kissen – Kissen	cushion, pillow
das Fenster – Fenster	window
das Mädchen – Mädchen	girl
das Möbel – Möbel	furniture
das Zeichen – Zeichen	sign (indication)
das Muster – Muster	pattern, model
das Büchlein – Büchlein	booklet

• neuter nouns with the prefix **Ge-**, often collective nouns [➤19g(iv)]:

das Gebäude – Gebäude	building
das Gebirge	mountain range
das Gebüsch	bushes, undergrowth
das Gehäuse – Gehäuse	casing; snail shell

(iii)   *-e group*

This group is sometimes combined with Umlaut. The group includes:

• a great many masculine nouns, especially one-syllable words. Of those which could add Umlaut, about half do, including all those in paragraph 19g(ii). For example:

der Arm – Arme	arm
der Hund – Hunde	dog, hound
der Ort – Orte	place
der Punkt – Punkte	point, full stop/period
der Tag – Tage	day

der Schuh – Schuhe	shoe
der Arzt – Ärzte	doctor
der Rock – Röcke	skirt
der Stuhl – Stühle	chair
der Anlaß – Anlässe	immediate cause
der Einwand – Einwände	objection
der Vertrag – Verträge	contract

• about a quarter of one-syllable feminine nouns. All have Umlaut:

die Hand – Hände	hand
die Stadt – Städte	town
die Wand – Wände	internal wall
die Wurst – Würste	sausage

• about three-quarters of those neuter nouns which are not in the no ending group. The only one with Umlaut is **das Floß – Flöße** 'raft':

das Bein – Beine	leg
das Brot – Brote	bread, loaf
das Ding – Dinge	thing, object
das Haar – Haare	hair
das Jahr – Jahre	year
das Ziel – Ziele	aim, objective

(iv)   *-er* group

This group is always combined with Umlaut where possible. The group includes:

• about a dozen masculine nouns, for example:

der Geist – Geister	spirit
der Irrtum – Irrtümer	error
der Mann – Männer	man
der Rand – Ränder	edge
der Ski – Skier	ski
der Strauch – Sträucher	shrub
der Wald – Wälder	wood, forest
der Wurm – Würmer	worm

• no feminine nouns.
• about a quarter of those neuter nouns which are not in the no ending group, mostly one-syllable, but also all those ending in **-tum** [➤19g(iii)] and eight others:

das Ei – Eier	egg
das Haus – Häuser	house
das Kind – Kinder	child
das Schild – Schilder	sign (notice)
das Gehalt – Gehälter	salary
das Geschlecht – Geschlechter	sex
das Gespenst – Gespenster	ghost
das Mitglied – Mitglieder	member

(v)   -s group

These are never combined with Umlaut. Not a native Germanic plural ending, but increasingly common. The group includes nouns from all three genders:

• large numbers of recent borrowings from English or French:

das Atelier – Ateliers	studio
der Bankier – Bankiers	banker
das Motel – Motels	motel
der Streik – Streiks	strike

• words ending in a consonant + a vowel other than **-e**:

das Auto – Autos	car
das Baby – Babys	baby
das Büro – Büros	office
die Party – Partys	(drinks) party
das Taxi – Taxis	taxi

• abbreviations (initials or shortened words). The **-s** is sometimes left off in speech:

der LKW – LKW(s)	truck
die Uni – Unis	university

• family names [➤19d(ii)].

 Noun plural endings have no effect whatsoever on the other parts of the noun phrase (determiners, adjectives, etc.). These are governed by very different rules, which are discussed in Chapters 23 and 24.

21c   Double plurals

A few nouns have different plurals with different meanings. For example:

das Band – Bande	fetters, bonds, chains	**das Band – Bänder**	ribbons

die Bank – Banken	banks (financial)	**die Bank – Bänke**	benches
der Block – Blöcke	blocks (large chunks)	**der Block – Blocks**	blocks (apartments, pad of paper)
die Mutter – die Mütter	mothers	**die Mutter – die Muttern**	nuts (for bolts)
der Stock – Stöcke	sticks	**der Stock – Stockwerke**	storeys
der Strauß – Sträuße	bunches	**der Strauß – Sträuße**	ostriches
das Wort – Wörter	(separate) words	**das Wort – Worte**	words (speech)

21d   Plurals with no singular

Some of these have exact English equivalents, but others are singular in English. For example:

die Eltern	parents
die Ferien	vacation, holidays
die Leute	people (in general)
die Flitterwochen	honeymoon
die Lebensmittel	food
die Zinsen	interest (on capital)

21e   Singulars for plurals

(i)   In some English words the final '-s' is a false plural, that is, the thing itself is singular and there is often no singular form with the same meaning. The German for these words is often singular. For example:

die Brille	glasses, spectacles
das Fernglas	binoculars
die Hose	pants, trousers
der Inhalt	contents
die Kaserne	barracks
der Lohn	wages
die Mathe(matik)	math(ematics)
die Physik	physics
die Politik	politics
der Pyjama	pyjamas
die Schere	scissors
die Treppe	stairs
die Umgebung	surroundings
die Waage	scales

die Zange   pincers, tongs

(ii)   Conversely, some English singular nouns are plural in German.
           The German singular then often means 'piece or item of ...'.

die Auskünfte	information
die Fortschritte	progress
die Hausaufgaben	homework
die Kenntnisse	knowledge
die Möbel	furniture
die Nachrichten	news

22 The role of the noun phrase in the sentence: the four cases

22a What are cases?

(i) What do cases tell us?

All languages have ways of showing what role each noun phrase is playing in the sentence, for example, as subject [➤4b], as object [➤8d/e] or as part of an adverbial expression [➤28c]. In some languages, such as English and French, this is shown mainly by the position of the noun phrase. Position can be important in German too [➤4e], but the role of a noun phrase or pronoun is shown most clearly by its *case*. Each case has its own set of endings. English has similar forms in the possessive '*s*, as in 'a child'*s* toy', and in the pronoun forms 'I - me, she - her, he - him, we - us, they - them', but German cases are much more significant.

(ii) German cases

German noun phrases and pronouns have four cases: *nominative*, *accusative*, *genitive* and *dative*. These are traditional names which are useful labels. Each case has a number of uses. Most of these are dealt with in other sections of this *Handbook*, but they are summarized for ease of reference in paragraphs 22c to f below.

22b Case endings on nouns

The case of a noun phrase is most commonly shown by a determiner [➤ch.23] or possibly by an adjective [➤ch.24], not by the noun itself. The only case endings added to nouns are detailed below.

(i)

Weak masculine nouns add **-(e)n** to all cases except the nominative singular [➤22g(i)]. Eight other irregular masculine nouns add both **-en** to all cases and **-s** to the genitive singular [➤22g(ii)]. One neuter, **das Herz**, also follows this pattern, except that it does not change in the accusative singular.

Mit meinem Kollegen ist bestimmt etwas los. Er ist nicht mehr mit ganzem Herzen bei der Arbeit. Am Telefon sagt er statt seines Namens bloß „Huh?". **Mich behandelt er wie einen Idioten. Ich würde lieber mit einem Affen arbeiten.**	There is certainly something the matter with my colleague. His heart is no longer in his work. On the telephone, instead of his name, he just says "Huh?". He treats me like an idiot. I would rather work with an ape.

(ii)   Other masculine nouns, and all neuter nouns, add **-(e)s** to the genitive singular. The **-e-** is used mainly to aid pronunciation. It must be used after **-s, -ß, -sch, -x** and **-z**.

Während des Mittagessens bin ich trotz des schrecklichen Wetters rausgegangen. Mein Wagen stand am anderen Ende des Parkplatzes.	During lunch I went out, despite the terrible weather. My car was at the other end of the parking lot.

(iii)   Short masculine and neuter nouns may add **-e** for the dative singular, though nowadays this is mainly confined to set phrases.

Im Laufe der Zeit bin ich mit dem ganzen Konkurrenzkampf unzufrieden geworden. Nur zu Hause fühle ich mich wohl.	In the course of time I have become discontented with the whole rat-race. Only at home do I feel at ease.

(iv)   All nouns except those which add **-s** for their plural [➤21b(v)] must end in **-n** in the dative plural. This means that any noun plural which does not already end in an **-n** must add one for the dative.

Mit Büros und Hotels hätte ich lieber nichts mehr zu tun. Ich möchte gern mehr Zeit mit meinen Kindern und meinen Freunden verbringen.	I would rather have nothing more to do with offices and hotels. I should like to spend more time with my children and my friends.

22c   *Uses of the nominative case*

This is the basic form of the noun, the form listed in dictionaries. It is used:

(i) for the subject of the sentence [➤4b]:

Mein ältester Bruder Martin hat Graphik studiert.	*My eldest brother* Martin studied graphic design.

(ii) for the complement of joining verbs such as **sein, werden, bleiben** [➤8c]:

Er ist *ein sehr kompetenter Zeichner.*	He is *a very competent draftsman/draughtsman.*

(iii) for certain noun phrases used in isolation, as when addressing people or in exclamations:

Aber Herr Ganz! Was für *ein interessanter Entwurf!*	Well, Mr Ganz! What *an interesting design!*

22d Uses of the accusative case

This has the same forms as the nominative except in the masculine singular. It is used:

(i) for the direct object of transitive verbs [➤8d]:

Mein Bruder leitet *ein ziemlich großes Team.*	My brother leads *a fairly large team.*

(ii) for free-standing adverbial expressions of time, value or measurement, that is, those not governed by a preposition:

***Jeden Morgen* fährt er *mehrere Kilometer* zur Arbeit.**	*Every morning* he drives *several kilometers* to work.

(iii) after some prepositions always [➤27b(i)]:

***Ohne den Wagen* wäre der Weg für ihn viel länger.**	*Without the car* the journey would be much longer *for him.*

(iv) after some prepositions to indicate motion towards a place [➤27b(iii)]:

Am Wochenende fährt die Familie *in die Berge* **oder** *ans Meer.*	On the weekend the family drives *into the mountains* or *to the seaside.*

(v) for many common greetings and wishes:

Guten Tag! Alles Gute! Vielen Dank! Einen Augenblick! Guten Appetit!	Good morning/day! All the best! Many thanks! One moment! Enjoy your meal!

22e Uses of the genitive case

The genitive has a range of uses, but it is now less used in speech, where it is more normal to use a prepositional phrase (especially with **von**). It is, however, widely used in written German, and it is not hard to find everyday texts in which it is the most common case.

• Except with proper names and certain set expressions, the genitive almost always follows the noun it depends on. To put it first sounds old-fashioned or mock-solemn.
• The main uses of the genitive are:

(i) to express possession:

Martins **Haus/Das Haus** *meines Bruders* **ist sehr schön gelegen.**	*Martin's/My brother's* house is very beautifully situated.

(ii) to define the scope of the preceding noun:

Es liegt auf der anderen Seite *der Stadt* **am Rande** *eines Wald(e)s.*	It lies on the other side *of town* on the edge *of a wood (woods).*

(iii) after nouns of quantity [➤3d]:

In seinem Garten steht eine Gruppe *uralter Eichen.*	In his yard there is a clump *of ancient oaks.*

(iv)   after certain prepositions. A few of these are common, but a
large number are only used in official or commercial writing
[➤27b(iv)]:

Dank *seiner Ausbildung* hat Martin ein gutes Gefühl für Design. Während *des vergangenen Jahres* hat er den Garten neu angelegt.	Thanks to *his training*, Martin has a good sense of design. During *the last year* he redesigned the yard.

(v)   after a few verbs and adjectives, including some set expressions after the verb **sein** [➤8d(iii), 24g(i)]. Most of these are little used in colloquial German:

Er bedurfte *der Hilfe* eines Fachmanns nicht – *dessen* war er sicher. Danach war er *sehr guter Laune/guter Dinge*.	He did not need *the help* of a specialist – *of that* he was certain. Afterwards he was *in a very good mood/in high spirits*.

(vi)   in some set adverbial expressions:

Eines Tages hat er mir gesagt: „*Letzten Endes* braucht man diese Fachleute nicht." *Meines Wissens* hat er nicht sich selber gemeint!	*One day* he said to me, "*When it really comes to it* you don't need these experts." *To the best of my knowledge* he didn't mean himself!

22f   Uses of the dative case

The dative case is common in both speech and writing. It is used:

(i)   for indirect objects [➤8e]:

Er hat *mir* das Bäumchen gezeigt, das meine Nichte *ihm* geschenkt hatte.	He showed *me* the sapling which my niece had given *him*.

(ii)   as the only object of certain verbs [➤8d]:

Sie wollte *ihm* dafür danken, daß er *ihr* bei ihrer Prüfungsvorbereitungen geholfen hatte.	She wanted to thank *him* for helping *her* with her examination preparations.

(iii) after some prepositions always [➤27b(ii)]:

Bei *der Prüfung* ist sie mit *sehr guten Noten* durchgekommen.	She passed *the examination* with *very good grades*.
Seit *letzter Woche* arbeitet sie als Forschungsassistentin.	Since *last week* she has been working as a research assistant.

(iv) after some prepositions to indicate position [➤27b(iii)]:

Das Labor(atorium) befindet sich in *der Stadtmitte*, hinter *der Hauptpost*.	The lab(oratory) is in *the town center*, behind *the main post office*.

22g   *Masculine nouns with irregular case endings*

(i)   *Weak masculine nouns*

The so-called 'weak masculine' nouns add the ending **-(e)n** to all cases (singular and plural) except the nominative singular. Almost all these nouns refer to humans or animals. The nouns which belong to this group are:

(A) all masculine nouns ending in **-e** except **der Käse**, **der Charme** and the eight nouns listed in paragraph 22g(ii). For example:

der Biologe – Biologen	biologist
der Junge – Jungen	boy
der Matrose – Matrosen	sailor
der Neffe – Neffen	nephew

(B) some native German nouns which do not end in **-e**. Note that **Herr** adds **-n** in the singular and **-en** in the plural. Especially in colloquial speech, there is a tendency for many of these nouns to have the normal endings in all or part of the singular. For example:

der Bär – Bären	bear
der Bauer – Bauern	peasant, farmer
der Bayer – Bayern	Bavarian
der Herr – Herrn – Herren	gentleman
der Mensch – Menschen	person, human
der Nachbar – Nachbarn	neighbor
der Narr – Narren	fool
der Oberst – Obersten	colonel
der Ochs – Ochsen	ox
der Papagei – Papageien	parrot
der Spatz – Spatzen	sparrow
der Untertan – Untertanen	subject (politics)

(**C**) a large number of nouns brought in from other languages, especially those ending in **-and, -ant, -arch, -at, -ent, -ist, -krat** and **-nom**. For example:

der Elefant – Elefanten	elephant
der Automat – Automaten	slot machine
der Student – Studenten	student
der Telefonist – Telefonisten	telephone operator
der Demokrat – Demokraten	democrat
der Astronom – Astronomen	astronomer

Note Weak masculine nouns do not have the **-n** ending in the singular if they are used without a determiner [➤ch.23]. This avoids confusion between singular and plural.

| **Das Verhältnis zwischen Professor und *Assistent* ist immer sehr wichtig.** | The relationship between professor and *assistant* is always very important. |

 Do not confuse weak masculine nouns with adjective-nouns like **der Deutsche – ein Deutscher** or **der Beamte – ein Beamter**, which have the variable endings of adjectives [➤24d].

(ii) Eight masculine nouns ending in **-e** add **-n** in the accusative and dative singular and the whole of the plural, and **-ns** in the genitive singular. One neuter, **das Herz**, also follows this pattern, except that it does not change in the accusative singular.

der Buchstabe – Buchstaben(s)	letter (ABC...)
der Friede –Frieden(s)	peace
der Funke – Funken(s)	spark
der Gedanke – Gedanken(s)	thought
der Glaube – Glauben(s)	belief

das Herz – Herzen(s)	heart
der Name – Namen(s)	name
der Same – Samen(s)	seed
der Wille – Willen(s)	will, intention

Note   Three of these nouns have alternative nominative singulars ending in
-n which are now more usual: **der Frieden, der Funken** and **der
Samen**. Indeed, it is helpful to think of them all as following the same
pattern as **der Wagen** 'car', but without the **-n** in the nominative
singular.

Specifying nouns: determiners

23a What are determiners?

You will not find the word *determiner* in older grammars but it is a very useful term, which takes in some of the most common words in any language.

• Unlike ordinary adjectives, determiners do not describe nouns but are used to place them in a context. They say whether they are assumed to be known or not, to whom they belong, how many there are and so on.
• Determiners come first in the noun phrase. In German they are the main indicators of the noun's gender, number and case.
• Most determiners have corresponding pronouns, which replace the whole noun phrase [➤ch.25].
• Numerals are also determiners, but it is convenient to discuss them separately [➤ch.30].

23b Case endings on determiners

In most noun phrases it is the determiner which best shows the case. With the exception of the three forms **die** and **das** 'the' [➤23d] and **ein** 'a(n)' [➤23e], all determiners have the same set of standard case endings (also known as 'strong' case endings). These are shown in paragraph 23c(i), taking **welcher?** 'which?' as a model. Note that:

• in the singular, the feminine has only two forms, the neuter three and the masculine four. Only the masculine has a separate accusative;
• the masculine and neuter are the same in the singular genitive and dative;
• for all determiners, adjectives, and pronouns, the plural case endings are the same for all three genders.

23c Which ...? What sort of ...? Interrogative determiners

(i) Welcher ...? *Which ...? [➤6d(iii)]*

This determiner is used very much as in English, to ask someone to choose from a known collection.

| **Entschuldigen Sie!** *Welches* **Hundefutter kaufen Sie am meisten? – Immer das billigste.** | Excuse me. *Which* dog food do you buy most? – Always the cheapest. |

Case endings

In the following table the standard case endings are shown in italics.

	Masculine	*Feminine*
Nominative	welch*er* Mann?	welch*e* Frau?
Accusative	welch*en* Mann?	welch*e* Frau?
Genitive	welch*es* Mann(e)s?	welch*er* Frau?
Dative	welch*em* Mann(e)?	welch*er* Frau?

	Neuter	*Plural*
Nominative	welch*es* Kind?	welch*e* Leute?
Accusative	welch*es* Kind?	welch*e* Leute?
Genitive	welch*es* Kind(e)s?	welch*er* Leute?
Dative	welch*em* Kind(e)?	welch*en* Leuten?

Note 1) In the masculine and neuter genitive singular **welchen** is often used instead of **welches** when the noun has the ending **-(e)s**.

2) Before an adjective, **welche** ...? may be used without any ending. The adjective then has the standard (strong) ending. This only occurs in formal written German.

(ii) *Was für (ein) ...?* What kind of ...? [➤6d(iv)]

This asks someone to describe something more closely. The **ein** is used with singular countable nouns (that is, anything you can count) and has its normal case endings [➤23e]. The case of the whole phrase is decided by its function in the sentence, not by **für**.

| *Was für* **Haustiere haben Sie? –** **Einen Schäferhund, einen Dackel und einen Gecko.** | *What sort of* pets do you have? – An alsatian, a dachshund and a gecko. |

Especially (but not only) in speech, the phrase is often split and the **für (ein) ...** put later in the sentence.

Einen Gecko? *Was* **ist das denn** *für ein* **Hund? – Kein Hund, eine Eidechse.**	A gecko? *What kind of a* dog is that? – Not a dog, a lizard.

(iii) Wieviel …? Wie viele …? *How much/many …? [➤6d(viii)]*

This determiner is used to ask about quantity. It may be spelled as one word or two, but the single word **wieviel** is used almost always in the singular and increasingly in the plural; it has no case endings. [Compare **viel(e)** in paragraph 23g(ix).]

Wieviel Futter/*Wie viele* **Dosen Futter kaufen Sie pro Woche? – Eine ganze Menge.**	*How much* pet food/*How many* cans of pet food do you buy per week? – A great deal.

➤   *What* a beautiful lizard! Interrogatives used as exclamations: ➤26a.

23d Already known: the definite article 'the'

(i)
When the definite article is used we know precisely what the noun phrase refers to, because it has already been mentioned, because it is closely defined or because it is obvious. It often answers the question **Welcher …?** 'Which …?' [➤23c(i)].

Im (In *dem***) 17. Jahrhundert war** *das* **Schloß** *das* **Landhaus** *der* **Familie Borkewitz.**	In *the* 17th century *the* castle was *the* country house of *the* Borkewitz family.

(ii) Case endings

Note the irregular **die** in the feminine and plural and **das** in the neuter. All other cases have the standard endings.

	Masculine	*Feminine*
Nominative	**der Mann**	**die Frau**
Accusative	**den Mann**	**die Frau**
Genitive	**des Mann(e)s**	**der Frau**
Dative	**dem Mann(e)**	**der Frau**
	Neuter	*Plural*
Nominative	**das Kind**	**die Leute**
Accusative	**das Kind**	**die Leute**

Genitive	des Kind(e)s	der Leute
Dative	dem Kind(e)	den Leuten

(iii) Uses of the definite article

Especially with nouns referring to concrete objects and people, German uses the definite article much as English does. At other times, though, German uses the definite article where English would not, and in ways which are impossible to tie down exactly. If in doubt, it is safer to use the article.

Set phrases with verb (+ preposition) + noun are particularly variable and must be learned as you meet them [➤8g]. Otherwise, as a rule of thumb:

(A) the article is more likely to be used to refer to something in general. It is almost always used before infinitive-nouns [➤10a(iii)];

(B) the article is less likely when talking about something in a particular situation. It is often left out in idioms with **sein** 'be' and after prepositions which are not linked to a verb.

In the following passage German usage is sometimes the same as English, sometimes not.

Zu der Zeit *war* im ganzen jetzigen Deutschland *Krieg. Das Volk* wollte *in Frieden* leben, aber *der Frieden* kam nicht. *Die Treue* und *die Ehrlichkeit* schienen verlorengegangen zu sein. *Die Pest* tötete Tausende, in allen Dörfern litten *(die) Leute* an *Unterernährung*, sogar *der Kannibalismus* war nicht unbekannt. *Im Winter* fehlte *Brennstoff. Die Geschichte* kennt keine schlimmere Zeit – wer *Geschichte* studiert, wird das schon wissen.	At that time *there was war* in the whole of what is now Germany. *The people* wanted to live *in peace*, but *peace* did not come. *Loyalty* and *honesty* seemed to have been lost. *(The) plague* killed thousands; in every village *(the) people* were suffering from *malnutrition*; even *cannibalism* was not unknown. *In winter* there was no *fuel. History* knows no worse period – anyone who studies *history* will already know that.

➤ Personal names ➤19d. Geographical names ➤19e. Weights and measures ➤23e(iii). Languages ➤19f(ii).

(iv) Shortened forms of the definite article

The definite article can be shortened in two ways. Both distinguish **der** 'the' from **der** 'this, that' [➤23f(i).]

(A) In informed speech, for example, **der, den, dem** and **das** become **d'r, d'n/'n, d'm/'m** and **'s.**

(B) In speech and writing shortened forms are commonly used after certain prepositions.

an + das → ans   an + dem → am   in + das → ins   in + dem → im
auf + das → aufs   von + dem → vom
bei + dem → beim   zu + dem → zum   zu + der → zur

Note   In speech other compounds with **das** are common, for example: **durchs, übers, ums, unters**. Except in certain set phrases like **ums Leben kommen** 'die', these are less used in writing.

23e   *Unknown individuals: the indefinite article 'a(n)'*

(i)   A noun phrase with the indefinite article emphasizes the type of person or thing being referred to, rather than the individual. The phrase often answers the question **was für (ein) ...?** 'what sort of ...?' [➤23c(ii)].

Hier sehen wir das Porträt *eines* Herrn aus dem 18. Jahrhundert. Er war *ein* leidenschaftlicher Jäger.	Here we see the portrait of *a* gentleman from the 18th century. He was *a* very keen hunter.

(ii)   *Case endings*

ein has no ending in the masculine nominative and neuter nominative/accusative. All other cases have the standard endings. Because **ein** has no plural, its opposite **keine** 'no ...' is given in the table.

	Masculine	*Feminine*
Nominative	ein Mann	eine Frau
Accusative	einen Mann	eine Frau
Genitive	eines Manns	einer Frau
Dative	einem Mann(e)	einer Frau

	Neuter	*Plural*
Nominative	ein Kind	keine Leute
Accusative	ein Kind	keine Leute
Genitive	eines Kinds	keiner Leute
Dative	einem Kind(e)	keinen Leuten

Note   All possessives (for example, **mein** 'my', **unser** 'our', **ihr** 'her, their') have the same endings as **ein** [➤23h].

(iii) Uses of the indefinite article

German usage is similar to English except that:

(A) no article is used after a linking verb [➤8c] to refer to someone's job, profession, nationality or religion. **ein(e)** is used if there is an adjective before the noun – being a doctor is a profession, being a *bad* doctor is not!

Seine Frau war *Österreicherin*.	His wife was *Austrian*. She was *(a)*
Sie war *Katholikin*, während ihr	*Catholic*, whereas her husband
Mann *Lutheraner* war.	was *(a) Lutheran*.
but	but
Sie war *eine begabte Malerin*. Er	She was *a gifted painter*, but he
war aber *ein ziemlich schlechter*	was *a fairly bad hunter*!
***Jäger*!**	

(B) the definite article is used in phrases of measurement (weights, frequency, etc.). **pro** 'per' is another way of saying this.

Der Honig kostet sieben Mark	The honey costs seven marks *a*
***das* Glas, die Pralinen kosten 15**	jar, the chocolates cost 15 marks
Mark *das* Pfund und die	*a* pound and the postcards 90
Ansichtskarten 90 Pfennig *das*	pfennigs *a* piece.
Stück.	
Wir bekommen hier Tausende	We get thousands of visitors *a/per*
von Besuchern *pro* Woche.	week here.

23f Pointing and showing: demonstrative determiners 'that, this' etc.

Demonstratives are like a strong definite article. They point to something near to or far from the speaker in time or place, or to something of a certain kind.

• Except after the **allerlei** group [➤(vi) below] and some usages with **solch-** [➤(v) below], adjectives following demonstratives have the **-e/-en** endings [➤24b(ii)A].

(i) *der* 'this, that'

This is the most common demonstrative in German. Colloquially it is often reinforced with **da** after the noun. It has exactly the same forms as the definite article [➤23d(ii)], but in speech it is always stressed and is never shortened as **der** 'the' usually is [➤23d(iv)]. This makes the difference between **zu der Zeit** 'then' and in **dem Augenblick** 'at that moment', and **zur Zeit** 'now' and **im Augenlick** 'at the moment'.

In *dem* **Zimmer (da) sehen Sie ein prachtvolles Himmelbett.**	In *that* room (there) you can see a magnificent four-poster bed.

(ii) *dieser* 'this'

dieser has the standard case endings [➤23c(i)]. It is used very much like the English 'this', except that in speech **der ... (hier/da)** is often used instead.

In *diesem* **Bett soll Albrecht der Bär geschlafen haben.**	Albrecht the Bear is said to have slept in *this* bed.

(iii) *jener, derjenige* 'that'

jener is used mainly in formal written German, but **derjenige** is used in both speech and writing. It is mainly followed by a relative clause [➤5b] defining who or what is being spoken of, as in English 'those people who ... '.

derjenige etc. is always written as one word, but the two halves are treated separately: **der-** has its normal case endings and is never shortened; **-jenige** has the **-e/-en** adjective endings, for example **diejenige, dasjenige, denjenigen, demjenigen**; (plural) **diejenigen**.

Aber *diejenigen* **Historiker, die** *jene* **Zeit studiert haben, glauben diese Geschichte nicht.**	But *those* historians who have studied *that* period do not believe this story.

(iv) *derselbe* 'the same'

This classes people and things together. The two parts are treated separately, as with **derjenige**, except that the **der** part does combine with prepositions [➤23d(iv)]. It is then written as two words. 'The same *as*' is **derselbe** *wie* [➤comparatives 24e(ii)].

Dieselbe **Geschichte wird von so vielen Schlössern erzählt!**	*The same* story is told of so many castles!

| Im *selben* Zimmer steht ein sogenannter Bibliothekarsstuhl. | In *the same* room stands a so-called librarian's chair. |

(v) *solch-, so ein* 'such (a)'

These determiners place people and things in a certain class. They are used in various ways. Note that adjective endings vary according to the construction chosen:

• adjectives take the **-e/-en** endings after **solcher** and after any part of **ein** which has standard case endings [➤24b(ii)A];
• adjectives have the standard case endings after **so** and after endingless **ein** and **solch** [➤24b(ii)B].

(A) In the singular the possibilities are:

• 'such (a) ...' (without an adjective): **(ein) solcher** ... or, more colloquially, **so ein** .... In formal usage **solch ein** ... is an emphatic alternative; here **solch** never takes an ending.

| *Ein solcher* Stuhl dient zugleich als Stuhl und als Trittleiter. | *Such a* chair serves both as chair and as step-ladder. |

• 'such (a) ... ' (with an adjective): **(ein) so** ... or, much more formally, **(ein) solcher**....

| *Ein so* schönes Beispiel wie dieses ist selten zu finden. | *Such a* fine example as this is seldom to be found. |

(B) In the plural the possibilities are:

• 'such ...' (without an adjective): **solche** ... is normal in both speech and writing.

| *Solche* Möbel wurden nur auf Bestellung hergestellt. | *Such* furniture was only made to order. |

• 'such ...' (with an adjective): **solche** ... or **so** ... The latter is more colloquial, but there may also be a difference between the two, as shown in the example. In literary writing endingless **solch** + adjective is also used.

Solche geschickten Schreiner ...	Skilled cabinet makers *like these* ...
So geschickte Schreiner ...	Cabinet makers *who were so* skilled ...
... wurden hoch bezahlt.	... were highly paid.

(vi) **allerlei, allerhand, vielerlei** 'all sorts of', **einerlei** '(all) the same', **keinerlei** 'no ... at all', **zweierlei** 'two kinds of', **usw.** 'etc.'.
None of these add endings. Any adjectives have the standard case endings [▶24b(ii)B].

| Sie sehen, wir haben hier *allerlei/allerhand* faszinierende Sachen. Wir haben sogar *zweierlei* patentierte Wasserklosetts aus dem 19. Jahrhundert! | As you see, we have *all sorts of* fascinating things here. We even have *two kinds of* patented water-closets from the 19th century! |

23g How much? How many?: the indefinite quantifiers 'some, all' etc.

Like the indefinite article, these quantifiers do not identify specific individuals. Some refer to the whole or none of some thing or group, others to some part or some members of it.

(i) For singular and plural materials (money, food, work materials etc.), phrases without an article are used much as in English. They are also used where English might have 'some, any'; here **etwas** can add emphasis.

| Hast du *Geld*? Ich habe schon *Bier* für die Party gekauft, aber wir brauchen noch *Gurken* und *(etwas)* Wein. | Have you *any money*? I've already bought *(some) beer* for the party, but we still need *gherkins* and *(some) wine*. |

(ii) **kein ...** '*no ..., not a(ny) ...*'

This has exactly the same endings as **ein**, except that it has plural forms [▶23e(ii)].

(A) In general, **kein** is used instead of **nicht (ein)** as the negative of **ein**/no article (+ adjective) + noun. If in doubt always use **kein**.

Wir haben auch *kein* frisches Brot, *keinen* Käse und *keine* Würstchen! Hoffentlich haben unsere Gäste *keinen* Hunger.	We do not have *any* fresh bread, (*any*) cheese or (*any*) sausages either! I hope our guests are *not* hungry.

(B) Note the use of **noch kein** to mean 'not yet' or 'not even'.

Von Carl haben wir *noch keine* Antwort gehabt.	We have*n't* had a reply from Carl *yet.*

(C) nicht (ein) is used in several contexts:

• in verb + noun constructions where the meaning is 'not' rather than 'no' or 'not a(ny)':

Weißt du, er fährt *nicht* Auto, nur Moped, und das ist kaputt.	You know, he does*n't* drive a car, only a moped, and that's broken.

• to stress the idea of 'not a single one', though **kein einziger** can also be used:

Stimmt. Das letzte Mal wollte *nicht ein* (kein einziger) Freund ihn mitbringen.	You're right. Last time *not one* friend would give him a lift.

• starting a sentence with an **ein** or article-less phrase and placing **nicht** later emphasizes the negative:

Eine andere Möglichkeit, zu uns zu kommen, hat er ja *nicht.*	After all he does*n't* have *any* other way of getting to us.

(iii) *aller, all der* 'all (the)'

These are used in various ways. Note that adjectives take the **-e/-en** endings [▶24b(ii)A] after all constructions with **all-**.

(A) In the singular, endingless **all** is normally used before other determiners. Before an adjective, **aller** with standard case endings is used, but this is rare outside set phrases (**mit allem modernen Komfort** 'with all modern conveniences'). Singular **all/aller** is far less common than the English 'all', which is usually expressed by **der ganze ..., mein ganzer ...** 'the whole ..., my whole ...' etc.

| Fast (*all* der Wein) der *ganze* Wein ist schon weg, und wir haben (*all* unser Geld) unser *ganzes* Geld ausgegeben. | Almost *all* the wine is gone, and we've spent *all* our money. |

(B) In the plural, **alle** (+ other determiner) + noun is the commonest usage, though **all die** and occasionally **alle die** are also used. Note that **alle** is *never* followed by a genitive, so **alle Kinder** means both 'all children' and 'all (of) the children'.

| Wo kommen *alle* diese Leute nur her? Haben wir *alle* Einwohner des Viertels eingeladen? | Just where do *all* these people come from? Did we invite *all (of) the* local residents? |

(iv)   *jeder* 'each, every', *jeglicher* 'any at all'

These both have standard case endings [➤23c(i)]. **jeder** can only be used in the singular. **jeglicher**, an emphatic alternative used mainly in formal written style, also has plural forms. (**jedweder** is another emphatic alternative which is rare even in formal writing.)

| Das nächste Mal kann *jeder* Gast eine Flasche mitbringen. So vermeiden wir *jegliche* Probleme. | The next time *every* guest can bring a bottle. In that way we'll avoid *any* problems. |

(v)   *beide* 'both, the two'

beide has the standard case endings [➤23c(i)]. Any following adjectives end in **-en**. **beiden** can also be used after another determiner, as in **seine beiden ...** 'both his .../his two ...'.

| Ich bin froh, daß wir deine *beiden* Brüder eingeladen haben. *Beide/Die beiden* jungen Leute mag ich gern. | I'm glad that we invited your *two* brothers. I like *both (the)* young people. |

(vi)   *einig-* 'some'

This refers to a fairly small amount or number. It has the standard case endings throughout, but following adjectives have different types of ending in the singular and the plural.

(A) The singular **einiger** is used mainly with abstract nouns ['some' with materials: ➤23g(i)]. Following adjectives have the **-e/-en** endings [➤24b(ii)A].

Es tut mir leid, daß wir sie seit *einiger* **Zeit nicht gesehen haben.**	I'm sorry that we haven't seen them for *some* time.

(B) The plural **einige** is common, though it is often left out where English might have 'some'. Following adjectives have the same endings as **einige**.

Einige **ältere Verwandte haben ihnen gegenüber (***einige***) Bedenken, aber ich finde sie sympathisch.**	*Some* older relatives have *some* misgivings about them, but I find them likeable.

(vii) *manch*- *'many (a)'*

This has the sense of 'a fair amount but some way short of all'. It is more common in writing than in speech.

(A) In both singular and plural, **mancher** is most often used with standard case endings. Following adjectives then take the **-e/-en** endings [➤24b(ii)A].

Mancher **junge Mann ist ...** *Manche* **jungen Leute sind ...** **... viel ausgelassener als sie.**	*Many a* young man is ... *Many* young people are ... ... much more boisterous than them.

(B) Endingless **manch** is common in the singular:

• before adjectives, which then have the standard case endings [➤24b(ii)B].
• in formal writing, before **ein**. Following adjectives then have the **-e/-en** endings except after endingless **ein**.

Manch (ein) **alter Mensch hat eine wilde Jugend gehabt.**	*Many an* old person had a wild youth.

(viii)   *etlicher* 'quite a lot of', *etliche* 'quite a few', **mehrere** 'several'

These have the standard case endings, as do any following adjectives [➤24b(ii)B].

Etliche gutbürgerliche Leute haben ein untadeliges Leben geführt – und bereuen es später! Ich kenne *mehrere* Rentner, die das nun nachholen wollen.	*Quite a lot of* solid middle-class people have led a blameless life – and regret it later! I know *several* pensioners who are now trying to make up for it.

(ix)   *viel* 'much/many', **wenig** 'little, few'; *ein wenig, ein bißchen* 'a little' (singular); *ein paar* 'a few', *ein oder zwei* 'one or two' (plural).

With one exception [➤(A) below], following adjectives have the standard case endings [➤24b(ii)B].

(A) In the singular, endingless **viel** and **wenig** are normally used. **viel-** and **wenig-** with singular case endings occur in some set phrases and in formal writing; any following adjectives then have the **-e/-en** endings.

Recht *vielen* Dank für die Party! Wir haben *viel* Spaß gehabt. Ich bin nur erstaunt, daß ihr so *viel* Arbeit in so *wenig* Zeit gemacht habt.	Very *many* thanks for the party! We enjoyed ourselves *a lot*. I am just amazed that you did so *much* work in so *little* time.

(B) In the plural, **viele** and **wenige** with standard case endings are the rule.

Es bleiben nur noch *wenige* unersättliche Gäste. *Viele* Leute sind nach Hause gegangen.	Only *a few* insatiable guests remain. *Many* people have gone home.

(C) Both **viel-** and **wenig-** can be used after **der** or another determiner, when they take the usual adjective endings.

Das viele Essen und *die vielen* Getränke sind alle – *unser weniges* Geld auch!	*The quantities of* food and *the many* drinks are all gone– so is *what little* money *we had!*

(D) ein wenig, ein bißchen, ein paar and **ein oder zwei** remain unchanged in all cases.

Übers Wochenende müssen wir mit *ein paar* **kleinen Würstchen,** *ein wenig/ein bißchen* **altem Käse und** *ein oder zwei* **Gurken auskommen!**	Over the weekend we shall have to get by on *a few* small sausages, *a little* stale cheese and *one or two* gherkins (pickles)!

(x)   *irgendein ..., irgendwelcher ... 'just any ..., any ... at all, some ... or other.'*

These are used in the same way as **ein** (singular only) and **welcher** (singular and plural).

Ich glaube, in *irgendeinem* **Schrank findest du** *irgendwelche* **Büchsen. In der Gefriertruhe ist noch** *irgendwelches* **Fleisch**.	I think you'll find *some (sort of)* cans in *some* cabinet *or other*. There is still *some kind of* meat in the freezer (chest).

23h   Belonging together: possessive determiners 'my, our' etc.

Possessives are used to show that the noun belongs to somebody or something. Which possessive is used depends on the possessor, but they add the endings belonging to the same gender and case of the thing possessed.

(i)   *Forms of the possessives*

The following table shows the two nominative forms of the possessives, with their subject pronouns. Note that the **-er** in **unser** and **euer** is part of the word, not an ending; especially in speech, the **-e-** is often dropped before case endings. [Use of second persons **du/ihr** as against **Sie**: ➤25b.]

		Singular				Plural	
First person	ich	*mein, meine*	my	wir	*unser, uns(e)re*	our
Second person	du	*dein, deine*	your	ihr	*euer, eu(e)re*	your
	Sie	*Ihr, Ihre*	your	Sie	*Ihr, Ihre*	your
Third person	er	*sein, seine*	his, its	sie	*ihr, ihre*	their
	sie	*ihr, ihre*	her, its			
	es	*sein, seine*	its			

Note   All these possessives have the same case endings as **ein** [➤23e(ii)]. Following adjectives have the **-e/-en** endings except when the possessive has no ending, that is, when it is **mein**, **dein**, **sein**, **ihr**, **unser**, **euer**.

(ii)   *Use of possessives*

Possessives are used in German very much as in English, except that the definite article is normally used instead of a possessive:

(A) when referring to clothes or parts of the body. A dative pronoun is often added for clarity [➤8e(iii)].

Hänschen, steck *die* Finger bitte nicht in *den* Mund! Zieh *das* Hemd an, and kämme *dir die* Haare! Hast du *die* Zähne geputzt?	Hänschen, please don't stick *your* fingers in *your* mouth! Put *your* shirt on and comb *your* hair! Have you brushed *your* teeth?

(B) with the adjective **eigen** 'own'.

Hoffentlich hast du diesmal *die eigene* Zahnbürste gebraucht.	I hope you used *your own* toothbrush this time.

However, possessives are used to avoid ambiguity, especially with the subject of the sentence.

Hänschens Mutter sah ihn an. *Sein* Gesicht war nicht sehr sauber, *sein* Hemd war zerrissen, und er hatte *ihren* Pullover an!	Hänschen's mother looked at him. *His* face was not very clean, *his* shirt was torn, and he had *her* sweater on!

(C) dessen can be used for 'his' and **deren** for 'her' when **sein** and **ihr** would be ambiguous [➤25g(i)].

Sie dachte an ihre Schwester und *deren* Sohn. Ob der stubenreiner war als ihr Sohn?	She thought of her sister and *her* (sister's) son. Was he more well-mannered than her son?

24 Describing nouns: adjectives

24a What do adjectives do?

Adjectives describe nouns. They can do this either as part of a noun phrase [➤24b] or as a separate element in the sentence [➤24c]. The former are known as attributive adjectives, the latter as predicative adjectives. Only attributive adjectives have added endings.

➤ A bad writer writes *badly*: adverbs formed from adjectives ➤28b(i).

24b Accompanying the noun: adjectives within a noun phrase

(i) Noun phrases can consist of any combination of determiners, adjectives and nouns. The adjectives in the phrase add endings according to the following rule:

• If either the determiner or the noun has a case ending, then the adjective has the so-called weak endings:
-e in the nominative singular of all three genders and in the feminine and neuter accusative singular,
-en in all other cases, singular and plural.
• Otherwise, the adjective has the same standard (strong) case endings as determiners [➤23c(i)]. **-e** and **-en** are of course also two of the standard endings, so in some cases it makes no difference.

(ii) The following tables show how this works. You can see that in practice adjectives end in **-e** or **-en** unless they come first in the phrase or the determiner has no ending.

(A) Adjectives ending in **-e/-en** (shown here in small capitals). In the table **der** etc. stands for all determiners with standard case endings. Parts of **ein, kein** or the possessives have been given where they too have these endings.

	Masculine	*Feminine*
Nominative	**der** rotE **Wein**	**die/meine** frischE Milch
Accusative	**den/einen** rotEN **Wein**	**die/meine** frischE Milch
Genitive	**des/keines** rotEN **Weins**	**der/meiner** frischEN Milch
Dative	**dem/seinem** rotEN **Wein**	**der/meiner** frischEN Milch

	Neuter	*Plural*
Nominative	da*s* hellE Bier	d*ie*/dein*e* kaltEN Getränke
Accusative	da*s* hellE Bier	d*ie*/eur*e* kaltEN Getränke
Genitive	de*s*/unser*es* hellEN Bier*s*	der/Ihr*er* kaltEN Getränke
Dative	de*m*/eur*em* hellEN Bier	de*n*/ihr*en* kaltEN Getränke*n*

(B) Adjectives with standard case endings.

Note the three cases where **ein, kein** and the possessives have no ending and so make no difference to the adjective ending. In the masculine and neuter genitive singular, the noun almost always has the case ending **-s**, so the adjective ends in **-en**.

	Masculine	*Feminine*
Nominative	(sein) rot*er* Wein	frisch*e* Milch
Accusative	rot*en* Wein	frisch*e* Milch
Genitive	[rotEN Wein*s*]	frisch*er* Milch
Dative	rot*em* Wein	frisch*er* Milch

	Neuter	*Plural*
Nominative	(unser) hell*es* Bier	kalt*e* Getränke
Accusative	(Ihr) hell*es* Bier	kalt*e* Getränke
Genitive	[hellEN Bier*s*]	kalt*er* Getränke
Dative	hell*em* Bier	kalt*en* Getränke*n*

In einem modernEN Zoo sind viele gefährdet*e* Tierarten zu sehen. Das heutig*E* Leben ist oft langweilig, und bei schön*em* Wetter zieht ein selten*es* Tier oder ein exotisch*er* Vogel Tausende von neugierig*en* Besuchern an. Wir sehen eine Gruppe afrikanisch*er* Schimpansen an und fragen uns, was für interessant*e* Gedanken sie wohl haben. Unsere nächstEN VerwandtEN schauen zurück und stellen sich dieselb*E* Frage!

In a modern zoo there are many endangered species to be seen. Life nowadays is often boring, and in good weather a rare animal or an exotic bird attracts thousands of inquisitive visitors. We look at a group of African chimpanzees and wonder what sorts of interesting thoughts they have. Our closest relatives return the gaze and ask themselves the same question!

(iii)   Some further points on the endings of adjectives within the noun phrase.

(A) If there is more than one adjective they all have the same ending. [Use of commas: ►2d(ii).]

Im nächsten, engeren Käfig sind ein Dutzend große und kleine südamerikanische Vögel.	In the next, narrower cage are a dozen large and small South American birds.

(B) Sometimes the noun is 'understood' (omitted because obvious), but this does not affect the rest of the phrase. Adjectives still have the same endings and (unlike adjective nouns, ►24d) are not spelled with a capital.

Die großen (Vögel) sind meistens Kraniche, die kleinen sind Finken. Der größte ist ein Storch.	The big *ones* are mostly cranes; the small *ones* are finches. The biggest (*one*) is a stork.

(C) Some adjectives brought in from other languages (mainly colo(u)rs) do not take endings.

Die Finken sind *prima* kleine Vögel, mit *orange* und gelben Schnäbeln und roten, *rosa* und sogar *lila* Federn.	The finches are *great* little birds, with *orange* and yellow beaks and red, *pink* and even *mauve* feathers.

(D) Adjectives made by adding **-er** to town names or numerals: ►24f, 30a(iv).

► You *lucky* people: adjectives after personal pronouns ►25b(iii). Something/nothing *special*: adjectives after indefinites ►25h(ii) and (iv), 24d(iii).

(iv) *The spellings of some adjectives*

(A) hoch 'high' changes to **hoh-** before case endings and in the comparative (**höher**).

Auf einem *hohen* Felsen hockt eine Gruppe Paviane.	On a *high* rock a group of baboons are squatting.

(B) Adjectives in **-el, -auer** and **-euer** drop the **-e-** before case endings and in the comparative, and so do foreign adjectives in **-er**.

Das alte Männchen hat ein *dunkles* Fell und einen etwas *sauren* Gesichtsausdruck.	The old male has *dark* fur and a rather *sour* expression.

(C) Some adjectives end in an **-e**, which is often dropped in speech though not usually in writing. Case endings are added to the stem without the **-e**. For example:

Irgendwie macht er einen *müden, trägen* Eindruck. Er schaut *trübe* vor sich hin und grunzt *leise*. *Blöd(e)* ist er aber nicht, nur *böse*!	Somehow he gives the impression of being *tired* and *lethargic*. He gazes *dully* into space and grunts *quietly*. He is not *stupid* though, just *cross*!

24c   At a distance: adjectives as separate elements

Adjectives which are not part of a noun phrase never have case endings in German. They usually describe the subject and are linked to it by a verb like **sein** 'be', **bleiben** 'remain' or **werden** 'become' [➤8c]. They can also describe the object, as in the second last sentence in the example given below, or form a free-standing phrase, as in the last sentence.

Viele Tiersorten sind *gefährdet*. In Zoos sind sie wenigstens *gesund* und *sicher*. Ihre Käfige sind aber oft *klein* und *kahl*, und ihr Bewegungsraum ist sehr *begrenzt*. Die aktiveren Tiere finden dieses Dasein *frustrierend*. *Verwirrt* und *verzweifelt* rennen sie unaufhörlich hin und her.	Many animal species are *endangered*. In zoos they are at least *healthy* and *safe*. However, their cages are often *small* and *bare*, and their room for movement is very *limited*. The more active animals find this existence *frustrating*. *Confused* and *desperate* they run ceaselessly to and fro.

24d   Adjectives used as nouns

(i)   All German adjectives can be used as nouns. These *adjective-nouns* are spelled with a capital and almost always take the normal adjective endings [➤24b(ii)]. Some typical adjective-nouns are:

der/die Abgeordnete	elected representative
der/die Angestellte	employee
der Beamte/die Beamtin	official (male/female)
der/die Deutsche	German
der/die Fremde	stranger
der/die Reisende	traveller

(ii)   Masculine adjective-nouns are often confused with weak masculine nouns [➤22g(i)]. The following table shows where they differ. [Nouns of nationality: ➤19f.]

Singular

	Adjective-noun: 'German'	Weak masculine: 'Frenchman'
Nominative	**der Deutsche –** **ein Deutscher**	**der/ein Franzose**

Plural

Nominative/ *Accusative*	**die Deutschen –** **zehn Deutsche**	**die/zehn Franzosen**
Genitive	**der Deutschen –** **zehn Deutscher**	**der/zehn Franzosen**

In both adjective-nouns and weak masculine nouns, all other cases end in **-en**.

A further difference is that many weak masculine nouns have a feminine form ending in **-in** [➤19g(ii)], thus: **der Franzose – die Französin, der Löwe – die Löwin** 'lion/lioness'. The only feminine adjective-noun in **-in** is **die Beamtin** 'official'.

(iii)   In speech, adjective-nouns sound just like a noun phrase with the noun understood [➤24b(iii)], but they have much more general meanings.

(A) Masculines and feminines usually refer to representatives of a whole class of people.

Die *Grünen* sind meist gegen Zoos. Trotzdem besuchen sowohl *Erwachsene* als auch *Jugendliche* sie gern. Zu Hagenbecks Tierpark in Hamburg kommen *Fremde* aus aller Welt, *Reisende* auf der Durchfahrt und viele andere.	The *Greens* are mostly against zoos. All the same, both *adults* and *young people* like visiting them. *Strangers* from far and wide, *travellers* passing through and many others come to Hagenbecks Zoo in Hamburg.

(B) Neuters refer to general ideas or qualities. They are often used after indefinites like **alles, nichts, viel, wenig** [➤25h(ii) and (iv)].

Wenn man *nichts Besonderes* zu tun hat, wird man dort immer *etwas Neues* finden, mit sehr *viel Interessantem* aus allen Ländern.	If you have *nothing special* to do you will always find *something new* there, with *much of great interest* from every country.

Note   A number of neuter adjective-nouns are almost always spelled with a small letter, for example:

Er ist alles *andere* als gescheit.	He is *anything* but bright.
Akten, Berichte und *ähnliches.*	Files, reports and *the like.*
Wir wollen es im *einzelnen* besprechen.	Let's discuss it in *detail.*
Ich hätte das *gleiche* getan.	I should have done the *same.*
Wir tun alles *mögliche/* alles Mögliche.	We are doing everything *imaginable/* everything we can.
Das *übrige* wissen Sie schon.	The *rest* you know already.

Others are written with a small letter only in certain set phrases:

im *allgemeinen*	in *general*
im *großen und ganzen*	on *the whole*
vor *kurzem*, aufs *neue*	a *short while* ago, *anew/again*
Ich halte Sie auf dem *laufenden.*	I'll keep you *informed.*

➤   The best thing *that* ever happened: relative clauses after neuter adjective-nouns ➤25j(vi).

24e   *More and most: comparative and superlative*

Note   For ease of reference, this section deals with both adjectives and the adverbs formed from them [➤28b(i)]. Unless otherwise stated, all references to adjectives apply also to their adverbs.

Most adjectives can be used to make comparisons: for this we use the *comparative* form. If we are comparing more than two people or things, then we use the *superlative*.

(i)   *Formation of comparatives and superlatives*

(A) Almost all German adjectives add **-er** for their comparative and **-(e)st** for their superlative. These forms then add the normal adjective endings when they are part of a noun phrase [➤24b].

Unsere elektrischen Handwerkzeuge sind die *erfolgreichsten* auf dem Markt. Wir haben einen *höheren* Umsatz als viele *bekanntere* Marken.	Our electrical hand-tools are the *most successful* on the market. We have a *higher* turnover than many *better known* makes.

Note   In a very few instances **mehr** and **am meisten** can be used for comparatives and superlatives (for example, with participles which are not normally used as adjectives). Normally, *mehr* **faul** *als* **dumm** means 'lazy *rather than* stupid', and *meist* **faul** means '*mostly/usually* lazy'.

Unser *meist gekauftes* Modell ist ein elektrischer Schraubenzieher.	Our *most purchased* model is an electric screwdriver.

(B) About 20 common one-syllable adjectives (and **gesund**) have Umlaut in the comparative and superlative. Note the irregular forms in **groß**, **hoch** and **nah**.

alt 'old'	**älter**	**ältest-**
arm 'poor'	**ärmer**	**ärmst-**
dumm 'stupid'	**dümmer**	**dümmst-**
gesund 'healthy'	**gesünder**	**gesündest-**
groß 'big, great'	**größer**	*größt-*
hoch 'high'	*höher*	**höchst-**
jung 'young'	**jünger**	**jüngst-**
klug 'clever'	**klüger**	**klügst-**
kurz 'short'	**kürzer**	**kürzest-**
lang 'long'	**länger**	**längst-**
nah(e) 'near'	**näher**	*nächst-*
scharf 'sharp'	**schärfer**	**schärfst-**
schwach 'weak'	**schwächer**	**schwächst-**
stark 'strong'	**stärker**	**stärkst-**
warm 'warm'	**wärmer**	**wärmst-**

(C) Three adjectives have completely different comparatives and superlatives. **minder** 'less' is used only as an adverb and **mindest-** usually means 'slightest'; otherwise, **weniger** and **wenigst-** are used.

gut 'good'	**besser**	**best-**
viel 'much/many'	**mehr**	**meist-**
wenig 'little/few'	**minder**	**mindest-**

(D) Two non-adjectival adverbs have a comparative and superlative. **Das mache ich *gern*** is the usual way to say 'I *like* doing that' [➤29a]. **eher/am ehesten** often refers to preferences rather than time.

gern 'willingly'	**lieber**	**am liebsten**
bald 'soon'	**eher**	**am ehesten**

Die Werkzeuge sind *eher* für den Amateur gedacht als für den Profi. Sie werden *am liebsten* von Bastlern gekauft.	The tools are intended for the amateur *rather* than the professional. They are bought *most (willingly)* by do-it-yourself enthusiasts.

(E) **-est-** is used in the superlative for ease of pronunciation, especially with adjectives stressed on the last syllable, or ending in **-s, -x, -z, -sk** and often **-d, -t** and **-sch**.

leisest-, laxest-, wildest-, amüsantest-, raschest-	quietest, laxest, wildest, most amusing, swiftest

(F) Half a dozen adjectives of position have only comparative and superlative forms. They are only used before nouns.

der äußere/innere	outer/inner
der äußerste/innerste	outermost, utmost/innermost
(also **äußerlich/innerlich**)	(external/internal)
der obere/untere	upper/lower
der oberste/unterste	uppermost, top/lowest, bottom
der vordere/hintere	front/back
der vorderste/hinterste	foremost, furthest front/back

(ii)   Using comparatives

(A) The comparatives of some adjectives (and one adverb) can mean **ziemlich ...** 'fairly ...'. Thus **eine ältere Dame** is not as old as **eine alte Dame**. For example:

alt	old	**älter**
dick	thick, fat	**dicker**
dunkel	dark	**dunkler**
dünn	thin	**dünner**
groß	big, great	**größer**
hell	light	**heller**
jung	young	**jünger**
klein	little, small	**kleiner**
neu	new	**neuer**
oft	often	**öfters**

(B) Superiors and inferiors are compared using **(noch) ~er als ...** '(even) more ~ than ...' and **weniger ~ als ...** 'less ~ than ...'.

Unsere Produkte sind *billiger als* die Konkurrenz, aber nicht *weniger verläßlich*.	Our products are *cheaper than* the competition but no(t) *less reliable*.

(C) Equals are compared using **(genau)so ~ wie ...** or **(eben)so ~ wie ...** '(just) as ~ as ...'.

Auf der letzten Industriemesse hatten wir *genauso viele* Interessenten *wie* im vorigen Jahr.	At the last industrial fair we had *just as many* inquiries *as* the year before.

(D) 'More and more ~ ' is **immer ~er**.

Die Nachfrage wird *immer größer*, also haben wir *immer mehr* Arbeiter anstellen müssen.	The demand gets *greater and greater*, so we have had to employ *more and more* workers.

(E) 'The more ~ ..., the more ~ ...' is **je ~er ...**, **um so ~er/desto ~er ....** (**desto** is more used in written German.) The first half of the sentence is a subordinate clause; the second part is the main clause. Note the positions of the verbs in each half of the sentence.

Je länger die Rezession dauert, *um so (desto) häufiger* machen die Leute selber ihre Hausreparaturen, *um so mehr* brauchen sie unsere Werkzeuge.	*The longer* the recession lasts, *the more frequently* people do their own house repairs and *the more* they need our tools.

(iii)   *Using superlatives*

Superlatives have several forms.

(A) der ~ste etc. and **mein ~ster** etc. are used when an adjective describes a particular noun.

***Unsere beste* Zeit ist im November, wo *die meisten* Leute ihre Weihnachtsgeschenke kaufen.**	*Our best* time is in November, when *most* people buy their Christmas presents.

(B) am ~sten is used:

• after **sein** 'be' in the sense of 'at its most ~'. It is also often used instead of **der ~ste** etc. [➤(A) above]:

Dann ist die Nachfrage *am größten* und unser Umsatz *am höchsten.*	That is when demand is *(at its) greatest* and our sales volume *(at its) highest.*

• for the normal superlative of adverbs:

Unsere Leute arbeiten *am schnellsten*, weil sie *am besten* bezahlt werden.	Our people work *(the) fastest* because they are paid *(the) best.*

(C) Any superlative adjective can mean 'extremely ~'. It must be followed by a noun, often with no article.

Auch während des *schlechtesten* Wetters kommen sie zur Arbeit, manchmal nur mit *größter* Mühe.	Even during the *worst* weather they come in to work, sometimes only with *the greatest* difficulty.

(D) There are various emphatic superlative adverb forms:

• A few consist simply of the stem, ending in **~st**:

äußerst	extremely	**längst**	long since
herzlichst	most cordially	**meist**	mostly, usually
höchst	highly, extremely	**möglichst ~**	as ~ as possible

• **aufs ~ste** 'most ~ly' is used in formal written German:

Wir möchten ihnen allen *aufs herzlichste* danken.	We should like to thank them all *most warmly.*

• There are several common adverbs in **~stens**, usually meaning 'at (the) ~st':

höchstens	at (the) most	schnellstens	with utmost speed
meistens	mostly, for the most part	strengstens	very strictly
		wenigstens	at least,
mindestens	at (the) least		at any rate

24f Adjectives formed from other parts of speech

(i) Adjectives formed by using a suffix

As in English, adjectives are often made from nouns and verbs by adding a *suffix*. Unless otherwise stated, the suffixes listed below are all added to nouns. An Umlaut is frequently added if the suffix has an **-i-** in it, but not normally otherwise.

• **~bar** '~able, ~ible' can be used with any suitable verb, sometimes with change of stem.

| **hörbar, machbar, sichtbar, trinkbar** | audible, feasible, visible, drinkable |

• **~(e)n, ~ern** 'made of ~'. **~ern** does usually add an Umlaut.

| **bleiern, eisern, golden, hölzern, kupfern, silbern** | leaden, iron, golden, wooden, copper, silver |

• **~er** makes adjectives from names of towns and villages where English would normally just use the name. These adjectives are spelled with a capital and do not add case endings.

| **Bostoner, Edinburger, Hamburger, Pariser, Wiener** | Boston(ian), Edinburgh, Hamburg, Parisian, Viennese |

~er also makes adjectives from numerals [➤30a(iv)].

• **~haft** 'like a ~'.

| **heldenhaft, mädchenhaft, pöbelhaft** | heroic, girlish, uncouth (rabble-like) |

• **~ig** '~y' is a very common suffix which often means 'having the look or qualities of ~'.

| **freudig, grünäugig, rothaarig, staubig, traurig** | joyful, green-eyed, red-haired, dusty, sad |

~ig also makes useful adjectives from some phrases and adverbs of place and time.

| **damalig, dortig, ehemalig, einmalig, gestrig, heutig, hiesig, zweitägig** | (the) then, of that place, former, unique, yesterday's, today's, local, lasting two days |

• **~(i)sch** '~ish' makes adjectives from foreign words, from names of people and from countries and provinces, including their languages [➤19f]. Some towns have adjectives in **-isch**, usually in set phrases or meaning 'the dialect of ~'.

algebräisch, arithmetisch,	algebraic, arithmetic,
geometrisch, taktisch,	geometric, tactical,
beethovensch, kopernikanisch,	Beethoven's, Copernican,
shakespearisch,	Shakespearian,
baierisch, bremisch,	Bavarian, Bremen,
sächsisch, Kölnisch Wasser	Saxon, eau de Cologne

~isch also makes often uncomplimentary adjectives from some nouns referring to people.

heidnisch, kindisch, wählerisch	heathen, childish, choosy

• **~lich** '~ly' is a very common suffix meaning 'relating to ~'.

beruflich, glücklich, wöchentlich,	professional, happy, weekly,
zweitäglich	every two days

~lich '~able, ~ible' is used with some verbs.

möglich, verläßlich, verständlich,	possible, reliable, understandable,
wahrscheinlich	probable

~lich '~ish' can be added to colo(u)r adjectives.

bläßlich, bläulich, gelblich,	palish, blueish, yellowish,
rötlich, schwärzlich	reddish, blackish

• **~los** '~less, lacking ~'.

hilflos, ratlos, sinnlos,	helpless, at a loss, senseless,
ziellos	aimless/random

• **~mäßig** is much used in official writing to mean 'related to ~' or 'in accordance with ~'.

planmäßig, verhältnismäßig,	according to plan, relative,
verkehrsmäßig	relating to traffic

• **~sam** 'having the quality of ~'. Makes adjectives from nouns and verbs.

biegsam, grausam, gewaltsam,	flexible, cruel, violent,
ratsam	advisable

(ii) Adjectives formed by using a prefix

Two *prefixes* in common use are added to adjectives to modify their meaning:
• **un~** 'un~, in~, dis~' etc., meaning 'not ~' or sometimes 'not very ~'.

unehrlich, unerhört, unglaublich, unschön, untypisch, unweit	dishonest, scandalous, incredible, not very nice, untypical, not far

• **ur~** 'very' or sometimes 'typically'.

uralt, urdeutsch, urgemütlich, urverwandt	ancient, typically German, extremely cosy, cognate (words)

24g Adjectives governing phrases and clauses

A large number of adjectives can govern noun phrases or clauses in the same way as the verbs discussed in paragraphs 8d on. Usually:

• the adjective follows the noun phrase;
• the verb is **sein** or another linking verb [➤8c]. In fact, the adjective often acts as a verbal particle [➤16e(ii)], except that it is never written as one word with the verb.

The main constructions are given below with a few common examples and cross-references to the corresponding verb usages.

(i) Adjectives + noun phrases

(A) A few adjectives are used with the accusative [verbs: ➤8d(i)].

Ich bin es *gewohnt/satt*.	I am *used to* it/*fed up with* it.
Ich möchte es *los* sein/werden.	I should like to be/get *rid of* it.
Es ist nicht viel *wert*.	It isn't *worth* much.

(B) Many adjectives are used with the dative [verbs: ➤8d(ii)].

Das Baby ist der Mutter sehr *ähnlich*.	The baby is very *like (similar to)* its mother.
Er/Das ist mir *bekannt*.	I *know* him/about it.
Sie war mir sehr *behilflich/dankbar*.	She was very *helpful/grateful* to me.
Sie waren dem Kind sehr *böse*.	They were very *cross* with the child.
Was bin ich Ihnen *schuldig*?	What do I *owe* you (am I *owing* to you)?
In Mathe ist sie ihm *überlegen*.	In math(s) she is *better* than (*superior* to) him.

This group includes common idioms referring to feelings and sensations [➤8k] and a number of adjectives meaning 'all the same to ~', at varying levels of politeness:

| Das ist mir gleich/einerlei/egal/wurs(ch)t! | That's all the same to me! I couldn't care less! |

(C) Some adjectives are used with the genitive. Very few are used outside very formal written German [verbs: ►8d(iii)].

Ich bin der ganzen Hetze *müde.*	I am *tired* of the whole mad rush.
Der Verbrecher war des Verbrechens *schuldig.*	The criminal was *guilty* of the crime.
Ich bin dessen *sicher.*	I am *sure* of that.
Er ist dieser Ehre nicht *würdig.*	He is not *worthy* of this honor.

(ii)   *Adjectives + prepositions + noun phrases*

(A) Adjectives can be used with any of the prepositions used with verbs [►8g]. The following examples show how the construction works.

Wir Bauern sind vom Wetter *abhängig.*	We farmers are *dependent* on the weather.
Das Land ist *arm/reich* an Mineralien.	The country is *poor/rich* in minerals.
Er ist zu allem *bereit/fähig.*	He is *ready* for/*capable* of anything.
Sie war *blaß* vor Zorn/ *bleich* vor Furcht.	She was *pale* with anger/*pale* with fear.
Wir waren *böse/zornig/wütend* auf sie.	We were *cross/angry/furious* with them.
Sind Sie mit unserem Plan *einverstanden*?	Are you *in agreement* with our plan?
Wann werden Sie damit *fertig* sein?	When will you have *finished* (with) it?
Ich bin auf ihre Antwort *gespannt/neugierig.*	I am *eager/curious* to hear your answer.
Er ist/hat *schuld* an der ganzen Sache.	The whole thing is his *fault*.
Wir sind *stolz* auf unsere Kinder.	We are *proud* of our children.
Das ist *typisch* für diese Gegend.	That is *typical* of this area.

(B) With many adjectives of this type the noun phrase can be replaced by a **zu** + infinitive clause [verbs: ➤8h(ii)] or, if the subject changes, by a **daß** clause [➤8i]. As with the verbs, this clause is then normally introduced by an adverb formed from **da(r)-** + the preposition, though especially in speech the adverb is often left out.

Ich bin (*dazu*) bereit, Ihnen *zu helfen*.	I am ready *to help* you.
Wir sind stolz *darauf*, an diesem Projekt teilgenommen *zu haben*.	We are proud *of having* taken part in this project.
Sie sind nicht *damit* einverstanden, *daß* wir den Bericht *veröffentlichen*.	They do not agree *to our publishing* the report.
Wer ist schuld *daran*, *daß* du müde *bist*?	Whose fault is it *that* you're tired?

25 Representing nouns: pronouns

25a What pronouns do

(i) The word *pronoun* means 'in place of a noun.' Pronouns are used instead of nouns as a way of avoiding clumsy repetitions. Remember that:

• all pronouns take their gender (masculine/feminine/neuter) and number (singular/plural) from the noun they refer to;
• things can have any of the three genders, so **er/sie** can mean 'it' as well as 'he/she';
• all pronouns take their case from their function in the sentence they are in;
• unless they do not change at all, all third person pronouns have some form of the standard case endings [➤23c(i)].

(ii) The types of pronoun discussed in paragraphs 25f to 25(i) below have corresponding determiners in chapter 23, to which cross-references are given.

➤ 'We gave *it* to *her/it* to *the woman/her the money*': order of objects ➤4e(ii).

25b Personal pronouns

(i) These are the most neutral pronouns – they simply replace nouns without adding further information. They may refer to the person(s) speaking (first person 'I, we'), the person(s) spoken to (second person 'you'), or the person(s) or thing(s) spoken about (third person 'he, she, it, they').

	Singular			
	Nom.	*Acc.*	*Dat.*	*Gen.*
First person	**ich**	**mich**	**mir**	**meiner**
Second person	**du**	**dich**	**dir**	**deiner**
	Sie	**Sie**	**Ihnen**	**Ihrer**
Third person	**er**	**ihn**	**ihm**	**seiner**
	sie	**sie**	**ihr**	**ihrer**
	es	**es**	**ihm**	**seiner**
	Plural			
First person	**wir**	**uns**	**uns**	**unser**
Second person	**ihr**	**euch**	**euch**	**euer**
	Sie	**Sie**	**Ihnen**	**Ihrer**
Third person	**sie**	**sie**	**ihnen**	**ihrer**

Note 1) Apart from in the genitive, the third person pronouns have the standard case endings (usually without the **-e-**) [➤23c(i)]. Note the extended **-nen** of the dative plural and the shortened forms of the genitives **unser** and **euer**.

2) The genitives of personal pronouns are rare even in writing. They are avoided by rephrasing the sentence using, for example, verbs and prepositions (especially **von**) which do not take the genitive.

(ii) *You, you and you: second person pronouns*

German second person pronouns are more complex than English.

(A) The 'familiar' singular **du/dich/dir** and plural **ihr/euch**, and their possessives **dein** and **euer**, are used when speaking to members of your family, to close friends and fellow workers, to fellow pupils, students, sports club members etc., to anyone under about 16 – and to animals! Note that in letters, which is where they are most commonly written, they are spelled with a capital.

Lieber Max,	Dear Max,
wie geht's *Dir*? Hast *Du* meinen	How are *you*? Did *you* get my last
letzten Brief bekommen? Und	letter? And *your* sister? Do *you*
Deine* Schwester? Zankt *Ihr	still have such wonderful quarrels?
***Euch* immer noch so schön?**	Give her my best wishes all the
Grüße sie bitte trotzdem von	same. See you soon!
mir. Bis bald! *Dein* Tom.	*Yours*, Tom

(B) Sie/Ihnen and its possessive **Ihr** are used when speaking to all other adults (singular and plural). They are always spelled with a capital but are otherwise identical to the third person plural **sie/ihnen** 'they/them' and **ihr** 'their'. This is sometimes called the 'polite' second person, but it is simply the normal form of address to anyone not close to you. Foreigners do well to let native speakers make the first move in changing from **Sie** to **du**. (Note that **Liebe(r) Frau (Herr) ...**, followed by **Sie** etc., is perfectly acceptable if you know a person fairly well.)

Sehr geehrte Frau Dorsch!	Dear Mrs. Dorsch,
Ich freue mich schon darauf, *Sie*	I am already looking forward to
kennenzulernen und einige Zeit	meeting *you* and spending some
bei *Ihnen* zu verbringen.	time at *your* house/with *you*. I
Hoffentlich geht's *Ihrem* Mann	hope *your* husband is better
jetzt besser.	now.

(C) The plural **ihr** etc. is used to any group of people which includes someone you would say **du** to, for example, a close friend and her/his parents, or a group standing talking. It is also used with nationalities: **ihr Deutschen** 'you Germans'.

Ich höre von Max, daß *Ihr* **alle ein paar Tage bei** *Euren* **Freunden in den Bergen verbringen wollt. Das wird Ihrem Mann sicherlich guttun. Mit freundlichen Grüßen** **Ihr Tom Hartley**	Max tells me that *you* are all going to spend a few days with *your* friends in the mountains. I am sure that that will do your husband good. Yours sincerely, Tom Hartley

(D) 'I say **du** to you' is **ich duze dich**, and 'I say **Sie** to you' is **ich sieze Sie**. Among native speakers **duzen** is normally associated with first names and **siezen** with **Herr/Frau** + surnames. But circumstances may alter this, especially with people from other countries where different rules apply.

(iii)   *Adjectives after personal pronouns*

As a rule, adjectives after personal pronouns have the standard case endings [➤24b(ii)B]. In the nominative plural, **-en** is more common than **-e**.

Sind *wir älteren* **Leute wirklich konservativer als** *ihr jungen***? Oder umgekehrt?**	Are *we older* people really more conservative than *you young ones*? Or the other way round?

(iv)   *Prepositions and personal pronouns*

In general, German uses the same personal pronouns after prepositions as in any other position.

Tom ist eine Woche *bei uns* **geblieben. Er hat viel** *für mich* **getan. Unsere Kinder mochten ihn gern, und er hat oft** *mit ihnen* **gespielt.**	Tom stayed *with us* a week. He did a lot *for me*. Our children liked him and he often played *with them*.

The main exceptions are:

(A) A preposition + 'it' or + 'them' referring to things contracts to one word, **da(r)** + preposition, as in the English 'therein, thereon' etc. The **-r-** is inserted when the preposition begins with a vowel.

| Tom hatte ein schweizerisches Taschenmesssser. *Damit* konnte man allerlei machen. *Es* hatte zahlreiche Klingen. Unsere Kinder wunderten sich immer *darüber*. | Tom had a Swiss pocket-knife. *With it* you could do all sorts of things. It had numerous blades. Our children always marvelled *at it/them*. |

(B) da(r)- compounds cannot be formed with:

• the prepositions **außer, gegenüber, ohne, seit**. The normal phrases are:

außerdem	apart from that, besides
(ihm) gegenüber	opposite (it)
ohne (es)	without (it)
seitdem, seither	since (then), ever since

• prepositions taking the genitive. Some of these have equivalent adverbs or phrases; some others use **davon**.

an meiner/seiner/ ihrer Stelle (for **statt**)	instead of me/him/her/them etc.
trotzdem	in spite of that, all the same
währenddessen	during this, meanwhile
seinetwegen/ihretwegen/ unsertwegen	for his/her/their/our sake
deswegen	because of that
außerhalb/ innerhalb davon	outside/inside it
oberhalb/unterhalb davon	above/below it

25c Reflexive pronouns

Reflexive pronouns are simply personal pronouns which refer back to the subject of the sentence, as when you do something to yourself. In general, they are therefore treated just like any other personal pronoun. Their use with verbs is discussed in paragraph 8f.

Note   The examples below show how often German uses a reflexive where English does not.

(i) Use of reflexive pronouns

• In the first person (**mich/mir, uns** 'myself, ourselves') and familiar second person (**dich/dir, euch** 'yourself, yourselves') German uses the normal personal pronouns as reflexives.

Setz *dich* **einen Augenblick, Tom, und schaue** *dir* **die Zeitung an. Ich werde** *mich* **schnell anziehen und** *mir* **einen Kaffee kochen. Wir müssen** *uns* **beeilen.**	Sit (*yourself*) down a moment, Tom, and have a look at the newspaper. I'll get dressed quickly and make *myself* a cup of coffee. We must hurry.

- In the third person there is only one reflexive pronoun: **sich** 'her/himself, themselves'. This is used in both singular and plural, accusative and dative, including after prepositions.

Hat dein Vater *sich* **jetzt von seiner Krankheit erholt? Hoffentlich haben deine Eltern** *sich* **in den Bergen gut ausgeruht. Sie sollten** *sich* **wirklich einen neuen Wagen kaufen. So ein alter bringt immer Probleme mit** *sich*.	Has your father recovered from his illness now? I hope your parents had a good rest in the mountains. They really ought to buy *themselves* a new car. Such an old one always causes problems.

- If you use the ordinary third person pronouns **ihn/ihm, sie/ihr, sie/ihnen** 'him, her, them' then the action is being done to somebody else, not to the subject. (Compare the meanings of the next two examples.)

Kommt deine Schwester mit? Hat deine Mutter *sie* **an unserem Ausflug erinnert?**	Is your sister coming too? Has your mother reminded *her* about our outing?

- **sich** (still with small **s**) is also the reflexive pronoun for **Sie** 'you'.

Frau Dorsch, erinnern Sie *sich* **noch an den Tag, wo Sie** *sich* **den Fuß verstaucht haben?**	Mrs. Dorsch, do you still remember the day when you sprained *your* ankle?

➤   I've cut *my* finger: possessives and reflexives ➤8e(iii).

(ii)   *Reflexive pronouns used reciprocally*

The plural reflexive pronouns **uns, euch** and **sich** can also be used 'reciprocally', that is, when people do something not to themselves but to each other.

einander, which never changes, can be used instead of the pronoun, especially to stress the meaning 'each other'. It must be used with this meaning after prepositions, when the two are written as one word. Otherwise, it is used more in writing than in speech.

Max und ich, wir haben _uns_ auf einem internationalen Arbeitslager in Hannover kennengelernt. Seitdem haben wir ziemlich viel _miteinander_ zu tun gehabt.	Max and I met on an international work camp in Hanover. Since then we have had a good deal to do _with each other_.

 Do not confuse reflexives with the words we use to emphasize that it was the subject that did something, and not anyone else, as in **Sie hat es selber gemacht** 'She did it herself'.

25d The indefinite pronoun 'one'

(i) The *indefinite pronoun* **man** 'one' means 'people in general, you, they'. As such, it provides one alternative to the passive [➤15f(iii)].

Man **sagt manchmal, daß solche Arbeitslager nichts Wertvolles erreichen. Da hat** _man_ **aber unrecht.**	_People_ sometimes say that such work camps achieve nothing worthwhile. But _they_ are wrong there.

(ii) **man** can only be used as the subject of the sentence. In the accusative **einen** is used, in the dative **einem**. The reflexive is **sich** and the possessive **sein**.

Wenn es _einem_ **gelingt,** _sich_ **mit Leuten aus anderen Ländern gut zu verständigen, hat man** _seine_ **Zeit nicht verloren.**	If _one_ succeeds in communicating well with people from other countries, _one_ hasn't wasted _one's_ time.

 Do not confuse **man** with the quantity 'one' as in **einer aus der Gruppe** 'one of the group' [➤25h].

25e The impersonal pronoun 'it'

There are a number of constructions using the *impersonal* **es**. In some it has greater status in the sentence than in others.

(i)   **es** is used as an 'empty subject':
- in **es gibt** + accusative 'there is/are ...'. Note that **es gibt** has no plural;
- in constructions such as **es macht nichts** 'it doesn't matter', **wie geht es?** 'how are things?', **es gilt/geht um .../handelt sich um ...** 'it is a matter of';
- when talking about the weather or time;
- in constructions corresponding to English 'there is/was a ~(ing)'. Although empty of meaning, **es** is here the true subject and cannot be left out, even if some other word or phrase starts the sentence.

Es hat damals in Hannover viel geregnet. *Es* war auch kalt – einmal hat *es* sogar geschneit. *Es gab* aber viel zu tun, und abends *gab es* oft Partys. Eines Abends hat *es* an der Tür *geklopft/geläutet* – die Nachbarn meinten, *es* wäre Mitternacht, wir sollten bitte an sie denken! In solchen Fällen *gilt es,/geht es darum,/handelt es sich darum,* ihren Gesichtspunkt zu verstehen.	That time in Hanover *it* rained a lot. *It* was also cold – once *it* even snowed. But *there was* a lot to do, and in the evenings *there were* often parties. One evening *there was a knock/ring* at the door – the neighbors said *it* was midnight, could we please think of them! In such cases *it is a matter of* understanding/*you have to* understand their point of view.

(ii)   There are a number of idioms where **es** or **das** is the commonest subject but not the only possible one.

Hannover hat mir gut *gefallen. Es* ist uns *gelungen*, die Stadt ein bißchen kennenzulernen. *Es fehlte* uns leider/Leider *fehlte* uns das Vokabular, um mehr zu machen.	I *liked* Hannover. We *succeeded* in getting to know the town a little. Unfortunately we *lacked* the vocabulary to do more.

(iii)   The 'caretaker' **es** can start a sentence, taking the place of the true subject, which then follows it. This may be done for emphasis or to place the main information later in the sentence [➤4e(ii)]. The verb agrees with the true subject (which may be plural), not with **es**. Because it is not the true subject, **es** can be left out if the sentence is re-arranged.

Es fanden manchmal/Manchmal fanden längere Ausflüge statt.	Sometimes longer excursions took place.

(iv) **es** can be used as the caretaker subject of a passive or reflexive verb to refer to an activity in general [➤15e]. Again, **es** is left out if it does not start the sentence.

Es wurde dann/Dann *wurde* viel gegessen und getrunken. *Es ißt sich* in manchen deutschen Gaststätten sehr gut.	*There* was then a lot of eating and drinking. *You can eat* very well in many German inns.

(v) **es** or its emphatic alternative **das** is sometimes used as object or complement of the verb in cases where English would omit it or perhaps use 'so'. Note especially *ich* bin's 'it's *me*'. etc – in German the subject is always the person referred to, not **es**.

Das habe ich immer geglaubt, jetzt weiß ich *es* aber!	I have always thought *so*, but now I know!

(vi) **es ist/war** etc. + dative is used with idioms referring to feelings and sensations [➤8h].

25f *Which one? Interrogative pronouns*

These are the question words listed in paragraphs 6d(i) to (iii).

(i) *Wer?/Wen?/Wem? Was? Wessen ? 'Who(m)? What? Whose?'*

(A) As in English, **Wer/Wen/Wem?** can only refer to people. They have the full range of case usages, including after prepositions, but **Wessen ...?** is now usually replaced by some other construction, such as **Wem gehört ...?** 'Who does ... belong to?'.

Entschuldigen Sie, *wer* ist das da drüben? – *Wen* meinen Sie? – Anders gesagt, *wem* gehört die Jacke mit dem Astrachankragen?	Excuse me, *who* is that over there? – *Who(m)* do you mean? – To put it another way, *whose* is the jacket with the Astrakhan collar?

(B) Was? has no other forms in current use [➤(D)below].

Das ist Magnus Krössis. *Was* wollen Sie von ihm?	That is Magnus Krössis. *What* do you want with him?

(C) The verb **sein** is plural after **Wer?** and **Was?** if they refer to more than one person or thing.

Und die Leute um ihn – *wer sind* die?	And the people around him – *who are* they?

(D) After most prepositions **Was?** becomes **wo(r)-** + preposition (compare **da(r)-**, ➤25b(iv)).

***Wozu* wollen Sie das alles wissen?**	*What* do you want to know all this *for*?

(ii)   *Welcher?* 'Which one?'

This has the same meaning and endings as its determiner [➤23c(i)].

Ich interessiere mich für einen seiner Leute. – Oh, für *welchen*? Und warum?	I am interested in one of his people. – Oh, *which one*? And why?

(iii)   *Was für einer? Was für welche?* 'What sort?'

einer is used in the singular, **welche** in the plural. Both have the same endings as **welcher** and the same meaning as the determiner **Was für ein ...?** [➤23c(ii)]. The case of **einer/welche** is decided by their function in the sentence, not by **für**.

Ich bin Berater. – *Was für einer*? – Ich berate Kunden. – Nein wirklich? *Was für welche*? – Reiche.	I am a consultant. – *What kind (of one)*? – I advise clients. – You don't say! *What sort*? – Rich ones.

25g   *Pointing and showing: demonstrative pronouns*

Demonstrative pronouns have the same meanings as the corresponding determiners [➤23f]. With the exception of **der** [➤(i) below] they have the same standard case endings [➤23c(i)].

(i) **der** 'this one', 'that one'

der is the most common demonstrative pronoun. It has the same forms as the definite article [➤23d(ii)], plus **-en** in all genitives and in the dative plural.

	Masculine	Feminine	Neuter	Plural
Nominative	der	die	das	die
Accusative	den	die	das	die
Genitive	dessen	deren	dessen	deren
Dative	dem	der	dem	denen

(A) **der** is used alone as a more forceful alternative to **er/sie/es**. Its 'pointing' role is often reinforced with **hier** or **da**. The neuter **das** is the general purpose pointing word 'that'.

Und wer ist *die da*? – *Die*? *Das* ist Claudia. *Die* ist wirklich klasse.	And who is *that*? – *Her*?/*That one*? *That*'s Claudia. *She*'s really great.

(B) Followed by a genitive or **von** + dative noun phrase **der** translates English '~'s'. It can also be followed by other defining phrases.

Mein Wagen ist eine alte Kiste. Ich habe mir *den* meines Bruders/*den* von Max ausgeliehen, *den* mit dem Zweilitermotor.	My car is an old crate. I've borrowed my brother*'s*/Max*'s*, *the one* with the two-liter engine.

(C) Followed by a relative clause it translates English 'the one(s) who/which ...'.

Claudia unterhält sich gern mit intelligenten Männern – besonders mit *denen*, die schnelle Sportwagen haben.	Claudia likes talking to intelligent men – especially to *those* who have fast sports cars.

(D) When referring to things, **der** can make **da(r)-** + preposition compounds, like personal pronouns [➤25b(iv)], but with the stress on the **da-**. It does not do this before defining phrases or clauses [➤(B) and (C) above].

Mein eigenes Auto nützt mir nichts – damit komme ich nicht bei ihr an. Aber mit **dem** von Max – wer weiß!**	My own car is no good to me – with *that* I'll never get anywhere with her. But with Max's – who knows!

(E) **dessen** and **deren** can be used instead of the possessives **sein** and **ihr** [➤23h(iii)].

Meine Schwester hat sich gestern lange mit Claudia und *deren* Bruder unterhalten. Hoffentlich hat sie nur Gutes von mir gesagt.	Yesterday my sister talked for a long time with Claudia and *her* (Claudia's) brother. I hope she only spoke well of me.

(ii)   The other demonstrative pronouns

These are:

• **dieser** 'this one', **jener, derjenige** 'that one', **derselbe** 'the same one' and **so einer, solche** 'one(s) like that'.
• With the following few exceptions they have the same endings and uses as the corresponding determiners [➤23f].

(A) The short form **dies** 'this' is used to point to things nearby, though **das (hier)** is often used instead.

Dies (Das) hier sind meine Traumwagen.	*These (This) are my dream cars.*

(B) **so einer** is used in the singular and **solche** in the plural, both with the standard case endings [➤23c(i)]. '... as such' is ...**als solcher**, agreeing with the noun referred to.

Ich habe ein paarmal *solche* probegefahren. *So einen* möchte ich haben. Das Auto *als solches* sagt mir wenig – nur seine Wirkung auf andere!	I have test-driven *ones like that* a couple of times. I should like to have *one like that*. The car *as such* means little to me – only its effect on others!

25h   How much? How many? Indefinite quantities

Some *quantifiers* refer to the whole or none of something, others to some part or some members of it. All the determiners discussed in paragraph 23g can also be used as pronouns.

The following paragraphs deal with additional points relevant to these pronouns.

(i) *einer* 'one', *keiner* 'none'

These have the standard case endings [➤23c(i)]. **einer** has no plural.

	Masculine	*Feminine*	*Neuter*	*Plural*
Nominative	**einer**	**eine**	**ein(e)s**	**keine**
Accusative	**einen**	**eine**	**ein(e)s**	**keine**
Genitive	**eines**	**einer**	**eines**	**keiner**
Dative	**einem**	**einer**	**einem**	**keinen**

(A) einer usually means 'one of a number', when it is often followed by a genitive plural or a phrase with **von**. It can also mean 'someone' [➤**jemand**, (iii) below].

Einer meiner Söhne ist ein begeisterter Filmfan, aber Kinokarten sind teuer für *einen/ jemand*, der wenig Geld hat.	*One* of my sons is an enthusiastic movie fan, but movie house tickets are expensive for *someone* who hasn't much money.

(B) keiner is used like **einer**, with the opposite meanings of 'none of ...' and 'no one' [➤**niemand**, (iii) below].

Keine der Lokalzeitungen gibt die Programme für die Großstadt. *Keiner* (*Niemand*) im Dorf wußte darüber Bescheid. Wir haben meine Eltern gefragt, aber *keiner* (der beiden) interessiert sich für Filme.	*None* of the local newspapers gives the program for the city. *No-one* in the village knew anything about them. We asked my parents, but *neither* (of the two) is interested in movies.

(C) nicht einer means 'not one', usually implying **... sondern zwei** '... but two' etc. **kein einziger** is 'not a single one'.

Übers Wochenende hat er *nicht einen* sondern fünf Fernsehfilme gesehen! Dabei war *kein einziger* sehenswert.	Over the weekend he watched *not one* but five movies! And *not one* was even worth watching.

(D) The alternative form **der eine** has a plural **die einen** 'some'. The **ein-** has the **-e/-en** adjective endings [➤24b(ii)]. It usually refers to one of two people or things, or some of a group, often contrasted with **der andere, die anderen** 'the other(s)'.

Mein Sohn hat zweierlei Freunde: *die einen* **teilen seine Filmleidenschaft, die anderen nicht.**	My son has two sorts of friends: *some* share his passion for movies, (the) others do not.

(ii) ***alles*** *'everything',* ***alle*** *'everyone',* ***beides*** *'both things',* ***beide*** *'both people'*

These all have the standard case endings [➤23c(i)].

(A) The singular **alles** and **beides** generally refer to things and the plural **alle** and **beide** to people.

Alle **mögen aber** *alles,* **was mit Pop zu tun hat. Mein Sohn hat eben eine Platte und eine Cassette gekauft.** *Beides* **spielt er unaufhörlich.**	But *they all* like *everything* which has to do with pop. My son has just bought a cassette and a record. He plays *both* non-stop.

(B) The alternative forms **die beiden** and more emphatic **alle beide** are the usual translations for 'the two (of them)'.

Er hat einen Freund Antonio. *Die beiden/Alle beide* **sind Popfans.**	He has a friend Antonio. *Both/The two of them* are pop fans.

(C) **alles** may be combined with an adjective-noun taking the **-e/-en** endings, to mean 'everything ..., all the ... things'.

Alles Neue **fasziniert sie.**	*Everything new* fascinates them.

(D) The word **alle** is used colloquially to mean 'all gone'.

Sein Geld ist jetzt aber leider alle.	Unfortunately his money is now *all gone*.

(iii) ***jeder*** *'each one, everyone'*

jeder has standard case endings, but no genitive. The more emphatic **ein jeder** 'just anyone, anyone at all' has all the sin-

gular cases; the **jeder** (in **ein jeder**) has adjective endings
[➤24b(ii)]. **jedermann** 'everyone' is now used only in formal
writing and set phrases.

Jeder weiß, daß man so eine Aufgabe nicht *einem jeden* geben kann. Das ist bestimmt nicht *jedermanns* Sache.	*Everyone* knows that you cannot give a job like that to *just anyone*. It certainly isn't *everyone's* thing.

(iv)   *jemand* 'someone', *niemand* 'no one', *etwas* 'something', *nichts* 'nothing'

These do not now usually have case endings, though they are
possible with **jemand** and **niemand**. In colloquial speech
etwas is frequently shortened to **was** and **nichts** pronounced
nix. **wer** is sometimes used in place of **jemand**.

(A) Adjective-nouns after any of these words have standard
neuter singular case endings, though accusative **-en** is also
possible after **jemand** and **niemand**.

Niemand Vernünftiges hätte *sowas Dummes* gemacht!	*No sensible person* would have done *something so stupid*!

(B) irgend jemand/etwas stresses '*just* anyone/anything'.

Hat *irgendjemand* denn *irgendetwas Sinnvolles* gemacht?	Has *anyone at all* done *anything sensible*?

(v)   *einiges* 'some things', *manches* 'quite a lot', *vieles* 'a lot', *weniges* 'not much'

The neuter forms **einiges, manches, vieles** and **weniges**
refer to things (to be) done. All but **einiges** are rather formal.
The short forms **viel** and **wenig** are more usual.

Wir haben schon *viel(es)* getan – es bleibt aber noch *einiges* zu entscheiden. Mit *manchem* bin ich nicht einverstanden.	We have already done *a lot* – but there are still *some things* to be decided. There is *quite a lot* I don't agree with.

25i Belonging together: possessive pronouns

Possessive pronouns are unique in that they represent two different nouns at once: the 'possessor' and the 'thing possessed'. Like possessive determiners [➤23h], they take their form from the possessor, and their gender and number from the thing possessed. Take care not to confuse the two: one person can own several things, and several people can be joint owners of one thing.

Natürlich sind ihre Hunde bessere Hauswächter als *seine*. Sein Hundekorb ist bequemer als *ihrer*.	Of course their dogs are better watch-dogs than *his*. His dog basket is more comfortable than *theirs*.

(i) Use

The possessive pronouns are the same as the determiners except that they have the full standard endings [➤**einer**, 25h(i)]. In general their use is similar to English, but note two common exceptions:

Gehört dieser Hund *Ihnen*? – Ja, er *gehört mir*. Ein Freund von *mir* hat ihn mir gegeben.	*Is* this dog *yours*? – Yes, it*'s mine*. A friend of *mine* gave it to me.

(ii) Forms

There are three alternative forms of possessive pronouns: endingless **mein** etc.; **der meine** etc.; **der meinige** etc. In the last two the possessive has the **-e/-en** adjective endings. These forms are used only in elevated style, and then often as nouns.

Ich habe *das Mein(ig)e* getan, tun Sie jetzt *das Ihr(ig)e*. Sie verwech-seln offenbar *Mein* und *Dein*! Herzliche Grüße an Sie und *die Ihr(ig)en*.	I've done *my bit*, now you do *your bit*. You obviously confuse '*mine*' and '*thine*' (take what is not yours)! Best wishes to you and *yours* (your family).

25j Relative pronouns

➤ *Whoever/Whatever* it was, ...: ➤5a(ii).

(i)   Use

A *relative pronoun* 'relates' or links a noun to a 'relative clause', which always begins with a comma. They have exactly the same forms as the demonstrative pronoun **der** [➤25g(i)].

• The clause closely follows the noun and defines it or comments on it [➤5b].
• Because it comes before the clause, the noun is known as the *antecedent*.
• Relative pronouns follow exactly the same rules as other pronouns [➤25a], that is, their gender and number are the same as for the antecedent, but their case depends on their use within the relative clause.
• The examples below show that German can never omit the relative pronoun or put prepositions at the end of the sentence as English often can. The order must always be:
... antecedent (...), (preposition, if any) pronoun ...

Drüben steht *der Mann, der* unsren Wagen stehlen wollte! – Ist das *der Wagen, den* Sie von mir gekauft haben? – Ja, *der Wagen, mit dem* wir in Urlaub gefahren sind.	Over there is *the man who* tried to steal our car! – Is that *the car (which)* you bought from me? – Yes, *the car (which)* we went on vacation *in*.

(ii)   *dessen or deren?*

The choice of **dessen** or **deren** for 'whose' depends on whether the antecedent is masculine/neuter (**dessen**) or feminine/plural (**deren**). The noun which follows has no effect on this at all. Any adjectives in the phrase have the standard case endings [➤24b(ii)B].

Gestern bin ich einem Bekannten begegnet, *dessen* älteste Tochter Petra in meiner Klasse war. Wir waren in der Buchhandlung, mit *deren* neuem Besitzer ich befreundet bin.	Yesterday I happened to meet a man I know *whose* eldest daughter Petra was in my class. We were in the bookstore, *whose* new owner I am friendly with.

(iii) A relative clause may be separated from its antecedent, especially by verbs at the end of the clause, but it should follow as soon as possible.

Die arme Petra ist von einem Lastwagen überfahren worden, der bei Rot durch die Ampel gefahren ist.	Poor Petra was run over by a *truck* *which* drove through a red light.

(iv) **welcher** *as a relative pronoun*

welcher, etc. sometimes replaces **der,** etc. in formal writing.

Fahrer, *welche* (die) sich so benehmen, sollten ihren Führerschein verlieren.	Drivers *who* behave like that should lose their driver's license.

(v) **wer** *'anyone who'*, **was** *'what'*

wer and **was** can be used to mean 'anyone who' and 'what'. They normally begin the sentence. They may be picked up by **der** and **das** etc. in the main clause; this must be done if the **der/das** is in a different case from the **wer/was. was** may also have **das** as its antecedent.

***Wer* so handelt, mit *dem* will ich nichts zu tun haben/(*der*) ist zu allem fähig.**	*Someone who* acts like that I won't have anything to do with/is capable of anything.
***(Das,) Was* er getan hat, *dafür* müß er büßen/ist mir unbegreiflich.**	*What* he did he will have to pay for/is incomprehensible to me.

(vi) **was** *as a relative pronoun*

was is used as a relative pronoun in several instances. Note the different English equivalents [►also (v) above and (vii) below]:

(A) when it refers back to the whole idea expressed in the preceding sentence:

Manfred erscheint nie pünktlich zur Arbeit, *was* seinen Chef sehr böse macht.	Manfred never arrives on time for work, *which* makes his boss very angry.

(B) when the antecedent is a neuter pronoun or neuter adjective-noun [➤24d(iii)]:

Er vergißt *alles, was* man ihm sagt.	He forgets *everything (which)* you tell him.
Er hat auch *etwas Seltsames* an sich, *was* uns alle mißtrauisch stimmt. Er ist aber gutmütig – das ist *das Beste, was* man von ihm sagen kann.	He also has *something strange* about him *which* makes us all mistrustful. But he is good-humored – that's *the best (which)* you can say of him.

 wer and **was** can never be used instead of **der** and **das** as normal relative pronouns. Their commonest use is to ask the questions **wer?** 'who?' and **was?** 'what?' [➤25f(i)].

(vii) Prepositions + relative pronouns referring to things may contract to one word: **wo(r)-** + preposition [➤25f(i)]. This is now little used even in formal writing. **wo(r)-** compounds are, however, normal when the pronoun is **was** [➤(vi) above].

Manfred scheint immer Geld zu haben, *worüber* ich mich sehr wundere.	Manfred always seems to have money, *which* I am very surprised *at*.

(viii) *Alternatives to relative clauses*

German relative clauses can be rather clumsy constructions. Perhaps for this reason, they are much less used in speech than they are in French or English, though they are common enough in writing. A favorite alternative is the identical demonstrative **der** with a main clause, though there are others.

Wir waren alle da außer Greta, *die* verreist war.	We were all there except Greta, *who* had gone away.
or	or
... außer Greta. *Die* war verreist.	... except Greta. *She* had gone away.
Es war schade um Greta, *deren* Sprachkenntnisse uns nützlich gewesen wären.	It was a pity about Greta, *whose* knowledge of languages would have been useful to us.
or	or

... um Greta. *Ihre* Sprachkenntnisse wären uns nützlich gewesen.	...about Greta. *Her* knowledge of languages would have been useful to us.

Note   A relative clause cannot be replaced in this way if it defines the antecedent rather than just adding a comment.

Greta ist die Frau, *die* letztes Jahr bei uns gewohnt hat.	Greta is the woman *who* stayed with us last year.

25k   *Natural and grammatical gender: problems of agreement*

There are some nouns whose gender is different from the sex of the person they refer to. Most of these are neuter diminutives ending in **-chen** or **-lein**, but there are other examples [➤20b(iv)]. If a pronoun referring to one of these nouns stands close to it, then the grammatical gender tends to be used; with relative pronouns this always happens. The further a pronoun is from its noun, the more the natural gender is likely to reassert itself.

Plötzlich erblickte mich *das* Mädchen, *das* ich im Café gesehen hatte. *Es/Sie* kam zu mir herüber, und wir unterhielten uns eine Zeitlang. Dann fragte ich *sie*, wo *sie* wohne.	Suddenly the girl (*that*) I had seen in the café spotted me. *She* came over to me and we talked for a while. Then I asked *her* where *she* lived.

26 Giving vent to your feelings: exclamations and interjections

26a Exclamations

Exclamations express strongly felt wishes or emotions. Very often they are not complete sentences, though it is always obvious what the rest of the sentence might be. In writing they end with an exclamation point.

(i) Addition of modal particles for emphasis

Said with force, almost any utterance can be an exclamation. One or more modal particles are often used to add emphasis, especially **aber, bloß, doch, erst, ja, nur** [➤29c(iii)].

Du bist mir *aber/vielleicht* einer! Das ist *doch/ja* die Höhe!	You're a real/right one! That really is the limit!

(ii) Expressing emotions

welcher ...!, **was für (ein) ...!** 'what (a)' + noun phrase, and **wie ...!** 'how' + adjective or adverb express emotions such as delight, anger, surprise or fear. **was für** is more used colloquially than **welcher**. Unlike when the same words are used as questions [➤ch.6], if a verb is used it is put at the end.

Was für/Welches Wetter! Wie heiß/kalt es ist!	What weather! How hot/cold it is!
Was für ein seltsamer Kerl! Was für wilde Augen er hat! Wie mager er doch/ja ist!	What a strange fellow! What wild eyes he has! How thin he is!

(iii) If only

'If only!' wishes are often expressed by a free-standing conditional clause, either a **wenn** clause with the verb at the end or a clause starting with the conditional. [Simple conditional vs. **würde** + infinitive: ➤14d Note.]

Wenn er *bloß/doch/nur/erst* anrufen würde!	*If only* he would call/ring up!
Hätte ich *nur* mehr Zeit! Wäre ich *bloß* nicht so beschäftigt! Könnte ich *erst* früher nach Hause!	*If only* I had more time! *If only* I were not so busy! *If* I could *at least* get home earlier!

(iv) *Another way of expressing a wish*

Free-standing **zu** + infinitive clauses can also express wishes.

Ach, immer hier *zu bleiben*! Nie wieder ins Büro gehen *zu müssen*!	Oh *to remain* here always! Never again *to have* to go to the office!

26b *Interjections*

Interjections range from words or short phrases which are really cut-down exclamations through standard noises associated with various emotions to whatever may be wrung from you in the heat of the moment. This is an area where non-native speakers need to be cautious – there is always the risk of making yourself ridiculous or causing offence.

Note Interjections do not count in the word order of any following sentence.

(i) *Addressing people*

Frau Biel, Sie haben den ersten Preis gewonnen!	Mrs. Biel, you have won first prize!
Martin, wir sind reich!	Martin, we're rich!
Sie da! Was machen Sie da?	You there! What are you up to?

(ii) *Agreeing and disagreeing*

Ja! Nein!	Yes! No!
Doch!	Yes I have/do/am! (contradicting negatives)
Stimmt! Klar!	True! I agree!

(iii)   General emphasis

Abgemacht!	Agreed/Done!
Aber, aber! Was ist hier los?	Now, now! What's going on here?
Aber Leute, wir fahren in fünf Minuten los!	Hey there, we're leaving in five minutes!
Mensch, was machst du nur?	Man, just what are you doing?
Mensch, (da) habe ich mich aber getäuscht/geärgert!	Boy, was I wrong/angry!

(iv)   Warning

Aufpassen/Aufgepaßt! Vorsicht!	Look out! Careful!

(v)   Startled surprise

Du liebe Zeit!	Hell's bells!
Ach, du heiliger Bimbam!	Good heavens!
Auwei!	Oh dear!

(vi)   Swearwords

Scheiße! is probably the most used, even by people who would avoid its English equivalent.

Scheiße! Verdammt/Verflucht (noch mal)!	Shit! Damn(ation)!
Verflixt! Diese verdammte/verflixte Maschine!	Blast! This damned/blasted machine!

E

LINKING AND MODIFYING MEANINGS: PREPOSITIONS AND ADVERBIAL EXPRESSIONS

27 Linking noun phrases into the sentence: prepositions

27a What does a preposition do?

A *preposition* is a connecting word. It links the noun phrase which follows it to various other parts of the sentence. This chapter deals mainly with the cases which follow German prepositions. The various links which prepositions can make are discussed in the following paragraphs:

➤ *With* a quick movement I put my hand in my pocket: adverbial phrases ➤28a.
I was relying *on* bluff: linking verbs to noun phrases ➤8g.
His reaction *to* my action was to draw a knife: linking two noun phrases ➤19h.
He tried to stab me *with* it: prepositions + pronouns referring to things (**da(r)**- compounds) ➤25b(iv).
He was pale *with* fury: linking adjectives to noun phrases ➤24g(ii).

27b Prepositions and the cases they take

German prepositions can be grouped by the case of the noun phrase which they govern. The following paragraphs list only the more commonly used prepositions. Note that a few sometimes follow the noun phrase.

(i) Prepositions folowed by the accusative

Six common prepositions are always followed by the accusative:

• **bis** 'until, as far as, up to; by (a deadline)'. Always used with another preposition of motion except before place names, adverbs, and time phrases starting with a noun or a numeral (or equivalent).

Bis 1962 **wohnte ich in der DDR (Deutsche Demokratische Republik)**. *Bis nächsten Freitag* **muß ich einen Artikel darüber fertig haben.**	*Until 1962* I lived in the GDR (German Democratic Republic). *By next Friday* I have to have an article on it finished.

• **durch** 'through'. Also 'across' (especially after **quer** 'crosswise') and 'throughout', often combined with **hindurch**.

| Damals lief die innerdeutsche Grenze mitten *durch unser Dorf*. | In those days the inner-German border ran *through* the middle of *our village*. |

durch 'by (means of)' shows how something happened [➤passive15c]. Hence **dadurch** 'thereby, by that means'.

| *Durch diese Grenze/Dadurch* wurde das Dorf entzweigerissen. | The village was torn apart *by this border/by it*. |

• **für** 'for'. With periods of time **für** means 'for ... in all' [➤(ii) below, **seit**]. Note **dafür** 'but (to make up for it)'.

| Das war *für uns alle* eine traurige Zeit. Nicht einmal *für einige Stunden* durften wir die Verwandten im Westen besuchen. | That was a sad time *for us all*. We couldn't visit our relatives in the west even *for a few hours*. |

• **gegen** 'against, towards; (at) about (numbers, time)'. With motion it tends to imply forceful contact.

| An einem Oktobertag *gegen Mittag* bin ich mit einem Traktor *gegen die Grenzsperre* gekracht und bin durchgekommen. | One October day *at about midday* I crashed a tractor *into the border barrier* and got through. |

gegen 'in exchange for; compared to'. Note **dagegen** 'but (on the other hand)'.

| Ich hatte mein ganzes Hab und Gut *gegen den Traktor* getauscht. | I had traded all my wordly goods *for the tractor*. |

• **ohne** 'without'. Often used without **ein** or a possessive where English would use one. **ohne** cannot form **da(r)**-compounds [➤25b(iv)], but it can be followed by a clause [➤27c].

Ohne Traktor/Ohne ihn hätte ich es nie geschafft.	*Without a tractor/Without it* I would never have managed it.

• **um** 'round; at (clock time)'. With other time phrases it means 'around', often strengthened with following **herum**.

Schon *um viertel nach zwölf* war das ganze Dorf *um mich* versammelt.	Already *at (a) quarter past twelve* the whole village was gathered *around me*.

um 'by, at (so much); concerning'. Note **darum** 'for that reason, that's why' and **um ... zu** + infinitive 'in order to ...' [➤27c].

Ich wollte *um jeden Preis* bleiben. Es ging ja *um meine Freiheit*.	I wanted to stay *at any cost*. After all, it was a matter *of my freedom*.

(ii)   Prepositions followed by the dative

Nine common prepositions are always followed by the dative:

• **aus** 'out of (places and motives), made of (materials)'.

Als ich *aus dem Haus* kam, sah ich einen großen Schlüssel *aus Messing* auf dem Gehsteig liegen.	When I came *out of the house* I saw a large key *made of brass* lying on the pavement.

aus also describes causes and motives.

Aus Neugier hob ich ihn auf.	*Out of curiosity* I picked it up.

• **außer** 'except, apart from'.

Außer einem kleinen Kind war niemand zu sehen.	*Apart from a small child* there was nobody to be seen.

außer means 'out of, beyond' in certain expressions.

Der Bankomat war *außer Betrieb*. Ich war *außer mir* vor Wut.	The cash machine/automatic teller was *out of order*. I was *beside myself* with rage.

• **bei** 'near to, at the house/shop of'.

Beim Apotheker wollte ich Aspirin kaufen. Da sah ich das Kind *bei* der Tür stehen.	I wanted to buy some aspirin *at the pharmacist's*. Then I saw the child standing *by* the door.

bei often indicates the background to something. **beim** + infinitive noun means 'while ~ing' [►10a(iii)]. Note **dabei**, with its many idiomatic usages.

Bei heißem Wetter bekomme ich oft Kopfschmerzen. *Bei dieser Gelegenheit* waren sie besonders stark. *Beim Zahlen* konnte ich die Münzen kaum sehen.	*In hot weather* I often get a headache. *On this occasion* it was particularly severe. *As I was paying* I could hardly see the coins.

• **gegenüber** 'opposite'. Always follows a pronoun. It can follow nouns, especially people, but more usually it precedes them.

Mir gegenüber stand eine ältere Frau, Frau Gruber, die *gegenüber der Apotheke* wohnte.	*Opposite me* was standing an elderly woman, Mrs. Gruber, who lived *opposite the pharmacist's*.

gegenüber '(in relation) to, in the face of'.

Meiner Familie gegenüber war sie immer sehr nett gewesen.	She had always been very nice *to my family*.

• **mit** 'with, at (the age of)'. [**damit** 'so that' ►5a(ii)].

Sie hatte ihren Mann *mit 40 Jahren* verloren. Ich sprach einen Augenblick *mit ihr*.	She had lost her husband *at the age of 40*. I spoke *with/to her* for a moment.

mit 'by using ...' is more widely used than the English 'with', for example, for means of transport and parts of the body.

Ich wollte dann *mit dem Bus* nach Pasing fahren. Beim Einsteigen stieß ich *mit dem Kopf* gegen die Tür.	Then I wanted to go *by bus* to Pasing. As I was getting in I bumped *my head* against the door.

• **nach** 'after (time)'. In the sense of 'following after' **nach** is used as a verbal particle [➤16e(ii)].

Nach einer Weile **sah ich, daß Frau Gruber** *mir* **nachgekommen war.**	*After a while* I saw that Mrs. Gruber had *followed me*.

nach 'to (a place)'. Used with towns and neuter countries [➤19e(i)], and adverbs. Note also **nach Hause** '(to) home' ['at home' ➤**zu** below].

Sie war ganz *nach hinten* **gegangen. Ob sie auch** *nach Pasing* **(fahren) wollte?**	She had gone right *to the back*. Did she also want to go *to Pasing*?

nach 'according to, judging by'. In certain phrases **nach** may follow the noun phrase.

Nach meiner Ansicht/Meinung **benahm sie sich sehr seltsam.**	*In my view/opinion* she was behaving very strangely.

• **seit** 'since, for (time)'. Refers to a period leading up to the time spoken of [➤12a(iv)]; compare **für** [➤(i) above].

Seit einiger Zeit **folgte sie mir überall hin.**	*For some time* she had been following me around everywhere.

• **von** 'from; of; by'. Often used to replace the genitive [➤22e], and with the passive [➤15c].

Dabei hatte ich aber nur Gutes *von ihr* **gehört. Ich war** *von der ganzen Sache* **ziemlich verwirrt. Da sah ich** *vom Busfenster aus*, **daß wir in Pasing waren.**	All the same, I had only heard good *of her*. I was pretty confused *by the whole affair*. Then I saw *from the bus window* that we were in Pasing.

• **zu** 'to (place, person)', but note **zu Hause** 'at home'.

Vom Bus ging ich direkt *zur* **Post.**	From the bus I went straight *to the post office*.

Da trat Frau Gruber ein und kam *zu mir* **herüber.**	Then Mrs. Gruber entered and came over *to me*.

zu 'for (purpose), to (effect), (made) into' and many other idiomatic usages.

Zu meinem Erstaunen **sagte sie** *zu mir:* „**Polizei! Darf ich fragen,** *wozu/zu welchem Zweck* **Sie den Schlüssel da gebrauchen wollen?"** – „*Zu keinem!*" **erwiderte ich. „Ich habe ihn gefunden. Das macht mich doch nicht** *zu einem Verbrecher!*"	*To my astonishment* she said *to me:* "Police! May I ask *what/what purpose* you are going to use that key *for?"* – *"(For) none!*" I replied. "I found it. That doesn't make me *(into) a thief!*"

(iii)   *Prepositions followed by either the dative or the accusative*

Some prepositions are followed by the accusative to show movement into a position and by the dative to show the position itself. The dative is thus often the result of the accusative.

(A) The accusative is only used for movement to the position mentioned. The dative is used, for example, for walking along behind, next to or between other people (often followed by **her**), running up and down between two objects, or flying around over a place.

(B) With a number of verbs, the accusative is used if the movement is emphasized, the dative if the position is uppermost in the speaker's mind. For example:

Accusative	
Maria hielt die Hand an *den* **Mund. Sie klopfte heftig an** *das* **Fenster.**	Maria held her hand to her mouth. She knocked hard on the window.
Dative	
Der Einbrecher hielt eine Lampe in *der* **Hand. Da klopfte es an** *der* **Tür.**	The burglar was holding a flashlight in his hand. Then there was a knock at the door.

(C) In a few instances this leads to prepositions taking the accusative after the simple verb but the dative when the verb is linked to a verbal particle [➤16e(ii)]. For example:

Beim Einkaufen *binde* ich immer meinen Hund *an eine* Laterne. */... an einer* Laterne *an/fest.*	When I am shopping I always tie my dog (*on*) to a streetlamp.
Ich habe Ihre Zeichnung *an die* Klotür gehängt./... *an der* Klotür *auf*gehängt.	I have hung your drawing (*up*) on the bathroom/lavatory door.
Ich möchte mich lieber *auf das* Sofa legen/setzen./... *auf dem* Sofa *hin*legen/*hin*setzen.	I should prefer to lie/sit down on the sofa.
Ich habe Ihre Namen *in mein* Notizuch geschrieben./... *in* meinem Buch *auf*geschrieben.	I have written your names (*down*) in my notebook.

(D) If there is no reference to place, then **auf** and **über** are used with the accusative, the others normally with the dative.

(E) The accusative is normal with:

Ich baue/schließe an ... an.	I build/add onto ...
Ich beuge mich über ...	I bend over ...
Es grenzt an ...	It borders on ...
Es mündet in ...	It flows into ...
Ich schreibe es in ... (ein)	I write it in(to) ...
Ich sehe/blicke auf ...	I look/glance at ...
Ich stütze mich auf ...	I lean on ...
Ich verteile es an ...	I distribute it to ...
Ich bin in ... vertieft/verwickelt.	I am engrossed/involved in ...

(F) The dative is normal with all verbs of arriving and (dis)appearing, and with:

Ich befestige es an ...	I fasten it to ...
Ich bringe es an ... an .	I attach it to ...
Ich drucke es auf/in ...	I print it on/in ...
Ich notiere es in ...	I note it down in ...

(G) There are 10 common prepositions which may take either the accusative or the dative according to the rules described above. In the examples the accusative usages are in italics.

• **an** 'on (a vertical surface), by, at'.

Der Leiter des Jugendwettlaufs stand vorne am Tisch und heftete eine große Karte *an die Wand.*	The organizer of the youth competition stood at the table at the front and pinned a large map *to the wall.*

• **auf** 'on (a horizontal surface), at'. Note the use of **auf** + certain public places: **auf der Straße/dem Platz/dem Bahnhof** 'in the street/square/station'.

„So, Leute!" sagte er, „Wir fahren gleich *aufs Land*. Der Start ist auf dem Unterdorfer Kirchplatz.	"Right, folks!" he said, "We shall soon be driving *into the country*. The start is in the Unterdorf church square.

• **entlang** 'along' + accusative describes movement alongside or down the middle of something. Here **entlang** follows the noun phrase.

Ihr lauft zunächst *den Waldrand entlang*.	You run first *along the edge of the woods*.

entlang 'along' + dative describes position alongside something. Here **entlang** precedes the noun phrase.

Vorsicht! Entlang dem Pfad ist ein Stacheldrahtzaun.	Watch out! Alongside the path there is a barbed wire fence.

an + dative + **entlang** is a common alternative for either motion or position alongside something.

Ihr lauft weiter am Zaun entlang auf eine kleine Hütte zu.	You go on running along beside the fence towards a small hut.

• **hinter** 'behind, beyond'. Note **hinter** + dative + **her** '(running/shouting) after ..., (walking) behind ...'.

Geht *hinter die Hütte*. Hinter der Hütte hängen numerierte Zettel an einem Nagel.	Go *behind the hut*. Behind the hut there are numbered tickets hanging on a nail.

• **in** 'in'. With periods of time **in** + dative means 'after (so long from now)'. Note also **im Radio/Fernsehen** 'on radio/ television', **im 4. Stock** 'on the 4th floor'.

Bald biegt der Pfad links *in den Wald* ein. Im Wald wird er sehr glitschig.	Soon the path turns left *into the woods*. In the woods it gets very slippery.

• **neben** 'next to'. **neben** + dative can mean 'apart from' or 'compared to'.

Die nächsten Nummern findet ihr neben einer hohen Eiche. Ihr müßt euch dicht *neben die Eiche* stellen, um sie zu sehen.	You will find the next numbers next to a tall oak tree. You'll have to go and stand right *next to the oak* to see them.

• **über** 'across, over, above'.

Der Weg führt weiter *über eine schmale Holzbrücke*. Über der Brücke weht eine grünweiße Fahne.	The path leads on *across a narrow wooden bridge*. A green and white flag is flying over the bridge.

über + accusative can mean 'about (concerning)' or 'more than (a quantity)'.

Über diese Fahne haben wir schon gesprochen. Sie ist *über drei Meter* lang.	We've already spoken *about this flag*. It is *over three meters* long.

• **unter** 'under, among, less than (a quantity)'.

Die Zettel liegen unter einem großen Felsblock verborgen. Ihr braucht nur die Hand *unter den Felsblock* zu stecken.	The tickets are lying hidden under a large boulder. You only need to stick your hand *under the boulder*.

• **vor** 'in front of'. Note **vor mich/sich hin** 'to myself/oneself'.

Links vor der Ziellinie sitzt die Schiedsrichterin. Ihr legt eure Zettel *vor die Richterin* auf den Tisch.	The umpire will be sitting before the finishing line on the left. You put your tickets on the table *in front of the umpire*.

vor + a dative time phrase means 'ago'.

Vor einem Jahr haben mehrere vergessen, das zu tun.	A year ago several people forgot to do that.

• **zwischen** 'between'.

Für das Schlußfoto sitzt ihr zwischen euren Eltern. Setzt euch also *zwischen eure Eltern.*"	For the final photo you'll be sitting between your parents. So go and sit down *between your parents.*"

(iv) *Prepositions followed by the genitive*

Many prepositions are followed by the genitive, but only a few are used outside formal, especially official writing. The following are in common use, but even here some other phrasing is often preferred.

• **(an)statt** 'instead of'. The longer form is more formal.

Gestern haben Sie uns *statt der richtigen Stärke* 2,5-Millimeter-Blech geliefert.	Yesterday you delivered 2.5-millimeter sheet metal to us, *instead of the correct gauge.*

• **trotz** 'in spite of, despite'.

Trotz unserer ausdrücklichen Anforderung ist das jetzt zum dritten Mal geschehen.	*In spite of our explicit request* this is the third time this has happened.

• **während** 'during'.

Der Fehler ist erst *während der Verarbeitung* entdeckt worden, als eine Maschine klemmte.	The error was only detected *during processing*, when a machine jammed.

• **wegen** 'because of'.

Wegen dieses Fehlers hat die Maschine einen schweren Schaden erlitten.	*Because of this error* the machine suffered severe damage.

• Eight prepositions of place also take the genitive. The four **-halb** prepositions are probably used more than the others.

außerhalb	outside	**diesseits/jenseits**	on this/that side of
beiderseits	on both sides of	**innerhalb**	inside

| **oberhalb** | above | **unweit** | not far from |
| **unterhalb** | below | | |

27c   *Prepositions followed by clauses*

The prepositions listed below can be followed by a **zu** + infinitive clause. If there is a change of subject, **außer, statt** and **ohne** can be followed by a **daß** clause. The equivalent for **um ... zu** is **damit** 'so that' [➤5a(ii)]; do not confuse this with **damit** 'with it' [➤25b(iv)].

• **außer** 'apart from'.

Außer jede Sendung extra *zu* messen, wissen wir nicht, was wir noch tun können. *Außer daß* die Reparatur teuer sein wird, verlieren wir auch Zeit.	*Apart from* measuring every batch specially, we do not know what else we can do. *Apart from the fact that* the repair will be expensive, we are also losing time.

• **ohne** 'without'.

Ohne die Maschine auseinanderzunehmen, ... *Ohne daß* diese Maschine in Betrieb ist, ... können wir nicht weiterproduzieren.	*Without* stripping down the machine ... *Without* this machine being in operation ... ... we cannot go on producing.

• **(an)statt** 'instead of'.

Statt einen neuen Lieferanten *zu* suchen, ... *Statt daß* eine andere Firma uns versorgt, ... möchten wir lieber bei Ihnen bleiben.	*Instead of* looking for a new supplier, ... *Instead of* another firm supplying us, ... we would rather remain with you.

• **um** 'in order to'.

Um bei Ihnen *zu* bleiben, ...	*In order to* stay with you, ...
Damit unsere Produktion nicht leidet, ...	*So that* our production does not suffer, ...
... brauchen wir Ihre Kooperation.	... we need your cooperation.

28 Types of adverbial expression

➤ We *often* went *by bus to the seaside:* order of adverbials in the sentence ➤4c(ii).

28a   What is an adverbial expression?

Adverbial expressions (often shortened to '*adverbials*') mainly answer the questions listed in paragraphs 6d(v) to (ix). We say that they 'modify' meanings because they complete, alter or even contradict them. There are three sorts of adverbial: adverbs, adverbial phrases and adverbial clauses. They all play the same part in the sentence – you can often say the same thing using any one of them.

Vorher ...	*Beforehand ...*	(adverb)
Vor der Konferenz ...	*Before the meeting ...*	(phrase)
Bevor die Konferenz		
angefangen hatte, ...	*Before the meeting started ...*	(clause)
... hatte ich mit meiner	... I had spoken to my boss.	
Chefin gesprochen.		

28b   Adverbs

These are single word expressions, of various types.

(i)   *Adverbs formed from adjectives [➤ch.24]*

Most of these adverbs answer the question **Wie?** 'How?', though they can answer other questions. German has no special adverb suffix like the English '-ly', so these adverbs are the same as the adjective, without any ending. (Some English adverbs are also like this, for example 'fast' and 'late'.)

Ich hatte einen *dringend* gebrauchten Bericht *äußerst schnell* und nicht sehr *gut* verfaßt.	I had written an *urgently* needed report *extremely fast* and not very *well*.

Adverbs can be formed from many adjectives by adding **-erweise**. These express the speaker's attitude to the event described [➤29b(iii)].

> *Glücklicherweise* war die Chefin an dem Tag abwesend, aber *dummerweise* habe ich den Bericht datiert.
>
> *Fortunately* the boss was absent on that day, but *stupidly* I dated the report.

➤ We talk fast but he talks *faster/fastest* of all: comparatives and superlatives ➤24e.

(ii) Adverbs formed from nouns and verbs

The ending **-(s)weise** can be added to many noun and verb stems, mostly to express the sense of 'as a ~, in ~s, ~ by ~'.

paarweise/gruppenweise/ massenweise	in pairs/groups/masses
ausnahmsweise/beispielsweise	as an exception/example
pfundweise/stückweise/ stundenweise	by the pound/ piece (piecemeal)/hour
teilweise/versuchsweise/ zeitweise	partly/experimentally/temporarily
beziehungsweise (often shortened *to* **bzw.**)	or, and ... respectively

Note These adverbs are increasingly used as adjectives, but only with nouns which describe a *process*, many of them formed from verbs.

eine teilweise Verbesserung	a partial improvement
schrittweise Fortschritte	gradual progress
massenweiser Protest	massive protest

(iii) Other adverbs

Many of the most common adverbs, especially those answering the questions **Wann?** 'When?' and **Wo?** 'Where?', are not formed from adjectives. These are dealt with in paragraph 29b(ii).

28c Adverbial phrases

Sometimes a noun phrase [➤19b] acts as an adverbial, as in **er redet *die ganze Zeit*** 'he talks *the whole time*', but most *adverbial phrases* begin with a preposition [➤ch.27 for full details].

Auf den ersten Blick hat die Chefin gesehen, daß der Bericht *in aller Eile* verfaßt und lange *nach dem Termin* eingeschickt worden war.	*At first glance* the boss saw that the report had been written *in great haste* and sent in well *after the deadline.*

28d   *Adverbial clauses*

Unlike the phrases, adverbial clauses contain a main verb and are introduced by a subordinating conjunction [▶5a(ii)].

Als sie nach mir geschickt hat, hatte ich ziemlich Angst, *weil sie Unpünktlichkeit haßt.*	*When she sent for me* I was quite scared, *because she hates unpunctuality.*

29 **What adverbial expressions do**

29a *The role of adverbs in German*

German makes very extensive use of adverbs, often in expressions where English or French would normally use a verb. This is especially true of *nuance adverbs* like **ja, doch, wohl** [➤29c(iii)] and of adverbs which express a general attitude [➤29b(iii)].

Ich schwimme *gern*, aber ich spiele *lieber* Handball. *Allerdings* spiele ich nicht sehr gut. Ich bin *wohl* zu klein. Dafür kann ich *leider* wenig.	I *like* swimming but I *prefer* playing handball. *I must admit that* I don't play very well. *I suppose* I'm too small. *I'm afraid* there is not much I can do about that.

29b *What do adverbials affect?*

An adverbial expression may affect, or 'modify', the meaning of a verb, an adjective or the whole sentence.

(i) *Adverbials modifying verbs*

Adverbials modify verbs by supplying further information about the action or situation described, for example when, where, how or why it happened.

Ich will fit bleiben, *also* spiele ich *im Winter jeden Mittwoch im Freizeitzentrum* Handball.	I want to stay fit, *so in winter* I play handball *every Wednesday in the leisure center.*

(ii) *Adverbs modifying adjectives and other adverbs*

Adverbs which modify adjectives and other adverbs generally answer the question 'How?', though there are other types.

Ich spiele *höchst* energisch aber *nicht sehr* geschickt.	I play *extremely* energetically but *not very* skilfully.

> Meine *meist* älteren Mitspieler sind *gleich* ungeschickt. Nach *nur* wenigen Minuten sind einige *erstaunlich* müde.
>
> My *mainly* oldish team-mates are *equally* unskilled. After *only* a few minutes some are *astonishingly* tired.

(iii)   Adverbs expressing an attitude

Some adverbs express an attitude to the whole statement [➤also 28b(i)]. For example:

allerdings/freilich/zwar	admittedly
angeblich	allegedly
bestimmt	certainly
gern/lieber	like/prefer [➤24e(i)]
hoffentlich	I/we hope that
leider	I'm afraid, unfortunately
möglicherweise	possibly
natürlich	of course, naturally
ruhig	by all means
vielleicht	perhaps
zufällig	by chance

29c   What effect do adverbials have?

(i)   Negative adverbs

nicht 'not' is by far the commonest negative. It is used very much as in English, but 'not a/not any' is normally **kein** [➤23g(ii)], and 'not anywhere, not ever' etc. is **nirgendwo, nie** 'nowhere, never' etc. [➤(ii) below]. Here are some common negative expressions:

(gar) nicht	not (at all)	nicht mehr	no longer
auch nicht	not ... either	keineswegs	not at all
nicht einmal	not even		

(ii)   Adverbial expressions which answer questions

The question-words in paragraphs 6d(v) to (ix) are themselves adverbs. Each question-word has a corresponding group of adverbials.

> Die Konferenz findet *morgen früh um halb neun* statt, *bevor wir nach Frankfurt fliegen.* (**Wann?**)
>
> The meeting is *tomorrow morning at half past eight, before we leave for Frankfurt.* (*When?*)

Sie wurde *in aller Eile* arrangiert.	It was arranged *very hurriedly*.
Das Personal ist *telefonisch* informiert worden. (*Wie?*)	Staff have been notified *by phone*. (*How?*)
Sie wird *hier* stattfinden, *im Büro des Personalleiters*. (*Wo?*)	It will take place *here, in the personnel manager's office*. (*Where?*)
Unsere Vertreter kommen *aus ganz Europa*. (*Woher?*)	Our reps are coming *from all over Europe*. (*Where from?*)
Ich bedauere *sehr*, daß Sie nicht dabei sein werden. Es ist *äußerst* ärgerlich. (*Wie (sehr)?*)	I *very much* regret that you won't be there. It is *extremely* annoying. (*How (much)?*)
Frau Dr. Kraus kann nicht kommen, *weil sie krank ist*. Ich habe *also* ihren Stellvertreter eingeladen. (*Warum?*)	Dr. Kraus cannot come *because she is ill, so* I have invited her deputy. (*Why?*)

These are some of the commonly used adverbs which answer these same questions. Note how many are in fact compounds of other parts of speech, for example, **zuletzt, umsonst, überall, gleichfalls, beinahe**.

(A) Wann? 'When?': time. There are a large number of these.

erst mal/zuerst	first of all
dann	then (next)
zunächst	at first
zuletzt	in the end
damals	then (at that time)
jetzt	now
bald	soon
oft	often
manchmal	sometimes
selten	seldom
immer	always
nie(mals)	never
noch immer	still
noch nicht	not yet
schon	already
erst	not until, only
heute	today
heute früh/abend	this morning/evening
(vor)gestern	(the day before) yesterday

(über)morgen	(the day after) tomorrow
heutzutage	nowadays
sofort/(so)gleich	at once, immediately
neulich/vor kurzem	recently

(B) Wie? 'How?': manner, methods, means. This is a very broad group, which includes most adverbs made from adjectives [➤28b(i)] and phrases answering questions like **Mit wem?** 'With whom?' and **Womit?** 'With what?'. See also the adverbs which express an attitude to the whole statement [➤29b(iii)]. Other adverbs include:

ebenfalls/gleichfalls	likewise
rundheraus	bluntly
sonst	otherwise
unversehens	by mistake
umsonst/vergebens	in vain

(C) Wo? 'Where?': place. Adverbs of place are often used with prepositions like **auf** or **in** where English would have 'at the top of ...' etc.

hier	here
dort	there
da	there, here
oben/unten	at the top/bottom, upstairs/downstairs
vorne/ hinten	at the front/back
außen/innen	on the outside/inside
draußen/drinnen	outside/inside
mitten	in the middle
überall	everywhere
irgendwo	anywhere
nirgendwo/nirgends	nowhere
anderswo/woanders	somewhere else
oben auf dem Haufen	at the top of the pile
draußen vor der Tür	outside the door
mitten im Wald	in the middle of the woods

(D) Wohin? Woher? 'Where to? Where from?': direction. **hin/her** combine with adverbs of place [➤(C) above] to make adverbs of movement away from/towards the speaker. They are also used by themselves after prepositional phrases to emphasize the direction. Note the use of **von/nach oben** etc. to indicate motion from or towards a position.

hierher	(to) here
dahin	(to) there, away

dorther	from there
dorthin	(to) there
irgendwoher	from anywhere
anderswohin	(to) somewhere else
von unten her	from below
nach vorne hin	up to the front
zum See hin	to the lake
von der Gaststätte her	from the inn

(E) **Wie ... ?** 'How ... ?': degree. Adverbs of degree usually modify adjectives or other adverbs. Many of those made from adjectives are colloquial and are used mainly by certain groups or ages, for example, **unheimlich** 'incredibly (eerily!)', **echt** 'really (genuinely)'. More humdrum adverbs include:

äußerst/höchst	extremely
beinahe/fast	almost/ nearly
besonders	especially
bloß	merely
durchaus/überaus	totally/thoroughly
ganz	entirely, quite
genau	exactly
größtenteils	for the most part
kaum	hardly
nur	only (not of time)
recht	really
schlechthin	absolutely
sehr	very (much)
so	so (to such an extent)
ungefähr/etwa	approximately/ about
verhältnismäßig	relatively
ziemlich	fairly, quite
zu	too

(F) **Warum?** 'Why?': reason, cause. Reasons are usually given in phrases or clauses. The few adverbs of reason all have the general sense of 'therefore'. In approximate order of frequency they are: **also, darum, daher, deshalb.**

(iii)   *Nuances of meaning: modal particles*

Like many other Germanic languages, German has a range of very useful short adverbs which express the speaker's attitude to what s/he is saying. Adverbs listed in paragraphs above are not repeated in the selection below, though many of them are used in this way. English often has no real equivalents, so the translations given are only approximate.

Wo bleibt *denn* der Manfred? Er sollte von Bonn herüberfahren. Hat er *denn* keinen Führerschein?	Where has Manfred got to *then*? He was going to drive over from Bonn. Hasn't he got a driver's licence *then*?
– *Doch*! Er ist *doch* Rennfahrer! Das wissen Sie *doch*.	– *Yes of course*! He is a racing driver *after all*. You *know* that.
– Er ist *eben* vergeßlich. Wir müssen *eben* Geduld haben.	– He is *just* forgetful. We shall *just* have to be patient.
– Das ist *ja* die Höhe! Er hat *ja* versprochen, pünktlich zu sein.	– That *really* is the limit! *You know* he promised to be punctual.
– Hören Sie *mal*, Sie könnten ihn *mal* anrufen.	– Listen, you could *just* give him a ring.
– Das *schon*, aber *schon* der Gedanke daran macht mich wütend.	– *True enough*, but *just* the thought of it makes me furious.
– Wo kann er *wohl* sein? Er hat sich *wohl* verfahren.	– *I wonder* where he can be? He has *probably* lost his way.
– Er ist *zwar* intelligent, aber er ist nicht sehr höflich.	– He *may* be intelligent, but he is not very polite.

_F_
USING NUMBERS

Numerals

30a Counting: cardinal numbers

(i) *The forms of the cardinal numbers*

These are the German numbers which you should know. All the others follow the same patterns. Note especially the irregularities in the numbers shown in italics.

0 null	21 einundzwanzig
1 eins	22 zweiundzwanzig
2 zwei	23 dreiundzwanzig
3 drei	24 vierundzwanzig
4 vier	25 fünfundzwanzig
5 fünf	26 sechsundzwanzig
6 sechs	27 siebenundzwanzig
7 sieben	28 achtundzwanzig
8 acht	29 neunundzwanzig
9 neun	30 *dreißig*
10 zehn	40 vierzig
11 elf	50 fünfzig
12 zwölf	60 *sechzig*
13 dreizehn	70 *siebzig*
14 vierzehn	80 achtzig
15 fünfzehn	90 neunzig
16 *sechzehn*	100 hundert
17 *siebzehn*	101 hundert(und)eins
18 achtzehn	102 hundertzwei
19 neunzehn	200 zweihundert
20 *zwanzig*	

1000 tausend	1 000 000 eine Million
1001 tausend(und)eins	1 000 001 eine Million eins
1002 tausend(und)zwei	2 000 000 zwei Millionen
2000 zweitausend	1 000 000 000 eine Milliarde

777 777 siebenhundertsiebenundsiebzigtausendsiebenhundert-
siebenundsiebzig

Note 1) As the last example shows, numbers under a million are written as one word, but in practice, numbers above 19 with more than one part, like **vierunddreißig** or **hundertzehn**, are always written as figures.

2) Figures over 1000 are written with spaces every three digits, not commas [➤30c(iii)].

3) When taking down tens and units, it is quicker to write the unit down as you hear it, then insert the ten before it. Especially on the telephone, **zwo** is often used for **zwei**, to avoid confusion with **drei**.

(ii) Numbers as nouns

(A) eine Million and **eine Milliarde** are always treated as feminine nouns. Other numbers are also feminine nouns when they refer to the number itself and to things like buses and trams [➤20b(ii)]. They all add **-(e)n** for the plural.

In Erdkunde kriege ich normalerweise *eine Drei.*	In geography I usually get *a three*.
Dreimal hat er *zwei Sechsen* geworfen.	Three times he threw *two sixes*.
Das hat DM2 500 000 (zwei Millionen fünfhunderttausend Mark) gekostet?!	That cost 2,500,000 marks?!

(B) ein Dutzend is a neuter noun of quantity [➤3d]. The plurals **Dutzende, Hunderte, Tausende, Millionen** and **Milliarden** describe approximate numbers of people and things. The first three add **-n** in the dative and, if used without a determiner, **-er** in the genitive.

In dem Winter sind *Hunderte* von Menschen erfroren.	In that winter *hundreds* of people froze to death.
Die Neugierigen sind in *Tausenden* gekommen.	The curious came in *thousands*.
Das schlechte Essen hat den Urlaub *Dutzender* von Familien verdorben.	The bad food spoiled the vacations *of dozens* of families.

(iii) Numbers and case endings

(A) eins, which does not change, is used for counting and as a feminine noun [➤(ii)above].

• The pronoun **einer,** etc., refers to one of a group [➤25h(i)]. It has the standard case endings.
• The form **ein** is used before a noun, with the same endings as the indefinite article [➤23e(ii)], but always fully pronounced.

der eine ~ etc. also makes it clear that 'one ~' is meant, not 'a ~'.
• 'Only one' is **ein einziger ...** or **nur ein ...**

Unser Hänschen kann schon von *eins* bis hundert zählen. Er ist *eines* der begabtesten Kinder seiner Spielgruppe. *Nur ein* anderes Kind ist mit ihm zu vergleichen.	Our Hänschen can already count from *one* to a hundred. He is *one* of the most gifted children in his playgroup. *Only one* other child can compare with him.

(B) Other numbers do not normally have case endings except that:

• in writing, **zwei** and **drei** quite often have genitives **zweier** and **dreier**;
• in certain set phrases the numbers 2 to 12 have a dative in **-en**.

Die Liebe *zweier* junger Menschen – wie schön! Während die Erwachsenen *zu zweien und dreien* herumstanden, kroch Hänschen *auf allen vieren* zwischen ihren Beinen.	The love *of two* young people – how lovely! While the adults stood around *in twos and threes*, Hänschen crawled *on all fours* between their legs.

(iv)   *Numbers as measurements*

Adjectives are made from cardinal numbers by adding **-er**. They refer mainly to money and to years, though sometimes also to other measurements. They can also be used as nouns, if it is clear what they refer to. The adjectives do not take case endings, but the nouns have the usual noun endings [►22b].

Leute in den *Achtzigern* erinnern sich noch an die *zwanziger* Jahre. Die normalen *Zehner* und *Hunderter* waren wertlos. Vier *Neunziger* (*neunziger* Marken) bitte. Leider habe ich nur einen *Fünfziger*.	People in their *eighties* still remember the *twenties*. The normal *tens* and *hundreds* (*ten and one hundred mark notes*) were worthless. Four *nineties* (*ninety Pfennig stamps*) please. I'm afraid I've only got a *fifty* (*mark note*).

30b   Arranging in order: ordinal numbers

(i)   Formation of ordinal numbers

Ordinal numbers are formed simply by adding **-te** to cardinal numbers from 2 to 19, and **-ste** to all other numbers. First, *t*hird, seventh and eighth are irregular. Ordinals are always used after a determiner and have the normal adjective endings [➤24b(ii)].

1. der *erste*	11. der elfte
2. der zweite	12. der zwölfte
3. der *dritte*	13. der dreizehnte
4. der vierte	20. der zwanzigste
5. der fünfte	21. der einundzwanzigste
6. der sechste	30. der dreißigste
7. der *siebte*	40. der vierzigste
8. der *achte*	70. der siebzigste
9. der neunte	80. der achtzigste
10. der zehnte	90. der neunzigste
100. der hundertste	200. der zweihundertste
101. der hundert(und)erste	1000. der tausendste
103. der hundertdritte	1 000 000. der millionste

2345. der zweitausenddreihundertfünfundvierzigste

Note   As shown in the list above, in German ordinal numbers are written with a period after them [➤also 31b(iv)].

(ii)   Firstly, secondly

For 'firstly, secondly' etc. **-ens** is added to the stem of the ordinal numbers.

Ich komme nicht, *erstens* weil ich keine Zeit habe, *zweitens* weil ich nicht will.	I am not coming, *firstly* because I have no time, *secondly* because I don't want to.

(iii)   Second/third best

For 'second/third best' etc., superlative adjectives are added to the stem of the ordinal numbers.

Käthe ist der *zweitbeste* Läufer ihrer Klasse, aber im Schwimmen ist sie immer die *drittletzte*.	Käthe is the *second best* runner in her class, but in swimming she is always *third from last*.

30c *Dividing into parts: fractions and decimals*

(i) With the exception of 'half' [➤(ii) below], fractions are neuter nouns made by adding **-el** to the stem of the ordinal numbers.

• Before a noun they are spelled with a small letter, and any determiner takes its gender from the noun, not the fraction. Fractions + common measurements are often written as one word.
• **dreiviertel** 'three-quarters' is normally written as one word, but other similar fractions are two separate words.
• There is no **und** between a full number and a following fraction.

***Dreiviertel* des Essens und *neun Zehntel* des Weins waren weg. Wir teilten den Rest auf. Jeder bekam ein *drittel* Brot und eine *zehntel* Flasche Wein. Ein *Zehntelliter* ist nicht viel! Vom Obst blieben nur noch *zwei einviertel* Melonen.**	*Three-quarters* of the food and *nine-tenths* of the wine were gone. We shared the rest. Each of us got a *third* of a loaf and a *tenth* of a bottle of wine. A *tenth of a liter* is not much! Of the fruit only *two and a quarter* melons were left.

(ii) 'Half' may be a noun, adjective or adverb:

(A) The noun is **die Hälfte**. 'Half the/this/that/my ...' etc is usually **die Hälfte** followed by a genitive or **von** + dative.

Karl hat mir *die Hälfte* seines Brots/von seinem Brot gegeben.	Karl gave me *half* (of) his bread.

(B) The adjective is **halb**. 'Half a ...' is normally **ein halber ...** etc., taking the normal adjective endings. **das Halb** refers to the number itself.

Ich hatte noch *einen halben* Apfel übrig.	I had *half an* apple left over.

(C) The adverb is **halb**.

Das hatte ich *halb* vergessen.	I had *half* forgotten that.

(D) 'One and a half' is **eineinhalb** or **anderthalb**, followed by **zweieinhalb, dreieinhalb** etc.

Nach *viereinhalb* Tagen sind wir zu einem Dorf gekommen. Wir waren *eineinhalb* Monate unterwegs gewesen.	After *four and a half* days we came to a village. We had been travelling for *one and a half* months.

(iii) As in most languages other than English, German decimals are written with a comma, not a point/period.

Ich hatte *10,5* Kilo verloren.	I had lost *10.5* kilos.

Times and dates

31a *Clock times*

(i) *Hours and minutes*

The following list shows the everyday way of telling the time. Note especially:

• **(die) Uhr** means 'clock, watch' ('hour' is **die Stunde**).
• Half-hours are always reckoned as 'half way to the next hour', so **halb eins** is 'half past twelve', not 'half past one'. In South Germany quarters are often reckoned in the same way, but this is not general throughout the country.
• '25 past/to' is often reckoned as '5 to/past' the half hour.

1.00	**ein Uhr/eins**
1.05	**fünf (Minuten) nach eins/ein Uhr fünf**
1.10	**zehn (Minuten) nach eins/ein Uhr zehn**
1.15	**Viertel nach eins/Viertel zwei**
1.20	**zwanzig (Minuten) nach eins/ein Uhr zwanzig/ zehn vor halb zwei**
1.25	**fünfundzwanzig (Minuten) nach eins/ein Uhr fünfundzwanzig/ fünf vor halb zwei**
1.30	**halb zwei**
1.35	**fünf nach halb zwei/fünfundzwanzig vor zwei**
1.40	**zwanzig vor zwei**
1.45	**Viertel vor zwei/drei Viertel zwei**
1.50	**zehn (Minuten) vor zwei**
1.55	**fünf (Minuten) vor zwei**
2.00	**zwei Uhr**

(ii) *The 24-hour clock*

The 24-hour clock is normal in official and business contexts such as railroad timetables and announcements, times of meetings, opening and closing times. It is always spoken as 'hours . minutes (if any)'.

00.15	**null Uhr fünfzehn**
07.30	**sieben Uhr dreißig**
10.45	**zehn Uhr fünfundvierzig**
12.00	**zwölf Uhr**
13.12	**dreizehn Uhr zwölf**

17.26	**siebzehn Uhr sechsundzwanzig**
21.57	**einundzwanzig Uhr siebenundfünfzig**
24.00	**vierundzwanzig Uhr**

(iii) Clock time phrases

Note how ways of saying 'a.m./p.m.' vary according to how early or late it is.

Wieviel Uhr ist es?/Wie spät ist es?	What time is it?
Wieviel Uhr haben Sie?	What time do you make it?
Es ist (Punkt/genau) halb elf.	It is (exactly) half past ten.
Wann/Um wieviel Uhr fährt der Zug ab?	When/At what time does the train leave?
um zwölf Uhr (mittags)/um Mittag	at twelve o'clock (twelve noon)/ at noon
um vierundzwanzig Uhr/ um Mitternacht	at 24.00 hours/at (twelve) midnight
um zwei Uhr nachts/nachmittags	at two a.m./p.m.
um acht Uhr vormittags/abends	at eight a.m./p.m.
gegen acht Uhr morgens	at about eight a.m. or not quite eight a.m.
vorm./nachm.	a.m./p.m.

31b Days, months and years

All names of days, months and seasons are masculine.

(i) Days of the week

Sonntag	Sunday
Montag	Monday
Dienstag	Tuesday
Mittwoch	Wednesday
Donnerstag	Thursday
Freitag	Friday
Samstag	Saturday (used everywhere)
Sonnabend	Saturday (only in the North)
am Montag	on Monday, etc.
montags	on Mondays, etc.

(ii) Months and seasons

Januar	January

Februar	February
März	March
April	April
Mai	May
Juni	June
Juli	July
August	August
September	September
Oktober	October
November	November
Dezember	December
der Frühling	spring
der Sommer	summer
der Herbst	fall/autumn
der Winter	winter

Es ist/wird bald Winter.	It is/will soon be winter.
Der Juli/Der Sommer war wirklich heiß.	July/The summer was really hot.
Im November/Im Herbst regnete es jeden Tag.	In November/the fall it rained every day.
bis Anfang/Mitte/Ende Mai	up to/by the beginning/middle/ end of May
Wir fahren nächsten Juni in Urlaub.	We are going on vacation next June.
letzten/vorigen/ vergangenen Januar	last January

(iii)   Major festivals in Germany

das (der)Neujahr(stag)	New Year's (Day)
der Fasching	(pre-Lent) Carnival
der Aschermittwoch	Ash Wednesday
der Karfreitag	Good Friday
(zu) Ostern	(at) Easter
Ostermontag	Easter Monday
Pfingsten	Pentecost/Whitsun
(Christi) Himmelfahrt	Ascension Day
Mariä Himmelfahrt	Assumption of the Virgin Mary (15th August)
Allerheiligen	All Saint's
der Heilige Abend	Christmas Eve
(zu) Weihnachten	(at) Christmas

Frohe Weihnachten! Merry Christmas!
Zweiter Weihnachtstag Boxing Day
Silvester(abend) New Year's Eve

(iv) Dates

Days of the month are ordinal numbers, as in English [➤30b(i)]. They are always written as figures, with a full stop/period, never as words. Note that (for example) 'in 1993' is either just **1993** or **im Jahre 1993**. [Spoken versions are given in square brackets below to show the endings.]

Den wievielten haben wir heute? What's the date today?

Heute ist der 16. [sechzehnte] August.

Wir haben heute den 16. [sechzehnten] August.

The date today is the 16th of August.

Sie ist am 20. [zwanzigsten] April geboren. She was born on the 20th of April.

Sie hat am 20. April Geburtstag. Her birthday is on the 20th of April.

Er ist 1833/im Jahre 1833 gestorben. He died in 1833.

Sie fangen (am) Montag, den 6. September an. You/They start on Monday, September 6th.

Hamburg, (den) 28.3.91/(den) 28. März 1991 Hamburg, 28 March 1991 (at head of letter)

G

INDEX

INDEX

Note **(1)** The symbol Ⓓ indicates that this term is defined in the paragraph shown.

(2) The sign ➤ refers you to another part of the index.